BOY SOLDIER

A Memoir of Innocence Lost and Humanity Regained in Northern Uganda

NORMAN OKELLO AND THEO HOLLANDER

unbound

First published in 2021

Unbound
Level 1, Devonshire House, One Mayfair Place, London W1J 8AJ
www.unbound.com

Map illustrations © Nel de Vink

Text design by Ellipsis, Glasgow

A CIP record for this book is available from the British Library

ISBN 978-1-78352-811-0 (hardback)
ISBN 978-1-78352-812-7 (ebook)

Printed and bound by CPI Group (UK) Ltd, Croydon CR0 4YY

1 3 5 7 9 8 6 4 2

In memory of all those who died and suffered in the twenty years of insurgency in northern Uganda and southern Sudan

Contents

Foreword   xiii

Part I: A First Encounter
   A Bitter Start   3
   The End of Happiness   17
   Writing My Name   33

Part II: Becoming a Soldier
   Death March   51
   Palutaka   60
   My Life as a Soldier   74

Part III: Losing My Humanity
   The Person I Feared Becoming   99
   The Attack on Palutaka   124
   The Deserts of Sudan   142

Part IV: The Birth of a Monster

    Exorcism of the Civilian Mind   167

    The Birth of a Monster   179

    Invoking the Spirit of Vengeance   195

    The Girls of Aboke   206

    The Kitgum Massacres   235

Part V: The Life After

    Escape   261

    A Prisoner Again   274

    Still Trapped in the War   309

    The Return of Happiness   334

On the Fates of the People in this Book   369

Uganda: A History of Cyclical Violence   383

War in Northern Uganda and the

    Genesis of the Lord's Resistance Army   395

On Peace and Unending War   413

Acknowledgements   423

A Note on the Authors   427

Supporters   429

Locations mentioned in Norman's story

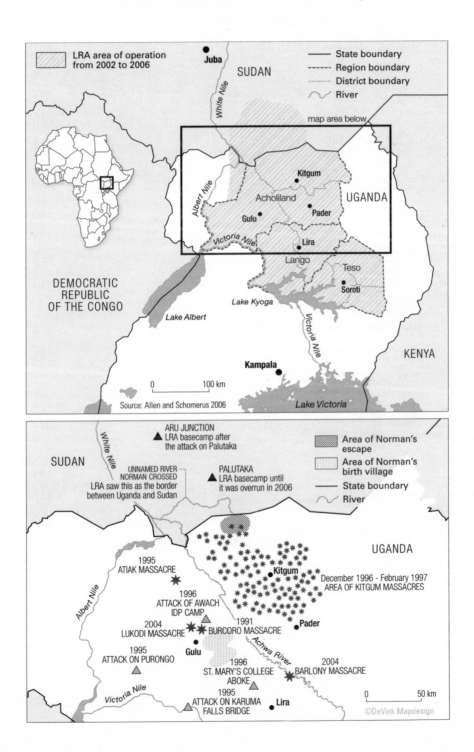

The LRA's shifting theatre of operation
between 2002 and 2014

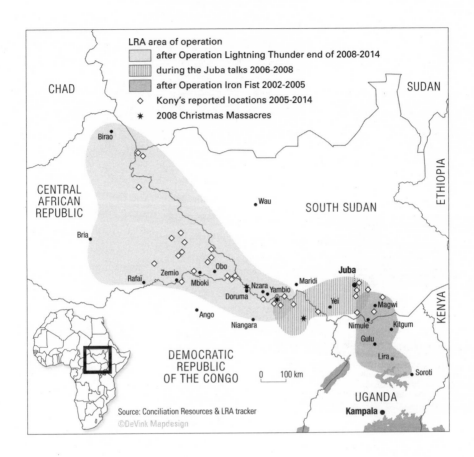

Source: Conciliation Resources & LRA tracker

©DeVink Mapdesign

Foreword

This is Norman Okello's story. On New Year's Day in 1995, at the age of twelve, he was abducted from his village in northern Uganda and forced to become a soldier in the Lord's Resistance Army (LRA), one of the most brutal guerrilla armies ever to have emerged from Africa's troubled history. For decades, the LRA has been led by the charismatic but ruthless Joseph Kony, a man who claims to be God's spokesperson and a spirit medium, and Norman's account of a life of warfare, hardship and horror while serving under him is shocking almost beyond words.

I first met Norman Okello in the last weeks of the Ugandan dry season in March 2007. He was still heavily traumatised. He suffered from severe insomnia and nightmares and he had major trust issues. At times he would appear to behave irrationally. He would often get up in the middle of a conversation and start running as fast as he could, sprinting into the distance until his legs couldn't carry him any further. Norman told me that there were moments when he was engulfed by overwhelming rage, and to avoid lashing out at everything in sight, he needed to expel and exhaust his anger by running. There were dark reservoirs of violence that clouded his soul and he could easily upset and frighten people, which happened many times after his return from the LRA.

But Norman was also one of the kindest people I had ever met. He was enormously generous and had no desire to offend or harm anyone. His kindness was demonstrated in the way he cared for his fellow war victims and the way he treated me. He voluntarily committed himself to improving the lives of former child soldiers and he was always willing to help me out. He had a great sense of humour and I can't count the number of times that we laughed our asses off during long walks or drinks at the local bars. He was a master of gallows humour and self-deprecation.

I was nervous and unsettled before my first interview with Norman – it was the first time I had spoken at length with a former child soldier. I had read a substantial amount of literature on the insurgency in northern Uganda, including several accounts of former child soldiers. However, none of this prepared me for Norman's revelations. It was not only his story that disturbed me, but also the way he told it. Although his recollections were vivid and animated, his body language suggested that his mind dwelt in a shadowy netherworld. His eyes seemed far away, looking into a past that was way beyond my experience. What I heard were accounts of unimaginable strength and courage but also terrible violence and appalling atrocities. Norman's testimony gave voice to the life of a young boy who was forcibly abducted but who tried to cling to his humanity, even though all the odds were stacked against him, and through his words I caught a glimpse of the malignant nature of the LRA.

Norman worked for an organisation called the War Affected Children Association (WACA), and it was through this organisation that I came into contact with him. By May 2007 I had conducted several interviews with him and although by then I had interviewed many former child soldiers, mostly females, Norman's story continued to leave the greatest impression on me. It was not so much the narrative itself that distinguished his story from others – all the stories that I have heard in northern Uganda easily merit a book – it was the way he told it. Norman is a natural storyteller: he has an incredible gift for narrative, capturing so well the telling detail, the arc of events, and the nuances of place, character and emotion.

It was not until April 2008 that Norman overcame his fears and suspicion and finally opened up to me. He began to recount his own role in the horrors that had unfolded: in his narratives, 'they did' was replaced by 'I did'. Later that year, we decided to visit some of the places that featured in his story. We travelled through the central north of Uganda, from Nwoya to Kitgum and from Lamwo to Lira. We crossed the border to present-day South Sudan, visiting Palutaka and Pajok in Eastern Equatoria. The locations helped trigger Norman's memories and revive details that otherwise would have been lost.

When I met Norman again in September 2009, he told me he no longer suffered from insomnia and that his traumas were much less severe. The process of writing this book has had a healing effect. As Norman put it himself: 'Remembering the past helps you to forget.' Of course, Norman will never forget what happened, but at the time of the last interview, twelve years after his escape, he had finally been able to lay his horrible memories to rest. For the first time since his very early childhood, he could say, in all honesty, that he was happy, and that life was treating him just fine.

What Norman and I hope we have achieved with this book is to detail his story as comprehensively as possible – from his early childhood and the true beauty of this part of Africa to his terrifying LRA missions, which contribute to the blackest pages of human history. Norman gives this war a face and a voice from the perspective of victim and aggressor, because Norman was both. His gradual loss of humanity entailed a struggle with the most basic of human instincts – the will to survive.

Ten years have passed since this book was written. The last entry into Norman's story is from 2009. The epilogue, however, provides a more up-to-date description of what happened to some of the people in this book and to the overall context. If this book is inaccurate about any names, dates or places, it is either because Norman's memory faltered at those points or because I misinterpreted them. For that, we apologise. I hope this story will grip you in the same way it gripped me after my first interview with Norman.

Dr Theo Hollander
January 2019

Part I
A First Encounter

A Bitter Start

It was a hot and dry night on New Year's Eve in 1994. December is always in the middle of the dry season, when the desert winds blow over Uganda, making it extremely hot. While the world was celebrating the transition to a new year, we were lying in the tall grass, hiding from a terrible menace that had terrorised the northern parts of my country for over half a decade. By now I had grown used to sleeping in the tall grass, but that didn't mean that I liked the whole mess we were in. New Year's Eve was no exception. For us, there was no feast, no nice big meal, no nothing. The only fireworks that we were likely to see this night were mortar fire and bullets flying around.

My part of the country, named Acholiland after the dominant tribe, wasn't a good place to grow up as a child, at least not after the war prevented us from living normal and dignified lives. The war had started in the mid-eighties, and by the mid-nineties the only places of relative safety in Acholiland were the bigger cities of Gulu and Kitgum, if only you could afford a place in the city. My parents weren't so fortunate. They couldn't afford a place in the city, and as I had no relatives living there either, I was destined to sleep in the tall grass. At least there was safety in hiding.

3

So, there I was, lying in the tall grass. I knew that my family were close to me – my father, mother and my younger siblings – but we didn't speak a single word all night. Even a whisper sounded like a thunderstorm on a clear day. We tried really hard to avoid all contact with the rebels. Every night we went to our hiding places, moving with absolute caution. We never hid in the same place for long, because if you stayed somewhere too long, the tracks would reveal your position to the rebels. In the mornings, after I woke up, I was always on guard and moving with great care. We didn't really live in the village any more, but in the thick bush surrounding it. Only for a few daily occasions did we come home, for example when my mother had made dinner. But as soon as we had eaten, we would disappear into the bushes again. Out of the twenty-four hours in a day, we spent a maximum of two or three in the village. The rest of the day I was in hiding. My daily routine was a constant game of hide and seek in which my life was at stake.

Our New Year's Eve passed in a complete and awful silence. Luckily, we were spared the deadly fireworks that everybody in northern Uganda dreaded. The next day I woke up and began the new year with my daily routine. First, I went to a stream nearby to wash my face. I would make sure that I never washed my face twice in the same spot, as it was extremely difficult not to leave any tracks on the riverbank. It was better to have your tracks spread out, instead of having them all concentrated on one place. My vigilance was highest in the morning hours when I went to the stream, because I never knew what I might run into. Not only was Acholiland infested with rebels, but you could also run into wild animals, like snakes, baboons or even leopards.

After I washed my face and drank a little, I went to the gardens to help my father in the field. The gardens were very small these days and always surrounded by thick bush. We had constructed this on purpose so that it would be difficult to spot us from a distance. The negative result of this construction was that we always had to fight the bush, which was constantly threatening to grow over our plots and destroy what we had sown. Usually we worked on the plots for a few hours and afterwards we would go to the village, where my mother would prepare a small breakfast, but on this day, my mother was not at home because she had gone to the market in Gulu with my siblings to sell our surplus from the maize and groundnut harvest of a few days ago.

So instead of going straight back to the village, I first went to the field to hunt for some birds, which would be a nice addition to our breakfast. In the meantime, my father was preparing some sorghum and cassava. I took the catapult, which I had brought from my hiding place, and started looking for prey. Hunting was always one of my favourite occupations. You had to be a good spotter to see all the birds around you, and when you located one, you had to sneak towards it without making any noise, aim and shoot. I always got a great rush from actually hitting one, which wasn't an easy task at all. I soon found some birds, and started to stalk them, crawling as close as I could without frightening them. I was just about to take my first shot when something startled the birds.

'You will never hit those birds, *kadogo*, you are way too slow.'

It was Francis, an older boy that I knew from school. Kadogo was a Swahili nickname that we always used for younger people. Francis came from a village not very far from mine, and he was on his way home. Like me, he had also been hunting, but he hadn't been able to kill anything. We joked a bit and decided that we might have more luck if we hunted together. Francis pointed to another tree that had a number of yellow birds. We both shot our stones simultaneously, but, as we often did, we both missed our target. Francis went home while I hunted on for another half hour, returning to our hut in the village empty-handed. It was here, at around eleven o'clock on 1 January 1995, that my true hell began.

As I sat down with my father to eat, gunfire erupted nearby. As we fled our hut, where we were hiding from the brutal sun, we saw people from the village nearby running towards us, carrying the message everyone in Acholi dreaded: 'The rebels are coming! The rebels are coming!'

I saw an old man, whose face was bleeding heavily, running for his life, and some women appeared, also fleeing the rebels, some with young toddlers in their arms and small babies tied on their backs. The peaceful morning suddenly dissolved into chaos as the gunfire became louder and everyone ran in different directions away from it. My primal instinct took over and I too started to run. I fled towards the bush with the speed of a leopard, not even sure where I was going or where I would hide. My father, my uncle and my cousin, who was mentally disturbed, were following me, and the four of us quickly ran past the papyrus. While we were running, my dad said he knew a good hiding place and took the lead. I think we kept on running for another two kilometres until we finally came to a terrain where the bush was very thick and still untouched by the wildfires. We would take cover from the rebels and hope they wouldn't find us.

Once we were lying on the ground, I could finally take the time to listen to the gun battle that was unfolding about three kilometres behind us. I could clearly hear that this wasn't the rebels attacking a village with unarmed civilians. When the rebels attack harmless civilians, they usually prefer to use axes, machetes and bayonets, both to make the terror more overwhelming and to conserve their bullets, but the battle that I heard unfolding behind me was one of massive gunfire. My guess was that the rebels had walked into a National Resistance Army (NRA) ambush, and this guess was confirmed when we saw an army helicopter flying over after some time. The helicopter didn't take an active part in the battle, as we heard no bombs being dropped. It probably came to pick up the wounded and bring new supplies, because after just a few minutes, we saw it flying over again, away from the battle. The fight went on for a long time, providing a further indicator that the forces fighting each other were substantive. The battle finally lost its intensity after about three long hours, erupting only sporadically over the course of another half hour.

For all that time, we lay there in complete terror; the four of us didn't say a single word. I started to think about the rest of my family. I wondered what had happened to my mother and my siblings, as well as my other relatives in our village. Could my mum and my siblings have run into the rebels earlier that day while they were going to the market? Town was in the direction where the gunfire came from, so it was not impossible that they had. The fear for my own life started to make place for a fear about the fate of my loved ones. Again, as I had many times before, I thought about how much I hated the rebels. They had taken away almost everything that I valued in life: the wealth and status of my family, my ability to go to school, my best friends, my ability to play games, and so many other things. Silently, I wished that the NRA would wipe out the rebels for ever, right on that spot three kilometres away. I really wished they would kill every single last one of them so that my family and I could rebuild our lives. But at the same time, I realised that this was wishful thinking: the rebels would continue to spread havoc for many years to come. The NRA hadn't been able to wipe them out during my lifetime. Although I was young, I knew that the rebels had their safe havens in Sudan where the NRA couldn't follow them. The best I could hope for was that the NRA would win this battle.

The gunfire lost its intensity only when the sun was descending. Although the fighting was over, we continued to lie in silence for another half hour. Total serenity surrounded us, and it was as if the attack was just a bad dream. From far away we could hear the faint screams of people in terrible pain, but those were the only sounds that suggested anything had happened. About an hour after the battle had died down, my father and uncle silently started to argue about whether we should go back to see if the NRA had won. My uncle was getting nervous, but my father overruled him, insisting that we should stay. Yet, as another hour passed in silence, we all started to become curious whether everything was safe again. Even if the rebels had won, they would have moved on by now. We planned how we would return to the village: my father and my uncle would scout ahead, and I would follow them from a distance with my cousin. We agreed that whenever my dad or my uncle saw any sign of danger, they would make a sign with their arms. At that point, my cousin and I would make a run for it and find a good place to hide. With this plan in mind, we left the safety of our hiding place.

My dad went ahead, followed by my uncle. My cousin and I pursued at a distance of around fifty metres. Slowly we zigzagged towards the village to check if everything was clear. When we came close to the road connecting our village to the main road, my uncle suddenly made the sign we agreed on. The moment I saw it, my cousin and I immediately fell down flat to hide in the tall grass and started to crawl away. I was terrified at the thought that the rebels would now take my father away from me as well, but this thought soon dissolved when my uncle told us that it was a false alarm. They had run into some distant relatives from the next village who were also going back to see if it was safe. Like us, the distant relatives hadn't encountered any rebels so far, so it appeared that the area was clear. Either the NRA had won the battle, or the rebels had moved on. After some small talk, which is the custom in this region, even in the face of war, the distant relatives went towards their village, and the four of us continued on our way. As we were nearing the neighbouring village, we saw that some of our relatives had already returned and were peeling the groundnuts our villages had collectively harvested a few days ago. Upon this sight, we decided to abandon the bush and walk the last kilometre on the path.

Several minutes later, it happened again. After my uncle and my dad walked through a little curve in the road, they suddenly stopped. As they stopped, my cousin and I instantly hid in the bush next to the road. I waited for a minute while I kept on observing my dad and my uncle. It seemed as though they were conversing with somebody, but, due to the bushes, we couldn't see who this person was. My cousin and I were waiting for the sign, but it never came. A minute went by, and still no sign. Since neither my uncle nor my father raised his hands, we naturally assumed that nothing was going on and that they had again run into some relatives. So we decided to walk up to them to see what was going on. It was only when we came very close that I realised, after years of being so damned cautious, how foolish this decision was.

At the sight of all the guns and the eyes full of bloodlust, I froze. Just like my dad and uncle, my cousin and I had walked straight into an ambush and were now surrounded by several rebels, all of them eager to shoot us. The rebels had probably seen us coming from a distance, but their good camouflage had made it impossible for us to see them until it was far too late. Only a fraction of a second after I had spotted the rebels, there came the most terrifying whisper I had ever heard.

'If you even dare to make a single movement, I am going to cut off your head – understand?'

I knew he meant it. This was probably the same thing they told my dad and uncle, which explained why they hadn't been able to raise their hands. We all knew perfectly well that this rebel wasn't joking. If a rebel said he would cut your head off if you didn't obey, he would surely do so. By now, we had heard enough stories to prove this. Silently, my father had hoped that we would run away the moment he stopped walking, but instead I walked straight through the doors of what would become my greatest hell.

I realised that it was too late to run away now: they finally had me. Around me, I saw seven rebels; three of them were somewhat older, about seventeen or maybe eighteen, and the rest were about my age. They all wore uniforms, even the young ones who could barely fit into them, and they had long dreadlocks, a common trait of the rebels. I saw that the bayonets on their guns and the machetes were stained with fresh blood, a sight that instilled terror. The worst thing about the rebels wasn't the weapons per se, but rather their eyes, which declared a willingness to use them. It felt as if I was looking straight into the devil's eyes. They looked at me with so much anger and aggression. The only thing I saw in those eyes was hatred and lust for blood. I knew that these people were not only capable of killing me, but they were also eager to do so.

I felt the hard butt of a gun in my back as I was smashed to the ground, and I felt a stinging pain in my side as the rebels began kicking me in my stomach and in my face. I saw that the others were getting the exact same treatment. The rebels immediately started tying us up with ropes so that we wouldn't have a chance to escape. To this day I still remember how the blood stopped circulating to my limbs as the rebels savagely tied me up. They told me that they would kill me if I tried to run. But how could I? I even had a hard time breathing because the ropes were so tight. The only thing that was on my mind was the question, 'Will I live, or will I be killed?', a question that would resurface many times in the years to come.

After the rebels had tied us up, they started to drag us to some kind of assembly point. They didn't care that the ropes were hurting me as they dragged me. I was bleeding from the top of my head, and I still felt a sharp pain in my side. But I did not dare complain. I didn't even dare to drop a single tear because I feared the rebels would cut out my eyes the moment I started to cry. As they were dragging me, totally paralysed by fear, I realised that some of the demons who were doing this to me, the personifications of evil, were not much older than I was. Of course, I knew the rebels liked to abduct children. Sometimes these children were seen again several years later, when they were butchering their own village without remorse and regret. I wondered what witchcraft could make children kill their own parents. I don't know what scared me more: whether I would survive this day, or whether they would also turn me into a man-eating demon that would boil young toddlers, behead respected elders and kill relatives.

As we arrived at the assembly point, I saw that they had also captured other people from my village. I pretended that we had never seen each other before. All this time, my dad, uncle, cousin and I hadn't spoken a single word to each other. It was better that the rebels didn't know that we were related. As soon as we reached the assembly point, one of the rebels started questioning me. This boy was barely older than I was, but he made me tremble with fear. He first questioned me about my dad. As he started, others joined in. They wanted to know who he was and if we were related. They threatened to kill me if I didn't tell them the truth. But I didn't tell them anything. I knew all too well what they could force me to do if I did.

In northern Uganda, regional news spreads like wildfires through an age-old rumour system. When something happens in Atiak today, it will be heard all the way in Kitgum only two or three days later. We called this mouth-to-mouth rumour machine Radio Kabi. I remember one specific rumour about a boy from a village not far from ours who was abducted in 1992. Six months later, this boy had returned to his village accompanied by other rebels, and together, they had slaughtered the entire village, including his family and other members of his clan. Something had transformed him from an innocent boy to a ferocious demon, intent on a killing spree.

At this moment, I didn't know what the future would bring me, but I decided that I would not become such a child. Because I didn't want to shoot my family, I told the rebels nothing but lies.

'Who is this man over here?'

'I don't know, sir. I have never seen him before.'

'You are lying. We can clearly see the resemblance between you and him. Now I ask you again, WHO IS THAT MAN?'

They were pointing at my father.

'Sir, I really don't know, I have never seen him before; he must be from another village.'

An older rebel joined in. 'Well, what a brave little fellow we have here. Now tell us, boy – we all see the resemblance between you and that man. I will ask you the question once more, and this time you better tell the truth, because I will not be so kind.'

To emphasise his point, this rebel kicked me really hard in my stomach. As I fell over, he asked the question again. Several seconds later, I still couldn't answer because I was struggling to breathe. When the oxygen filled my lungs again, I gave him my answer. 'Sir, as I told you before, I really don't know this man. This is the first time in my life that I have seen him.'

Even though I was extremely frightened, I continued to give him the same answer. All this time, I knew that they knew I was lying. But I kept on insisting that I didn't know my father. My father, in the meantime, was doing the same. My last answer hadn't satisfied the rebels and they started to beat me with big sticks. My father remained quiet during my ferocious beating. Not even once did he object to my punishment. It might seem very odd behaviour for a father, but we knew that this was the right thing to do. I have never been angry about this. If I had told them the truth, there was a big chance that they would have ordered me to do the unspeakable. Thus, as they continued to interrogate me about my father and my uncle, I continued to deny that I knew them. When they had enough of my lies, they changed the subject.

'Tell me, where do you live?'

I pointed to the opposite direction, because I didn't want the rebels to know where I lived. Once more, the story came to mind about the boy who had returned from the bush only to slaughter his own village. If the rebels didn't know where I came from, they could, at least, not force me to do such horrible things. It was at this point that my cousin really started to cause a lot of trouble for me.

'Sir, he is lying to you. His village is over there.'

He pointed in the right direction. I knew that my cousin didn't counter my arguments to have me killed. My cousin had mental problems, couldn't think straight, and on top of that he was reeling with fear. I knew I was in trouble now.

'DO YOU KNOW WHO THE FUCK WE ARE?! I have killed people for far lesser reasons than this. What is it? Don't you value your life? If you want, I can make you sleep here for ever. I will teach you what happens if you lie to me.'

At that point the rebel took his big stick and hit me with it five times. The first hit was right on my nose, and I started to bleed heavily. It was at that point that my cousin started to cry really loudly. Maybe this was my luck. The noise that my cousin made really irritated the rebels, including the one that was hitting me, and as a result, they started to shift their attention towards him. My poor cousin got such a bad beating. Within seconds, he was bleeding like me, but, somehow, I was happy that he was getting a beating. I was terrified at the thought of what would happen if he told the rebels the truth about my father as well. Somehow it was for the best. The rebels were happy that they had managed to shut him up, and I was happy that he didn't speak any more. While they were still beating him, a senior rebel came to the assembly point, clearly agitated by all the noise. The moment he arrived on the scene, he told the soldier that was hitting my cousin to immediately stop what he was doing.

'These boys will get their beating, don't you worry about that. Now, take these people to the main assembly point and make sure that they remain quiet. Kill them if you have to.'

They stopped questioning me. They took us to another assembly point, where we found the main group of the rebels, and I realised that almost everybody from my area had been taken hostage. I saw almost all the people from our village and the surrounding villages sitting there. The number of rebels at this location shattered me. I saw hundreds of them, and I realised that there was no chance on earth that I would be able to escape them.

When we came to the main group, I was separated from my father and uncle. This was one of the most difficult moments in my life. We realised that there was a chance this would be the last time we would ever see each other again, and yet we couldn't do anything that would reveal our bond. I wanted to scream out. I wanted to run to my father, hold on to him and never let go, but I knew I couldn't. I knew that I would risk both of our lives if I even blinked at him in a suspicious way. Only once did I look back at them and found that my uncle and father were both staring away from me and my cousin intentionally. It was very painful to leave my father without saying goodbye or showing any kind of emotion, but it was the right thing to do. I desperately hoped I would see them soon, but a chronic fear told me that this would not be the case. In the meantime, there were so many questions tormenting me: What would happen to me? Would I ever see another sunrise again? If I did, then what about tomorrow, would they kill me then or would they take me with them and also turn me into a demon like the ones who caught me? But I didn't dare ask any of them.

As they brought us to another area, I saw that they had also captured Francis. We looked at each other, but we both kept quiet. The three of us, Francis, me and my cousin, were taken to the senior rebel who had commanded the soldiers to stop beating us. This man was older than most of the rebels that I saw around. Most of them were still kids, not much older than me. Yet this man could have been my father. I was hoping that at barely twelve years old, I would still be too young to join the rebels. I really hoped that this older man would see this as well, but instead he confirmed my worst fears.

'Tomorrow we shall take you with us and you *will* become a soldier. Tomorrow morning we will write your name!'

The End of Happiness

The war had begun right after I was born. I had lived under its shadow for so long that it had become a part of me. Although the encounter I had with the rebels on the first day of 1995 was the most dramatic so far and would also have the most profound effect on the rest of my life, it wasn't the first encounter that I had ever had with them, nor the first time that the war had struck me and my family right at the core of our existence. The war had loomed over me and my family all of my life, and it had slowly deprived us of all our wealth, freedoms and means of proper existence. Eventually it even took away our happiness. However, this was after I had a small taste of Acholi life as it was before the war. Please let me start from the beginning.

My name is Norman Okello. I was born in 1982 in a small village near Gulu, the largest town in northern Uganda. My father was descended from a royal clan and at the time of my birth he still had considerable wealth, which continued to grow throughout my early childhood. My father had pursued a higher education but had not completed it because he had inherited the farm from my grandfather. This made him a wealthy man with much status in our small community. At the height of his wealth, my father possessed more than twenty cows and dozens of goats.

He met my mother when he was still in higher education in Lira District, south of Acholiland. Lira is where the Langi live. My mother was a Langi, which is a different tribe from the Acholi, but closely related and speaking a similar language. My parents always met each other at the borehole where they went to fetch water. Although my mother was illiterate, my father fell madly in love with her. After a long period of courtship, which is customary in these parts of Uganda, my father and mother married. My dad had to pay a dowry of two cows and several goats, which sealed the contract of marriage. While many marriages in Uganda are brokered by the parents to establish good relationships between clans or to add to a family's wealth, theirs was not a marriage of convenience; they really loved each other. Five years later, I was born.

Although I was the third-born in my family, my parents always considered me their firstborn, as my two older brothers had died of the measles before my birth. At that time, the measles was a very common disease in Uganda, killing many children in their first few years. But few people bothered to go to the hospital. They just prayed to God that it would go away, as my parents did when I was afflicted with the disease. My two older brothers and the two siblings that followed me weren't so lucky. They all died of the same preventable disease. When the first of my younger siblings died, I was still too young to remember. The second one, however, died under my guard. My parents spent most of the time away from the village, working in the gardens or herding the cows, so I was in charge of the babysitting. I had to carry my younger sister around with me all day, and I was the first to see that she was becoming ill. She had a terrible fever, and after a few days she got spots all over her body. This time, afraid of losing yet another child, my parents decided to take her to the hospital, but it was already too late. She died on the way. Four out of the first five children of my family had died of this horrific disease. I remember that we gave her a burial, but it is too long ago to recall any of the emotions that I felt at that time. Fortunately, all the siblings that followed did survive. First, there were my three younger brothers, Victor Ocitti, Jimmy Komakech and Johnbusco Peter, followed by my sister, Janneth Akech.

The Acholi tribe is divided into many clans and the clan I was born into was called Atuo. A long time ago, when Acholiland was still divided into chiefdoms, our clan was a royal clan within the Koc chiefdom. My father always told me that I was in line to become the next clan chief. Although everyone in our clan was a Christian, there were still remnants of our old religion, which some people continued to adhere to. For example, our clan had a clan goat. This goat was chosen by the clan to be our protector. When there was no rain for a long time, we would blame the goat. And when the rain came, we would praise the goat. This was a remnant of the old religion and the old traditions that were common in this land long before the white men came to bring Christianity.

The village was an extended one. This meant that everybody in the village was related. My uncle was my immediate neighbour, and the hut next to him belonged to my aunt. When my grandfather was still alive, his hut stood in the middle the village, but in 1995 this hut belonged to us. The families in Uganda are usually very big, and although everyone in my village was family, it was certainly not a small village, as there were a few hundred people living there. In Acholi culture, the men were supposed to only marry women from other villages and other clans. The land that surrounded the village belonged to everybody. We all sowed the seeds together and we shared the harvest. Money was not a factor in our village; it barely existed. Much more was done by trade and sharing. Only when some of the women went to the markets of Gulu or other towns would they sometimes return with money. The village was a thirty-minute walk to the main road that led to Gulu, which was another six hours from there.

I remember my early childhood as a happy time. Although the rebellion started not long after my birth, the first few years of the war were not too bad for us. Since our new president Yoweri Museveni came to power, we heard stories about violence committed by government soldiers. My dad sometimes talked with his neighbours about the terrible acts of slaughter that occurred in Namokora and many other places. We also heard about the many acts of theft, arrests and public torture. Because of this, my father warned me to stay far away from any men carrying guns or dressed in uniforms. But while this violence was unfolding in other parts in Acholi, none of it reached our village in the first few years of the war. The battles were often located far away from us, even up to Jinja, near the capital Kampala, and the rebel armies of that time didn't terrorise the local population that much. Life pretty much proceeded the way it had for hundreds of years in these regions.

As my family worked on the fields, I was mostly preoccupied with babysitting and playing games with my friends. We used to play all kinds of games. One of these games involved making music together. The percussion was always my favourite. We often went swimming – not that there was a river nearby. The stream was too small to swim in, but there was a pond where we would let our cattle drink. I went to this place very often to swim with my friends. The game that I played most, however, was football. We always made a football out of rubbish and banana leaves, and we improvised a goal. When this was done, all the children of my village would be divided in two teams and then we started to play. There was nothing organised about these games: no set lines, no timeframe, and the teams were rarely equal. Often it was impossible to tell which team had won, because all the kids, including me, constantly shifted to the team that had the ball. Yet on the few occasions that we could decide who the winning team was, I was extremely delighted if I belonged to it.

Hunting birds and edible rats was another favourite pastime. We made our own slingshots and catapults, which we used to kill our prey. The interesting thing about hunting was that you never knew what the day would bring. You never knew what you would catch, or if you would come home empty-handed. Sometimes we would take the dog with us. We had one dog in our home, both for hunting and protection, although for the latter he was not very good. When the dog saw a squirrel, he would hunt it, and we would run after the dog. For hunting the birds, we mainly used the slingers and catapults, but for the edible rats, we also used spears, and bows and arrows.

Still, the memories that I cherish most are the times that I went with my father to herd the cows. Whenever I grew tired of walking, my father would put me on the back of one of his cows. These were truly happy times. On the back of the cow I felt like a god, overlooking the bush on a mighty animal. Nowadays you see the cows again, but for a long time cows were absent from northern Uganda because of the war. It was mostly the government and raiders from neighbouring Karamojong who took them.

The cows occupied a central place in Acholi culture – they were a kind of currency. Whenever there was a conflict, a council of village elders would bring the two conflicting sides together, and in case of a fine, the loser had to pay it in cows. Dowries were also paid with cows and goats. Without the cows, there would be no marriages and no new generations of Acholi youth. Cows were also the primary means of trade, but as the war progressed, the cows slowly disappeared from the northern landscape due to cattle raids. With their disappearance, many aspects of Acholi culture dissolved, as people could no longer marry, settle disputes or trade in our traditional ways. I had the feeling that with the disappearance of the cows from the northern landscapes, our natural Acholi happiness also disappeared.

For us, our happiness also started to fade when they took away all our cows in a single event that happened while the web of the war was stretching and entangling us and our ways of life. While the disaster that occurred was certainly related to the war, it had a much older origin, one that was very common in Africa for as long as people could remember.

It happened when I was just five years old, I think during the dry season, because I remember that this specific day was very hot and in some places the grass had turned completely yellow. My father had gone to the gardens to work on the land and my mother and I had stayed behind to do some domestic work. Not long after my father left, we saw a big group of men appear from the bushes. I will never forget this moment because some of these men were naked apart from the rifles or clubs they were carrying. I had never seen such a sight before. Those who were not naked wore purple robes. The men talked to each other in very loud voices, but I didn't understand a single word of what they were saying. It was obvious that these men weren't from the Acholi tribe or any tribes related to the Acholi.

Although I had never seen one before, I immediately recognised these men to be Karamojong, highly feared cattle warriors.
My uncle used to tell me stories about them. About how they
purely lived on the blood and milk of cows and never ate anything.
Every day, the Karamojong would make a small cut in the veins of
a cow, from which they would tap the blood. The combination of
milk and blood was not only nutritious enough to keep them alive,
it also made them grow very tall. They would only slaughter a cow
on very special occasions. My uncle further told me that the
Karamojong had a very strange religion. He told me that they
believed deeply that all cows in the world belonged to them. In the
beginning of time, God had given them all the cows, and since that
time, many other tribes had stolen the cows away from them. So,
whenever the Karamojong set out to go on a huge cattle raid, they
were, in their opinion, not stealing any cows, but merely reclaim-
ing them. This unwarranted belief, in addition to their large stocks
of AK-47s, which some said were given to them by the government
to oppress the Acholi people, made them the most notorious cattle
raiders of the entire region.

As I saw the Karamojong coming from the bush, I knew we
were in big trouble. True to their reputation, they immediately
proceeded towards our cattle, ignoring us. As they were opening
the fences to release the cows, my father came running from his
garden and he started to argue with the Karamojong, who didn't
pay the slightest attention to what my father had to say. My mother
and I were in our hut, watching from a distance. I was really afraid
they would kill my father, and I only hoped that he would give up
and surrender the cows. After only two minutes the Karamojong
grew tired of my father's pleas and they knocked him to the ground
with a club. Then they tied him up and put a strap in his mouth so

that he couldn't say anything else. After that, there was nothing to stop them stealing the cows.

I was too afraid to do anything. It was obvious that the Karamojong were in no rush. They took their time to lead all the cows out of the fenced area where my father and I had put them the day before. After they were done, they entered our hut, where my mother and I were shivering in fear, but they never even touched us. They came in, stole some pots, pans and flour, and afterwards left towards the east, where I had been told their homeland was. We never saw them, or our cows, again. As soon as they left, we went to my father and untied him. Although his face was only bleeding a little bit, we could see from his body language that he was deeply wounded. Not because he was hit on his head, but because he had just seen all his wealth stolen from him. The Karamojong had taken away not only his wealth, but also his pride and status while he was lying half-conscious on the ground, unable to do anything to stop them.

Cattle raids were as old as the tribes of Africa, and although it was a cruel practice, it was part of our culture. Although the Karamojong were the most notorious, they were not the only tribe guilty of cattle raiding. Like most tribes, the Acholi had also been active in stealing other people's cattle. In the past, raiding cattle was one of the ways in which the men could show their masculinity and, in some tribes, stealing cattle was even used as an initiation rite for the young men. Up to this moment I had only heard stories of cattle raids and I always listened to them with great interest. The stories almost reflected a romantic picture of bravery and cunning. Never had I realised the huge impact it had on the bereft.

After this event, our lives changed. We used to be among the wealthiest of my village, but as we lost over two thirds of everything we possessed, we also lost our opportunity to flee the war zone while we still could. We were, of course, not unique in this. Other members of our village also lost everything, and my father sometimes told me that what was happening in the rest of Acholi was the greatest theft of Ugandan history, mostly perpetrated by the Karamojong cattle raiders, and the government who allowed them to roam free.

Eventually, the raiding of our cattle and our loss of wealth would have a great consequence on my life, but for now I only noticed the little things that changed. My father didn't laugh as much as he used to; we had to live with less food, and we rarely had any meat on the menu. I also played less with my friends, since my father forced me to help him in the field much more often. This and the events that followed robbed me of my life's joys.

It was not until 1990, three years after we lost our cattle, that our lives were really ruined. The end of all happiness began when the Lord's Resistance Army paid a visit to our village. The rebels came in the morning hours. While my mother was grinding the sorghum, a local grain that we used to make bread, my father and I went to the bush near our house to chop down some trees because we needed a new plot for our crops. Just as my father started hacking down a tree, we saw a young man come running from the bush while being chased by two soldiers who were carrying machetes.

From where we were, we saw the man running towards our hut, which he bypassed. The man was a distant relative from another village. The moment my father saw what was happening, he grabbed his axe and took off to chase the hunters. My father could not let a boy from our neighbouring village be hacked to death. While my father was chasing the two hunters, a bodyguard from the local council saw this whole ordeal happening from the side of the papyrus. As one of the few people in our village carrying a gun, he started shooting at my father, whom he had mistaken for a rebel. I watched as the bullets flew over my father's head. Almost an entire magazine was fired at my father, but luckily the guard was one of the poorest marksmen I had ever seen.

While the guard was shooting, the rebels entered our village from the east and shot that guard. Only one bullet struck him, but it hit him straight in the face. As I saw his brains being splattered over the papyrus behind him, I started feeling sorry for the man who had almost murdered my father. It all happened so fast. Before I knew it, the village was surrounded and the rebels disarmed my father, taking the axe away from him and holding him down at gunpoint. I never found out what happened to the young man they were chasing; I never saw him again.

I just stood there, nailed to the ground, not able to run anywhere. I was simply looking. From our hut my mum was screaming at me: 'What is happening, Norman? Who are these people? What do they want from us?'

I wanted to reply but I couldn't find the words.

I was standing there in shock, totally traumatised. My mother kept on screaming, but I was unable to answer. My younger sister, whom I carried with me all this time, stood beside me and grabbed my hand. Apart from this sign of life, she looked like she had been dead for several years. While my mother was still screaming at me, a soldier came to the hut she was in and ordered my mother out of there.

'Come out of the house right now! I will give you only one second and then I will light the house on fire with you in it, I kid you not,' he screamed.

My mother didn't take anything, not even the second that the man had given her. She immediately came out of our house. We all stood there, paralysed by fear, watching the village as the chaos was unfolding. On my left, I still saw the guard, whose brains were seeping out of his head, visible from even twenty metres away. All around me, I saw more rebels coming from the bush. They were entering the houses to force everybody out. After all the people were out, we were told to go to our grandfather's house. That was the main house, the biggest house of the village. When we arrived there after a two-minute walk, we found our grandfather in deep shock like the rest of us. After the rebels had assembled us, they started shouting the new rules to us.

'Why are you supporting the government? Why are you listening to your pathetic local councils? From now on we are in charge. Remember that. WE ARE THE LAW. You shall listen and you shall abide. From now on the local councils will be banished and all local leaders will be shot. Bicycles will also be forbidden. Anyone we see on a bicycle will lose their legs. If you have to go somewhere, go by foot. Any household that has a dog will be executed. We don't want to see a dog ever again in this country. As a token of our goodwill, we will not execute you today. Today it is just your village that will burn. But as you see your houses burning, remember that next time it will be your own flesh if you do not abide by our laws.'

After they had assembled us and told us all their rules, they started setting fire to our houses. Not a single one was spared. After the soldiers were done burning everything down, they grabbed our remaining goats, our sorghum and all the chickens, and took off. Just like that. I remember that we remained seated, unable to move. Everyone was in shock. Soon after the rebels had left, my grandfather spoke. He told us that we shouldn't remain in the village as the rebels could still return and carry out their threat to burn us alive. He said, 'We have seen what they are capable of; they might come back and do us even more harm. We should leave this village and hide.'

Everybody concurred, and after the sun went down we started to move with everybody from the extended family. We all moved to another village, not very far away from ours, but we never entered it. We decided to stay hidden in the papyrus. Then we saw the soldiers coming to that other village. It was as if we had taken the same route as the rebels. Immediately, when the villagers saw the rebels coming, the youth took off. They ran straight to the papyrus where we were hiding, giving away our position to the rebels. As some young men passed me, running for their lives, I also took off. Along with a friend, we followed the young men from the other village, not even sure why we were running and not aware that we were being followed by some rebels. I only became aware of this when the rebels knocked me down as they continued to follow those boys from the village. It was clear that they were not after me or my friend. So we stood up and decided to walk back to our families. When we came back, we saw that the soldiers had surrounded all the older people and they were questioning them. After a few minutes the soldiers who were chasing me and my friend came back, dragging one young man from the village behind him. They started to beat him seriously. The rebels also found a woman from that village who was hiding in the bushes and also started beating her like nothing I had ever seen before. Although they didn't hurt anybody from my village, the message was clear: from this time onwards, we would never be safe again.

After this terrible night, everything changed. All the people from my village started to send their children to town with the little wealth that they still possessed. But we possessed nothing. The rebels and the Karamojong had taken everything we ever had.

As I saw all my friends disappearing to the towns, it became very lonely for me. Only a few children stayed behind, but even with them I could no longer play the games that I used to play. Nothing remained the same. We were not allowed to make any noise any more during the whole day, every day. I wanted to play with my friends, but our parents had decided that the children should always be close to them, and not play with each other, because together we would make noise and wander off.

Because the rebels burned our house, we lost absolutely everything, including all our clothes; we only had what we were wearing. The days after the rebels paid a visit to our village, my father fixed the thatched roof again. In the meantime, we were sleeping in our hut, but under the open sky. At night we were always fighting the cold. In the months that followed, we gathered some extra clothes and blankets, gifts from people from neighbouring villages. Sometimes we would receive them out of charity, other times we would trade them for some food that still remained growing on our garden plots.

The rebels had made it clear. They meant business when they told us not to support the government and that their laws would be enforced with total terror. Everyone lived in fear and the rebels lost what little sympathy they had from the local population. This is also around the time when the rumours started to spread like wildfires throughout Acholiland. We heard the most terrifying tales of absolute brutality. We heard many stories of children being abducted and made to kill their loved ones. We even heard stories of mothers who were forced to boil their own offspring and eat them. Similar stories came from schools, where the rebels had surrounded a school, boiled the teacher, and ordered the students to eat the teacher. These stories were rumours that travelled from mouth to mouth, so it was hard to establish the truth. However, as the rumours kept on piling up, we all got scared. Some stories came to us from people who were abducted but managed to escape. They told the most horrifying accounts of the killings, the long walks and the camps in Sudan. I really didn't understand what was happening. Sometimes I wondered if I was still alive or had already died and gone to hell. This event, the burning of our village, really was the turning point in my life. After this we heard no more laughter in my village; all happiness had disappeared. Life passed in complete silence as we tried not to attract any attention.

The rebels became omnipresent in our region. I started to see them every week. Whenever I saw them, I would try to hide or to run away. But they didn't really seem interested in me. I still tried to go to school, but even that was becoming more dangerous, as my school was very far away and I always had to walk there. The stories about forced cannibalism really discouraged us from going to school, but still many pupils were attending. We were eager to learn and receive an education. That is, until the day that the rebels paid our school a visit. That day we were in class and we were singing a song in Acholi. The song was about how sending pupils to school would help our world develop. While we were singing, we saw the soldiers coming from the bush with their pangas.* All the children started screaming, 'Teacher, teacher; the soldiers are coming; the soldiers are coming!'

We all started running towards the one door, which was our only escape route. Even the teachers were running and pushing the

---

* A common word to describe a machete.

children aside. Some of my classmates fell at the doorstep, causing us all to get stuck in the doorway as everybody tried to push their way out. The next moment the head teacher came and pulled us out. We all started running. I never saw what happened to our school or my classmates. I just ran for several kilometres until my legs couldn't take me any further. After that, I never went back to that school.

About a year after the rebels of the Lord's Resistance Army paid that life-changing visit to our village, we received another visit from them. By this time, we had rebuilt our village, putting new thatched roofs on the huts so we no longer had to fight the cold at night. The rebels came in the middle of the night, when we were all sleeping. My uncle, my cousin and my auntie were also sleeping in our hut. They came to our hut and knocked on the door very loudly. They told us all to come out. I was sure that this time the rebels had come to kill me, or even worse, force me to kill my parents. My parents, auntie and uncle immediately came out, while my cousin and I were hiding in a dark corner of the hut. Luckily, the rebels never entered. They told my family that they needed a guide to take them to the next sub-county, and my auntie, to protect me and her son, immediately volunteered to guide them, just to get the rebels away from the hut we were hiding in as soon as possible. We never saw her again.

It was after that night that my father sat down to have a conversation with me. He was very sorry that he couldn't take me to town, like so many other parents were doing. He explained that he had no money to take me, or to feed or shelter me there. Since we didn't have family in town, I would starve to death if he sent me there. I could see despair on my father's face as he was telling me this; he felt so guilty. This is what he told me next: 'From now on, you are going to sleep in the bush. You will only sleep in the tall grass or in the bush, at least one kilometre away from the village. During the daytime you will hide, and you will be quiet. You will never let your presence be known. Only if we call you can you come out of hiding. Don't listen to any strange voices telling you something, only to ours.

Every time I heard something moving in the bush, I would freeze in terror. The smallest sound could totally paralyse me. From this time onwards, every day brought the same routine. My life, once so interesting, had evaporated into a life dominated by fear and boredom. There was no more joy. For the next few years, every night I would go to the bushes. In the rainy season I had to battle the cold, and in the dry season I had to be careful not to get caught in wildfires. My life became really miserable, but at least I managed to stay out of the hands of the rebels, until that fatal New Year's Day in 1995.

Writing My Name

I still felt the pain of leaving my father without even saying good-bye, as the two younger rebels were dragging us to yet another assembly spot. Once we got there, the commander ordered them to bind us to a tree and began to speak.

'We will take you with us and train you so that you'll become hardened soldiers. But I have some good news for one of you. To show that I still have some compassion in me, one of the three of you will be released, and it is up to you to decide who.'

At this point, my cousin, Francis and I looked at each other. I was really wondering if this was another one of his tricks. He asked us again: 'So, which of you wants to be released?'

There was only silence.

'If you don't want to be released, we can take all three of you.'

I was really wondering whether he was sincere, or whether he was just testing us. I thought that if I spoke right now, there was a chance that I would be executed. I knew that those who unsuccessfully tried to escape from the movement were always killed. Yet at the same time, if the commander meant what he said, now was the best and probably only opportunity to escape the brutal fate that lay ahead of me. I don't know where I got the nerve from, but I was the first of the three of us to speak. With a trembling voice I told the commander that my cousin and I were brothers and that for the sake of our parents he couldn't take both of us.

'Please, sir, you can't take both of us. Our parents need us on the fields, to help with the harvest and sowing of the crops. They can't live without both of us. Please, sir, I beg you . . .'

The moment I had said this, the commander stopped smiling and looked me deep in the eye, as if he was extremely angry. I was convinced that I had walked into a further ambush, albeit one that was psychological in nature. As the commander looked at me, I was convinced that he would draw his pistol any time now and shoot me on the spot. For half a minute, which felt like a lifetime, he looked into my eyes. Then he started to laugh as he told another rebel to release my cousin.

'So, all of a sudden you two are brothers, are you? We really need to work on that lying character of yours!'

Relief went through my body as I realised I would not be killed. But it was immediately followed by a feeling of sadness when I understood that the release of my cousin meant that I would still be taken and that I hadn't escaped my fate. Don't get me wrong: up to this day I am really happy that my cousin escaped the dreadful years that I went through, but like any other kid in that situation, I had silently hoped the commander would release me instead. Still, I knew that this was for the best. My cousin's mental problems meant they could never make a proper soldier out of him. I knew that if they took him instead of me, he wouldn't even last a day. The commander probably also realised this, and I suspect he had decided to release my cousin long before he asked the question. It was indeed a test. The commander gave us some time to say goodbye, and afterwards my cousin was untied. They gave him some food to make up for his beating and to keep him quiet, and afterwards they took him back to the other assembly point.

My cousin left as night was beginning to fall. In the meantime, Francis and I lay there tied up to a big mango tree. At around eight o'clock five rebels came. They untied Francis and dragged him away. I was told to get some sleep. Only minutes later I heard screams. Terrifying, bone-shattering screams. Although I was unable to see him, I knew what was happening to Francis as I heard sticks batter down on him. After a while he stopped scream-ing, and this frightened me even more. I anxiously tried to see what was happening, but the mango tree completely blocked my sight. Something told me that I would be next. I was waiting for them to start dragging me away, but they never did. That whole night I didn't close even one eye; I was so afraid.

My body was still aching from the beating I had received during the day, and they had tied me up so tight that I had trouble breath-ing. As it got darker, the rebels all went to their positions. Some of them put up small tents in which they went to sleep, while others went to the guarding posts where they would stay awake all night. I still couldn't believe their numbers; there were so many of them. Actually, I couldn't even believe that all this was happening to me at all. I was still hoping I would wake from this terrible dream.

That night was awfully quiet. They never brought Francis back, so I had no idea if he had survived his beating. Never had I ex-perienced a night that passed as slowly as this one, but eventually, like every other night before and after, the world made its round and the morning came. Even before the sun appeared in the sky, everywhere around me the rebels started to wake up. I saw the commander walking towards me. It was clear that he was coming for me. That is when he told me the news: 'Today, boy, today we are going to write your name.'

So there I was. From the corner of my eye I looked at the man who I considered to be my own personal nemesis. He was very tall and muscular. The moment he came to me, he ordered some boys to collect something in the bush. Afterwards he turned his attention to me. I still didn't dare to look him straight in the eye. I was waiting for him to take out his notebook and pen to write my name, but he never did. At this point, I still thought that the writing of the name would happen with pen and paper, but that couldn't have been farther from the truth. Only minutes later, the two boys returned with a lot of branches. They were told to untie me, and afterwards the writing of the name began. I honestly hadn't realised that writing my name would mean that I would be beaten almost to death. I had to lie down with my face towards the ground. The commander told me that this would teach me to never try to escape. Then, the order came: 'HIT HIM. HIT HIM LIKE YOU NEVER HIT ANYONE BEFORE AND DON'T STOP UNTIL I SAY SO!'

The three boys started to cane me ferociously. Never in my life had I felt so much pain. I think they gave me more than 120 strokes each, using long, bamboo-like sticks. The boys hit me as hard as they possibly could and just didn't stop. They kept on beating me and beating me. After a while, there was no place on my body left untouched by those dreaded sticks, but still they continued to beat me. Once on my buttocks, twice on my buttocks, then another time and another time and another time! I sincerely thought I was going to die, a feeling that would come back to me several times in the years to come.

After the beating had continued for more than five minutes, my body went numb. Although I still saw them hitting me, I didn't feel the pain any more. I saw the mouth of the commander move, probably to scream orders that they should hit me even harder, but I did not hear a single sound. It was like I was in a terrible dream from which I was unable to wake. Then I lost consciousness.

When I came to, I noticed that the rebels had stopped hitting me. Nonetheless I felt terrible pain. I couldn't sit because they had caned my buttocks; I couldn't lie down because they'd caned my back; and I couldn't stand or walk because they'd caned my legs and feet. I couldn't even grab hold of anything because they'd caned my arms and my hands. My whole body was covered with blood, and in most areas my flesh had burst open and deep wounds were visible everywhere. Apparently, these open wounds provided a feast for the flies: I was covered with these crawling and itching insects. But weak as I was, I didn't even have the strength to chase them away. I was sure that if no one treated these wounds soon, they would get infected and I would die.

After the beating was over, the commander ordered another rebel to take care of me and to attend to my wounds. He lifted me up and carried me to a tree, where he literally threw me in its shade. He boiled some water and afterwards he started to clean my wounds with hard strokes and a piece of dusty cloth drenched in hot water. Every time he even touched my body, I had the feeling I could melt into the earth, so excruciating was the pain. The boy told me his name was Gabriel, and that most of the rebels captured by this commander had undergone this treatment. He told me that if I survived, I would be taken into the rebel movement. *If I survive.* I had nearly been beaten to death, yet I lived. The casual way Gabriel said 'If you survive' scared me. At that point, I was more dead than alive, and my survival was not guaranteed. Gabriel told me that the writing of the name determined if one would live or be killed. Those who endured the beatings in stoic silence proved to be strong and ready to take on a rebel's life. I feared the worst for Francis, as he had screamed like a pig.

The boy told me that the commander had been very impressed with me. During my whole beating I hadn't screamed once; I hadn't even cried. I was probably too afraid. Honestly, I couldn't really remember anything of my own behaviour during the beating. I only remembered the pain. At that time, I didn't care about what the commander thought of me or even what positive repercussions his liking me might have. I just wanted to go home to my mum and dad.

The whole of the next day we stayed put. Only a few hours after the beating my body began to swell, causing me even more pain, which repeatedly caused me to lose consciousness, only to regain it minutes or maybe even hours later. In the moments that I was conscious, my mind dwelt upon my family. I wondered what would happen to my father. There was no way of knowing if the rebels would kill the entire village, or if they would let us be. I also wondered what had happened to my mother and siblings, who were supposed to return the evening before, but would have found our village empty. What would my mother do? Would she start looking for us in the papyrus? Would she start screaming our names and be captured herself? What would the rebels do with my father and all the other relatives who were at their mercy? Then my thoughts moved to my own immediate future. What on earth would happen to me? Would I also be taken to Sudan, where innocent children were turned into monsters? I didn't know. Somehow, I didn't want to think of what was ahead of me, because with every minute that passed, I had more difficulty imagining a happy ending.

In the evening one of the rebel girls gave me some food. She looked at me with contempt and told me that I had to eat separately because my body was filthy, and my soul was still unclean and unholy. The rebels never saw themselves as the mindless killers they were. They always referred to themselves as 'holies'. They were the holy warriors of the Lord, with the goal to liberate Uganda from its tyrannical and ungodly rule. Around me I heard the rebels talking about how they would overthrow the Ugandan government. This was the mission that God himself had given Joseph Kony. They said that the leader of the rebels stood in direct contact with the Almighty. The rebel girl, who wasn't much older than I was, shuffled some food in my direction and gave me my orders. I was supposed to eat this away from the others, I wasn't supposed to look at people and I was not allowed to talk to anyone, not a single word, at least not until I was initiated. That word, initiation, brought terror to my heart.

The next day, early in the morning, the commander gave everybody the order to move out. Afterwards the commander came to me and he told me to say goodbye to my father because I would never see him again.

'You didn't honestly think that your lies could fool us, did you? But you don't need to worry; we already wrote your name. This means that you are one of us now. We won't kill your father.'

The commander ordered two soldiers to escort me to my father. At this point I still couldn't walk, so I really needed them to support me, which they did. My father was still at the assembly point where we had been separated. The moment he looked at my battered face, tears sprang into his eyes. He stood up and wanted to run towards me, probably with the intent to hurt the rebels who were supporting me, but luckily, other relatives constrained him. As I was brought in front of him, I could no longer stop my tears from flowing over my cheeks. This time I knew that I would never see him again.

'Dad, I am leaving now and I don't think I will be back. Give my love to Mum and my brothers and sisters. I love you.'

Afterwards I stumbled towards my dad with my own strength and gave him a hug and a kiss. We were both crying our eyes out, and at this point I never wanted to let go. Yet the rebels who had been supporting me wouldn't let us. Our hug lasted only a few seconds, after which those evil demons pulled us apart.

'Bye now, Daddy. I will miss you.'

At that point my father turned mad. It took four of our relatives to restrain him. He started to scream at the rebel commander, who was watching this whole drama from a distance.

'Why don't you take me? This boy is way too young to be a soldier. Please take me and I will become the hardest-working soldier you've ever had.'

The commander looked at him without saying anything. Our relatives had great difficulty constraining my father, who was really struggling to get loose.

'Don't you hear me, damnit? Take me. This boy that you are taking, my son, is very stubborn, lazy and very weak. You should take me. I swear I will do everything you tell me. I won't disappoint you.'

In the meantime, they started to drag me away. As the distance between my father and me grew, his voice became less audible. But he continued to scream until I was well out of sight and until the wind could no longer carry his words far enough for me to hear them. One of the last things that I heard him screaming was that I should be brave, and that he would be awaiting my return, no matter how long it would take. When I could no longer see or hear my father, I stopped crying. I knew that I had entered a new phase in my life, and the only thing I could do was to take my father's advice to my heart. I had to be brave, otherwise I would not survive.

My two escorts were discussing that they had stayed on the same spot for too long, and that even though they had managed to grandly defeat the NRA only two days before, they would be back, and this time well-armed and supported by tanks, mambas,* gun-ships and even aeroplanes. Suddenly I realised that the NRA – which I had regarded as my saviour only two days earlier – was now my enemy. Once again, the cursed war had brought me to a dramatic crossroads in my life. Things would never be the same again. Gabriel, the boy who had tended my wounds the day before, was one of the boys who had been ordered to help me move. I put my arms over their shoulders while my legs dragged behind me. This clearly annoyed the boys.

'Boy, we might have been ordered to take care of you, but that does not mean that you are untouchable. If you don't start walking, we will leave you here for the blocking force, who will make you rest for ever!'

I knew that they meant what they said, so I really tried to walk. While I was moving, some of the dried-up wounds on my body cracked open and the blood started flowing again, attracting the disgusting flies. Although I was in excruciating pain, I had to keep up. Although I managed to walk a little bit, I had a lot of trouble moving my legs. But my escorts weren't interested in excuses. If I

---

* A South African armoured personnel carier (APC), usually mounted with a heavy machine gun.

delayed them too much, they would leave me behind and I would be shot. Those were the rules, clear and simple.

Luckily, we did not move very far that day. We only moved for about two to three hours, after which we got some more rest. By LRA standards, this was not really marching, but for me it felt like hell. I tried so hard to keep the pace, but I simply couldn't. I knew if I lagged behind too much I would be killed, so whenever I noticed that Gabriel and his companion started to become agitated, I tried extra hard to follow their pace. Yet I couldn't help delaying them. I could see the pure anger in Gabriel's eyes. He was ready to kill me. At a certain point two rebels came up to us and told Gabriel that I was pretending and that he should let me be, so that I would be shot. The boys actually started having a serious discussion about whether they should shoot me or if I should live. They were discussing this while I was only half a metre away from them, like I was some kind of cattle, unable to say anything while my fate was being sealed.

To my surprise, Gabriel came to my defence, as he was specifically ordered by the commander to take good care of me, and he would get a severe beating if I died on his watch. This didn't mean that we were friends, but it did save my life that day. I soon found out that in the LRA you didn't have any friends, only colleagues. Of course, there were people I liked and had cordial relations with; however, there were none I trusted with my secrets. I think that Gabriel detested me and that he would have rather killed me there and then than support me another step further, but like everybody else, he was afraid of the commander and he couldn't ignore a direct order.

After several hours of walking we had our first break. I asked Gabriel if I could please have some water to tend my wounds and he gave it to me. By now, almost all my dried-up wounds had cracked open and I was bleeding from all sides. The only thing I could do was to clean them with water.

After an hour's rest, we started moving again. Every step was hurting me. Gabriel had grown tired of me and he had asked the commander to be transferred to the advance group. This was the group scouting the terrain before the main body arrived. The LRA always moved in three groups. The front group would scout the area for any ambushes. The main group, which contained the majority of the soldiers, the commanders and the artillery, would follow. And lastly, the blocking force would come. They would guard the rear from any attacks and also kill the soldiers who weren't able to walk any more. The commander granted Gabriel's request and so I was left alone with the other soldier.

Without two people supporting me, it was very difficult to keep up. Sometimes, and little by little, I would fall behind. It didn't take very long before my escort grew tired of me and decided to leave me there. Then things really got tough. I had to walk on my own now and I could only do so by ignoring the pain. There was one voice in my head telling me to give up, but my will to live was too strong. I just carried on, ignoring the terrible pain. Whenever I lagged too far behind, someone would come to my aid and support me. I remember one boy who begged me to walk faster as he pushed me ahead. Most rebels, however, were passing me, leaving me to be killed by the blocking force. The only reason why I survived the first two days was because we didn't move very far.

Miraculously, after three days my wounds had already started to heal. Although the pain had not disappeared entirely, it was a lot less severe, and I could manage to walk on my own again. I hadn't seen Francis again, so I assumed that he was killed that evening when I heard his terrifying screams, although he might also have been in the blocking force or the advance party. Every evening I had to eat the rebels' leftovers, which I ate in isolation while under close guard. The rules that the rebel girl had told me still applied. I wasn't allowed to talk to anyone, eat with anyone or look anyone in the eye. Every day my thoughts focused upon my family. How were they doing? What were they doing to get me out of this hell? The more I thought about this last question, the more I realised that there was nothing that they could do. I was really left to fend for myself. The time had come to grow up.

Although I didn't notice it, the commander had watched me closely during these days and at the sight of my quick recovery, he decided that I was ready for the initiation process. In his eyes, I had proved to be strong enough to receive the honour of joining the holy ranks of the blessed warriors of God. On the morning of the fourth day, the commander told me that I would be baptised and that I would join the ranks of the holy warriors. Although I was happy that I would move up in rank, it was the word baptism that sent shivers up my spine. After I had found out that writing my name happened with huge sticks battering down on my body, I didn't trust anything they told me, especially if it involved some kind of ritual. I knew what a baptism was, but I was not sure if it meant the same thing for the rebels. For all I knew, it could mean that they would drown me in the River Nile. I was pleasantly surprised when it turned out to be very much like a normal baptism.

There were two small bottles. One was filled with holy water, which had been blessed by Kony himself and came straight out of Sudan. The other bottle was filled with holy shea oil, which they told me would prevent bullets from hitting me. The ritual was carried out by the commander himself and two altar boys, who were senior warriors and the personal guards of the commander. The boys were standing behind the commander; one was holding the water and the other the oil. They first started sprinkling the holy water on to me. Afterwards, the commander dipped his finger in the shea oil, and he started to make crosses on my body. First on my forehead, then the palms of my hands, my feet and my back. Then he drew a big heart on my chest. The last thing I had to do was to swallow a sip of the holy water. I imagined it was poisoned, but for really old water, it actually tasted quite nice. Then the commander spoke some blessings and suddenly my position within the rebel army changed. From that day onwards, I was no longer unclean, and I didn't need to eat separately from the rest. I was allowed to talk with others, although I didn't feel the urge.

I was baptised while the rest of the rebels surrounding us were cooking. When the ceremony was over, most of the cooking was done and I was invited to join some boys to eat. It felt good to be one of the holies. Since I had made an impression on the commander, he chose me to be his first escort. The commander was one of the few people who had joined the LRA voluntarily, and due to his good conduct, he was given the rank of captain. His specialty was the artillery department. As I became his first servant, he started to reveal the trade secrets of the artillery to me. Although my official training was still to come, he gave me preliminary training while we were marching from one place to the other. He was very loyal to the LRA and educated in the ways of the rebels, but he didn't like training people too much. He told me what to do. Duck! Run! Cover! He explained to me how to load and unload a gun, and how to take it apart and put it back together again, but he would only tell me things twice. Whenever he had to tell me something for the third time, he would slap me in the face really hard.

Whenever we were on the move, I would be right behind him. I always had to carry his load. His blanket, his tent, his gun and, most importantly, his chair. I had to make sure that whenever he sat down, the chair was ready. He never told me when or where he would sit down – I just had to guess. Whenever he sat down and the chair wasn't ready or if I had put it at the wrong spot, he would slap me. Whenever he went in the bushes for a long call, which we say when someone has to take a shit, I had to stand close to him, holding his gun in case of any attack. Only when he was in a meeting with other commanders did I leave his side, because I was not allowed to hear what was discussed in those meetings.

For two months we stayed in Uganda, attacking small, harmless villages and abducting children who were completely paralysed by fear, as I had been. Although I wasn't yet given a gun and most of the fighting was done by the advance force, I did witness some of the horror that we unleashed upon the local populations. I remember the day when we carried out an attack on a small trading centre, I think it was called Kamoro. It was a market day. We carried out our attack late in the morning, at around 11 a.m., which was almost the busiest time of the day. We burned down all the houses and captured many people. That day we didn't take any prisoners. The people we caught in their houses were locked in and left there to burn, while the ones we captured on the streets were shot. That was the first time I saw so many people being killed.

Back in those days, killing people was so common. Kony had set a law that there should be no crossing of the road. Anyone we caught crossing the road was killed, often by the most horrible means. Another law was that people were not supposed to work or move on a Friday. Thus, if we caught you crossing the road, you would be killed. If we caught you doing anything on a Friday, you would be killed. If you were even lying beside the road, you would be killed. Many people were killed in those days. Also, when we caught the local leaders, we would kill them because they had direct ties to the government. I remember one day when we found a local leader. We started beating him thoroughly. At a certain point, when the rebels had enough of bullying him, they cut off his hands. The boy who had encouraged me only a few weeks earlier to move faster, one of the people I owed my life to, placed the man's hands on a huge log, while another hacked them off with an axe. That poor old man. I saw how he was crying. Because of his tears, my new colleagues also cut off his feet, again using the axe. Before he bled to death, the commander ordered some holies to cut off his head using the same axe again. We had killed him as if he wasn't even human. I had seen animals being butchered with a lot more respect. The level of brutality we used on this man was sheer evil. I pitied his soul.

A few days later, I saw them put a bayonet in the throat of a young man. It was a Friday and we caught the young man working in the garden, probably to harvest the crops so that his children could eat. That was his crime. Blood was spraying out, as they had hit an artery. It was a terrible sight. At night, I saw the man again. While they were pushing him around, I saw that it was no longer him but me. Slowly I looked at myself as they stuck a bayonet in my throat. Then I woke up, drenched in sweat. Silently I hoped I would grow stronger so that I could bear these sights without being so frightened and traumatised. My life in the daytime was difficult enough as it was; I didn't need my nights to become equally gruesome.

As we moved on and carried out more attacks, we grew richer and richer. Besides setting up the chair, plundering became another one of my main tasks. Whenever the advance party had exterminated a village, I came in to take away all the valuables and all the food. I would always see the dead bodies lying around. The plundered goods that I had to carry were getting heavier, but I was also growing stronger as I was well fed and had recovered from my beating. The stronger I grew, the more confident I became that I might get an opportunity to escape very soon. This thought gave me a lot of courage and strength. But as with everything else in my life, this hope did not last. I had been with the rebels for two months when all my hopes of escape vanished.

Part II
Becoming a Soldier

Death March

Although I had suffered a lot during the two months that I was with the LRA in Uganda, it was nothing compared to what was about to unfold. I was slowly getting used to the hardships, like the killings and the marching, but none of these had prepared me for my first march to Sudan.

This march was something else. For four days we walked almost non-stop. Only on a few occasions did we rest, but never longer than half an hour. On the second day I got blisters on my feet and on the fourth day my feet even started to swell up. But there were no excuses. If you stopped, you would be killed. What made it even worse was that we completely ran out of water and food. My mouth was so dry that I couldn't even swallow any more, and my stomach ached from the hunger. All around me I saw people collapsing and dying. They fell down, unable to move, unable even to cry for help. I knew that I was also close to my end. I couldn't bear this much longer.

The march started somewhere on the border of Kitgum and Gulu District, close to the Achwa River. For the previous couple of months, the LRA had been abducting and looting in Uganda. As a result, our troops had swelled to more than 300 people, most of whom were new recruits. Like me, the other recruits were being trained while we were on the move. We were taught how to march, how to run, how and where to take cover, and how to kill. I had seen many killings, but, so far, I had never been forced to participate in murder. However, I had no illusions that I would maintain my innocence for much longer. Few returnees will publicly acknowledge their complicity in murder, but for those who stay in the LRA for some time, becoming a murderer is a fate difficult to avoid. For me, this day came on the first day of our march towards Sudan. We had just crossed the Achwa River when my commander called me and the other recruits to witness 'something important'. We were taken to a large open area in the bush where we all had to line up.

As we stood there, two soldiers appeared out of the bush, dragging another soldier behind them. The third soldier was tied up and he had this terrified look in his eyes. He was a tall, dark boy with long dreadlocks. I estimate that he was around eighteen years old. I knew who he was. Not that I knew him personally, but I had seen him before and I knew he was a senior soldier who had been with the LRA for a couple of years. He was even given a low rank, like corporal or sergeant or something. As I looked into his eyes, I came to realise what he apparently already knew. Today would be his last day in the LRA.

I still remember the exact words when the commander told us that we had to execute him. 'This is the living example. This is the example of what will happen to you when you try to escape. I want all of you to be part of his death so that you will never forget this lesson.'

Apparently, this boy had tried to escape. Now we had to kill him. We were given several clubs, stones and sticks. I was one of the few given an AK-47 with a bayonet attached to it. We had to line up so that everybody would have a turn to hurt him. A few fanatics made sure that they were first in line, which in retrospect wasn't such a bad choice. By the time it was my turn, the soldier was severely injured but he wasn't dead. I looked him in the eye and he looked back at me, revealing the terror in his eyes. From all sides I was being watched. The commander had high hopes for me, and he was curious what I was capable of. I took a deep breath and then plunged my bayonet into his body. I felt it glide into his chest and I still remember the gurgling sound he made, a sound that I am still anxiously trying to forget. After me, there were many more recruits. All of us had to participate. The fact that we were many relieved me a bit from the feeling that I was responsible for his death, but I had no illusions about what I had done. I had killed an unarmed man tied in ropes at point-blank range. I hadn't done it of my free will, but I had done it. I could have stabbed him in the arm and moved on, but instead I stabbed him in the chest, plunging my bayonet into his lungs. From this point onwards, I knew that I had lost my innocence and that I was no longer a child. I was a murderer and I had learned my lesson: whatever you do in the LRA, don't you ever try to escape!

Just minutes after the last recruit stabbed the already dead body, we started moving again. Hour after hour we moved. My feet started to hurt, and I was trying to erase the image of the dying corporal, but to no avail. All day long we walked through Kitgum District, and when day turned to night, we continued walking. It was late at night on the first day that we finally got our first rest after the killing incident. I tried to sleep, but my dreams were haunted by the corporal's eyes. It felt like he was taking his revenge in my dreams. No matter how desperately I tried, I could not lose the image of his last living moments. Although I was exhausted, the dream caused me to wake up again. I was too terrified to sleep. Long before sunrise, we started moving again and although my feet hurt, it was actually a relief to be on the move again. Idleness really is the worst thing for a traumatised mind. All day long we walked. I saw very few villages on the way. The ones we did see were abandoned. The civilians living there had either been killed by the advance party or they had fled. By now, we were in a group with over 300 combatants and recruits. While the LRA is a master in concealment, even they couldn't successfully hide a group this large. Wherever we went, rumours of our movement preceded us.

In the last few hours of daylight on the second day, I didn't see any signs of human beings or human civilisation any more. It was as if we were walking in a completely deserted landscape. At dusk we got to a river. I was told that this river marked the border of Uganda and Sudan, and I wondered if I would ever see Uganda again. We started crossing the river. One soldier swam across with a rope tied around his waist, which he tied to a tree at the other side of the river. This was our alternative bridge. The first to go were a few senior soldiers of another LRA group, who waited for us at the other side of the river. Then it was our turn. I was somewhere in the middle of the group of new recruits, which meant that there were at least a hundred in front of me and an equal number behind me.

When it was my turn to cross the river, I put the rope under my armpits and started dragging my body across. Although the water ran fast, I had no problem crossing. When I was at the other side,

I looked back for a last glimpse at Uganda. But they didn't give me much time to look.

'You there, I want you to walk over to that group immediately, and stop staring back at Uganda, or I will teach you the meaning of pain!'

Always these threats! Never was anything said in a nice way. He could have just told me to join the group. I wondered why every sentence in the LRA had to end with words such as pain, kill, suffer, and so on. I walked over to the other group and when we had enough people we marched on under the guard of a group of senior soldiers until we came to what they called the 'operation venue', a kind of field headquarters, where we were allowed some rest as we waited for the others to cross the river.

It was after the river crossing that things really started to get tough. Sudan is considerably drier than Uganda and decades of war had led to an exodus of civilians towards Uganda, Kenya and Ethiopia. The lack of human civilisation meant that there was no opportunity to plunder any settlements or raid any livestock. At the river, we filled our bottles with water and were told that this was the last water we could get before reaching our destination, so we had to use it sparingly. Also, our food rations were declining drastically, as we would not find any opportunity to replenish our stocks. We started our march again. We had been walking for most of the night and much of the morning when I noticed that the landscape had changed. The luscious green bush had given way to yellow grass. There was still enough vegetation, but it was the dry and thorny kind. I started to wonder how the plants managed to find water, because I didn't see any. Sudan was also much warmer. Even in the early morning sun, I already felt a pressing heat, which only continued to increase for the rest of the day.

Even before the sun reached its peak, the first victims started to fall. One boy was walking right in front of me. He was both older and taller than me. I noticed that at a certain point his pace slowed down, while his head started hanging and he couldn't manage to walk in a straight line any more, as though he were drunk. When I got very close to this person, I heard him whisper, 'Miya pii, miya pii,' which means 'give me water' in Acholi. At that moment I was still doing fine, and I still had some water to spare, so out of compassion I filled my bottle top with a few drops of water, and I gave it to him. I think it helped him a little, because after this he managed to walk a little bit faster. Yet after not even half an hour he started to slow his pace again. Actually, we all started to slow our pace, even the senior soldiers. I told him that he should take a minute of rest, but I think at that point he was already halfway into the spirit world, and he couldn't hear me any more. I forget how long he managed to keep up, but at a certain point I saw him fall over. As he tripped, he fell with his head against a rock, while all his luggage was still tied on his back. He hadn't even used his hands to break the fall. He was five metres in front of me when he collapsed. I wanted to stop to help him, but a senior soldier was behind me and we were told it was not our duty to look after the others. So instead of giving him some water, I passed him and never even looked back. Whether he lived or died, I don't know, but I never saw this person again.

It was not long after this when I also poured the very last drop of water out of my bottle and I learned what thirst really is. You must know that thirst spares no one. It doesn't discriminate. Thirst doesn't care if you are a woman or a man, a new recruit or an experienced soldier, a commander or a private. In the afternoon of the third day, everybody was thirsty, and everybody suffered.

Victims were picked at random. I also started to feel the consequences. My lips, mouth and throat completely dried up. At a certain point I tried to swallow, but I had even stopped producing saliva. At one point we walked past a rocky mountain and the rocks were even warmer than the sun in which they had been baking all day. It was as if we'd walked into an oven. In this place, it was especially the more experienced soldiers who suffered, as their footwear was not made to deal with this heat. Those rubber gumboots really started to boil, which made walking increasingly difficult. In contrast, I was wearing shoes made out of rubber car tyres, and although my feet were covered with blisters, I was still OK.

The second person that I saw collapsing was a very experienced soldier. When the senior soldiers collapsed, things became very dangerous, especially for us new recruits, as the soldiers started waving their guns around and threatening others that they would kill them if they did not give water. That was the same with this man. He walked over to a new recruit, maybe ten metres in front of me, and shoved his gun into his mouth, demanding water, which the recruit of course didn't have. He would have killed the kid if other soldiers hadn't intervened. They started asking for water from everybody and then they finally found a new recruit who had so bravely managed to spare a little for himself. This was divided among the soldiers, but to no avail. At a certain point the soldier collapsed. He fell on the ground, unable to move any further. At that point the other senior soldiers lifted him up and he was dragged on. I quickly learned that it was only the new recruits who were left for dead when they collapsed.

The next day, I saw four other people collapse from the thirst and the increasing hunger. On the fourth day we ran out of food as well, which was less of a pity than you would expect, because our mouths were so dry that we couldn't swallow the food anyway. At one point, I saw a girl lying on the ground. Her luggage was lying beside her, and a soldier was caning her with a thin but flexible stick. She was lucky. Out there you were lucky if you got a beating. A beating meant the difference between life and death, as a good beating would help you up on your feet again. The ones that did not receive a beating were the ones that were really in trouble, as they were left at the mercy of the blocking force, who could either kill them or leave them to die a lonely death. I was actually doing pretty well on the fourth day. In the morning, I had found some mud in a remnant of a puddle where there had been a flowing river once. With two hands I had grabbed the mud and started sucking all fluids out of it. I didn't care that insects laid their eggs there, I only cared for the moisture, and it helped. Different people had different techniques to cope with the thirst. I saw others drinking their own urine, but for me the mud was enough to give me the strength to last.

In the afternoon of the fourth day, the land started to become greener again and there was more shade to hide under. We were slowly climbing to a higher altitude and in front of us we saw some green mountains, which meant that there would be water soon. This gave me the strength to continue, strength that I desperately needed, as I was nearing my end. My feet started to swell and although the mud had helped me, my mouth was still dry, and my stomach ached with hunger. If we didn't reach our destination soon, I would surely collapse, just like all the others that I had seen falling on this horrendous trip. But once more I was lucky. It was when I was about to give up that I finally saw hope appearing on the horizon. The relief that I felt when I saw the camp was the greatest that I had experienced in LRA captivity so far. I would not give up now that redemption was so close.

Palutaka

When I entered the camp, people welcomed us by sprinkling water over us and giving us a few drops of water to drink. After walking in a bare landscape for the last few days, I was amazed by the number of people in this camp and how it bustled with life. Thousands of people were performing all kinds of activities. On the perimeter of the camp I saw people digging in the gardens. There were young boys, armed to the teeth, standing guard in an elaborate system of trenches. When we entered, I saw people carrying bamboo and grass. Others were sweeping their huts and carrying water. I saw one group of very young people running around the camp while they were being drilled by an older commander. I immediately realised that almost everybody was armed and that the average age of the people here was very young. I saw teenage mothers carrying their guns in one hand and their babies in the other, and hardened soldiers who weren't even eleven years old.

As we advanced deeper into the camp, I saw some huge stone buildings, similar to those in Gulu town. Not far from a large stone church there were tanks manned by people who looked very different from us. Later I found out that these were Arab soldiers of the Sudanese government, which was our main ally and arms supplier. Further on, I saw thousands of grass huts, all inhabited by more young and heavily armed people. I was completely amazed by the sheer size of it all.

We were led to a large open space in the middle of the camp, where another high commander was awaiting us. We were all lined up around him and then he started a speech. The commander introduced himself as Raska Lukwiya, a man who would later be indicted by the International Criminal Court (ICC), and he welcomed us to this camp, which he called Palutaka.

'This is Palutaka, our military base and your new home. The Spirit Lakwena is pleased to see that you have joined our holy movement and that you have shown yourself willing to take up arms to overthrow the tyrant who calls himself President of Uganda. You are now part of the Lord's army, which will create a Uganda that will be just and where the Acholi will be supreme; a country which shall be justly ruled by the Ten Commandments. God has chosen us to lead his army and rid the world of all evil, starting in Uganda. You are a soldier of the Army of the Lord now.'

I don't remember his exact words, but it was something like that. He lectured us in a way as if we all had joined the LRA voluntarily and that we would want nothing other than the honour of fighting for the LRA, or the 'Army of the Lord', as he called it. After his political propaganda speech, he told us about the rules in Palutaka.

'The Spirit knows you, and he knows your deepest thoughts. Those who only think about escaping will suffer the consequences. You are never allowed to leave the camp without specific permission. You are not allowed to take a shit without our permission.

Every Friday and every Sunday you are expected to attend Mass, unless you are specifically ordered to do something else.'

This speech continued for almost twenty minutes. All this time I was barely able to remain conscious. I had just survived the worst march of my life and I only wanted to lie down and rest. But this was not to be. After Raska told us the many rules of Palutaka, other commanders came and started to do a selection. Those of us who looked strong were put into four different brigades. The weaker ones were selected to become bodyguards of the lower-ranking commanders, such as captains or first lieutenants. I was among twenty who were selected to join Stockree Brigade, the brigade that I would serve for the rest of my stay in captivity.

After the selection, we were given to the artillery commander, Ocan, who brought us to Stockree Brigade's parade ground. Here we received another lecture from our direct commander, a lieutenant major this time.

'Don't you ever try to escape, because the Spirit will get you and you will die an awful death. Obedience is key. If you don't obey me, you will disobey your own life. We want you to be active all the time. Everything that you are ordered to do, you have to do it in full spirit. Never take your own initiative. If I catch you doing something I didn't order you to do, you will die.'

My mind started to buzz with all these new rules. There were rules for everything. I knew that in order to survive, I had better learn these rules quickly, but by the end of his speech I wasn't able to focus any more. During the previous four days I had only had a few hours of sleep in total, and I was utterly exhausted. The lieutenant kept on talking. I could see that he was happy to have several new recruits that he could boss around. As his monologue continued, I tried extremely hard to keep up the appearance that I was listening, but in truth, I was on the verge of collapsing. When I was barely able to remain standing any longer, I finally heard the words I had been waiting for.

'After one week your military training begins; until that time, you will have a week of rest. So now I order you to go to your huts and sleep.'

I had never been so happy to oblige an order from the LRA as this one. We were guided to our huts by a senior soldier. I shared a hut with three others, two senior soldiers and one other fresh recruit. As soon as he showed me which bed was mine, I literally collapsed. I think that I was asleep even before I hit the sack.

Long before the dawn the next day, yet another commander woke us up. He gave us a few minutes to get to the parade ground, where we were ordered to march again. My feet were still swollen from the day before and every step I took hurt, but I didn't complain. I wanted to make an impression on my new commander, and I figured that the best way to do this was by being obedient, and to excel in everything I did. Survival in the LRA meant that I had to adapt to their ways and do as they did. As we began marching, the rest of Palutaka started to wake up. All around me people came out of their huts.

As for everybody else in the camp, the day started with lining up. The unit commanders would first have a look at everyone to see if they were missing any faces, then they counted everybody and if there were none missing, we would start the morning march. It wasn't until we were nearly done marching that hundreds of other groups started their morning marches. Obviously our commander had a thing for waking up early. We marched for several hours and then we were given different tasks. As we came in with so many new recruits, new huts had to be built. So on that first day, many of the new recruits in my section were led to the bush to collect wood and to cut grass for the huts. Others started digging holes in the places where the huts were to be built. At around noon my section commander called me: 'Kadogo, I want you to collect all the rubbish around our compound and sweep the floor.'

I was given the easiest task and I did my job to the best of my abilities. When I was done, I was instructed to assist the others with building the huts. Maybe it was because I was small, but in the first week they never let me do any of the really hard work. I was ordered to fetch water, clean the compound, fetch some more water, bring the commander some food and clean the compound again.

Palutaka was at the foot of a green mountain and to collect water I had to go downhill where there was a stream, which was only a short walk from the outer perimeter of the camp. The first couple of times I was led by a senior soldier, but after that I was allowed to do this on my own. On my daily walks to the stream I got a good overview of Palutaka camp. I soon realised that it was divided into two military base camps. On one side there was the heavily armed military base of the Sudanese government army and on the other side was the LRA camp. The two armies mainly lived separately from each other, but in harmony. We traded with them and the officers especially had a lot of interaction, but junior soldiers were not allowed to interact with them. For me it was difficult to follow this order. Whenever I went to the stream, I met Sudanese Arabs who were also collecting water. Initially I had little contact with them, as I wasn't allowed to talk to them and didn't speak their language, but I could not keep this up for very long. I soon figured out the meaning of 'Salaam alaikum' and I learned to reply with 'Alaikum salaam'.

I think that the LRA camp was the larger of the two camps and I was continually amazed by the number of people there. I had never seen so many people in such a small location; only market day in Gulu could compare. The LRA numbered at least 5,000 soldiers, but it could easily have been double that. I had no way of counting all of them. The Arabs also had a considerable force.

On my way to the stream each day, I also got a good picture of life in Palutaka and the activities people were busy with. I saw that young soldiers were always digging trenches, and others held guard when there was no need to be vigilant. I would pass the gardens where the women were digging and sowing, with their babies tied on their backs. I always wondered what would happen to these babies. They were born in the camp and knew nothing about the other life that was denied them. It made me think about my own childhood: playing football with plastic rubbish; telling stories about the fox, the turtle and the hyena; and herding cows with my dad. I remembered the excitement and the fun that I had when I was doing these things and realised that they would never experience any of this. Instead, by the age of ten they would probably become the most dangerous killing machines that walked the face of this earth, completely unaware of the life they could have had.

My first week there passed very slowly. For three days we worked on building huts and the fourth day we were summoned to go to the assembly point of Control Altar, which was the main brigade of the LRA. It was prayer day. This was another strict rule within the LRA. Fridays and Sundays were rest days and days of prayer. Anyone who was caught doing any work on these days would be heavily caned. It was obligatory for all to be present at the sermons, and all of us happily obliged. On Friday, Joseph Kony himself would come to preach to us, and on Sunday it was another commander. The sermons had many similarities to those that I had witnessed in church at home: a choir, altar boys, holy water, and even the blood and body of Jesus. But there were also differences: these services were held under the open sky and the sermons had a very militarised nature.

At this first prayer service, I was seated quite far away from Kony, but I could still hear him clearly. He started praising the Lord like we used to do in our church, but his preaching was different. It was full of military propaganda and his own personal glorification. He claimed that he was the messenger of God, a prophet who was in direct contact with God. He stated that the strength of God was mirrored by the strength of his army and by the prophet leading that army. As I looked around, I saw that thousands had gathered around him. We all cheered for Kony, which was very impressive, thousands upon thousands all cheering together.

Many longed for the Friday prayers, and I also had to admit that the services were quite interesting. Kony could really talk. Not only did he talk long and loud, he also talked in a way that triggered something in me. He got me aroused and excited about our mission. When he told us that we were God's warriors, selected by the Lord himself in all his wisdom, it made me feel proud and worthy. Those moments that we were in prayer, I forgot all about my hardships and I felt as if I had a purpose, as if I mattered. It wasn't long before I started to cheer together with the thousands of others, trying to outdo some of the new recruits who sat close to me.

By the end of the week, several new huts were built, and I made sure that the compound was clean and free of any rubbish at all times. I realised that to survive here, I had to do more than oblige; I had to excel. I quickly learned which rules were flexible and could be broken, and which were sacred. I would have to look after myself and this meant that I had to break some rules and take my own initiative.

My first challenge of survival was a chronic lack of food. We had arrived in Palutaka with more than 200 new recruits and the gardens couldn't sustain so many new mouths to feed. This meant that food rations went down drastically, so we were all hungry. In the morning we never ate anything. We woke up, started to march, and then we went about our daily tasks. Only after we finished were we given our first and only food of the day. The food was brought by a senior soldier and the moment it came we all had to divide into groups of about ten people. We sat down in a circle around the frying pan with some beans and a pot containing watery soup. We all took a small handful of beans, beginning with the most senior soldier then proceeding to the left. We didn't just grab the beans and eat. We waited until everybody had grabbed something, then we compared hands to see if everybody had the same amount. If somebody had too much, he either had to put it back or he would be skipped the next round. When everybody was satisfied over the amount, we were allowed to eat. Then the second round followed in the same manner. The soup was divided in a similar way. We were all given a small slice of bread and again we showed each other how much we had. When everyone was satisfied, we would dip the bread in the soup and eat it. The amount of food that we were given was enough to keep us alive, but not enough to give us strength, so we were all growing weaker.

However, the biggest challenge to our survival wasn't hunger, but disease. Our constant state of hunger affected our immune systems and we had to be very careful not to fall sick. There were all kinds of diseases out there, like malaria and yellow fever, but the most common were diarrhoea and typhoid, which were especially deadly if one was weakened by a lack of food.

In that first week, one of the new recruits in my section complained about a headache and stomachache in the morning. He told the Mzee – a respectful Swahili word for elder, but the name we used for our section commander – that he didn't feel well and asked for permission to stay in his hut. Instead of caring for this boy, the Mzee gave him a terrible beating. Halfway through the march the boy started puking and he fell down. With another beating he was up and running again, but by now it was clear to everyone that he wasn't pretending. When he fell over again, the Mzee ordered a senior soldier to escort him to the sick bay, and this was the last time I saw him. Soon after I learned that for the most junior combatants, there was no sick bay in this camp. Going to the sick bay actually meant that they would walk the afflicted person to a distance far from the camp, where they would either kill them or let them die a lonely death. This ensured that the body wouldn't contaminate others.

I knew that the best way to avoid getting sick was by drinking plenty of water and supplementing my daily food rations with other sources of nutrition. Water was no problem. In Palutaka there was enough water, especially for me, since it was my task to fetch it. But getting enough food was a real challenge. Our rations did not provide us the extra strength that was needed to perform our rigorous daily activities. So we had to be creative, and I quickly found a way. I could see that the commanders always had enough to eat. On my marches to the stream I found the spot where they threw away potato and cassava peel. Although it was forbidden to take this peel, I quickly learned that this was a flexible rule that could be broken to increase my chances of survival. It seemed better to collect the peel and run the risk of a caning than to risk getting sick and being sent to the so-called sick bay. I taught myself how to collect the peel while no one was watching, and I would hide it in my pocket instead of eating it immediately. I would take it with me to the stream and eat there when I was alone, or to my hut and eat it in the middle of the night when everyone was asleep. In the first few weeks, getting this extra source of nutrition became a personal mission. It helped me a lot, especially in my second and third week in Palutaka, when the military training began.

On the morning of the seventh day in Palutaka we were awakened even earlier than usual and told that our military training had begun. Instead of the usual marching, that morning we had to run. For training we ran to the mountain, which was located much farther away than it appeared. After this, every morning started with running up and down it countless times. In the LRA nothing was ever easy. We were always pushed far beyond our limits and that was exactly what happened during the training.

After several hours of running up and down the mountain we would start a long march, only to return to the mountain when the sun was at its peak. In the afternoon we would receive a little training in combat, including what to do if we walked into an ambush, how to advance in the style of the LRA, and how to move when making a tactical retreat. We were told that during battle LRA soldiers would only lie down when they were shot dead. LRA soldiers were blessed by God and so there was no need to hide or take cover: 'If God and the Spirit believe in you and if you are truly a warrior of God, bullets will just bounce off your body, so there is no need to hide.'

Upon completion of the afternoon training we ate two handfuls of beans and drank some watery soup. I volunteered to fetch some water so that I could collect some more peel. Afterwards we all went back to the mountain for more evening exercise. This time we were given very heavy clubs to run with, to resemble a gun.

The extra food I managed to get really helped. While everyone else was growing weaker and having more and more difficulty climbing the mountain, I was doing fine. Every day I saw people fainting out of sheer hunger and exhaustion. Whenever someone fainted, the commanders would give them a beating and, without a chance to recover, they would be forced to rejoin the others. If they fainted again, they would receive what was called 'hot exercise' or 'hot training'. This could involve anything, like running up the mountain while carrying a heavy weight or running twenty times around a bottle and then climbing the mountain. Whatever it entailed, it always included the mountain and more caning. If they fainted again after the hot training, they would receive what was called special caning. In this case the commander would cane them on a very specific area of the neck using the cleaning rod of a gun. The person would have to lie down, and the commander would step on their head with his gumboots. Then he would cane the person's neck several times, and I promise you that it hurt. In short, it was better not to faint. I was spared all this special attention because I never fainted. I sometimes fell down from exhaustion or simply stumbled over my own legs, for which I received a mild beating, but I never fainted.

After three weeks, this training came to an end and we started our first gun training. They showed us two guns and identified one as an AK-47 and the other as an AK-49.

'Do you see the difference?'

I did. The AK-49 was much bigger and it had some different features. Also the sound was different. The AK-49 had a much bigger bang. They started to explain all the parts. Slowly they took the gun apart and with each new piece they told us its name, which we had to repeat.

'Retainer pin, hammer pin, trigger,' and so on.

After taking the gun apart we had to reassemble it again and to name the parts as we did so. Anyone who made a mistake was caned. There was always the caning. It was never as bad as the first time when they wrote my name, but still, they would make sure that it hurt and that a lesson was learned. For the next few days this exercise was repeated, until it became an integral part of our brains.

After several days we had our first and only target practice. They taught us how to hold the gun, how to aim, how to hold our breath when shooting, and finally, how to shoot. We used a big drum for target practice. The drum was a good distance away. They marked a red spot on it, and we were supposed to hit this target. Each of us received five bullets and we were warned that we would be caned if we missed. Because we were always short on bullets, these would be the only training shots that we ever got. The next time we shot, it would be for real. So I did what they had taught me. I aimed, held my breath, and when my hand was steady, I shot – miss. A second shot – missed again. In all five shots I never hit the red dot on the drum, but because every single bullet did hit the drum, they deemed it good enough. I received no caning that day. Everyone else also managed to hit the drum. The last day of our training was the first in which none of us received a beating.

Our training finished about a month after I had arrived in Palutaka and about three months after my abduction. On the last day of training, there was a blessing ceremony in which we were each given our own gun and both the combatant and his gun received a blessing, similar to the anointing ceremony. They placed the gun in my hands, took some white stuff and drew a big heart on my chest, followed by a cross on my body, back, lips, palms and feet. During the ceremony we were bare-chested and we clapped and sang a song about Jesus and God.

'Jesus has saved us . . .' *Clap . . . clap . . .*

'Nothing is impossible to God . . .' *Clap . . . clap . . .*

After they drew the heart and the crosses on my body, they sprinkled me with holy water while they said some words of blessing. Then it was my gun's turn. It got sprinkled and it also received words of blessing. In the meantime we kept on clapping and singing.

'Jesus has saved us . . . Nothing is impossible to God . . .'

We remained bare-chested until the white stuff slowly started to be absorbed into our bodies. This ceremony was meant to invoke the spirit of protection in us, and somehow it really worked for me. It was during this ceremony that I started to feel a change. I actually felt the power of the Spirit running through my veins. They also sprinkled my gun to invoke the Spirit in the gun, so that it would not jam or malfunction when I was fighting.

The gun that I was given was an AK-47, with a bayonet fixed on it and timber at the back so that I could put it against my shoulder. This gun was also called an SMG, sub-machine gun or a short machine gun. but we mainly called it Yugoslavia, because the guns came from Yugoslavia, or so we were told. I remember very well what they told me when they gave me the gun: 'This is your life, and this is your death. The moment you hold it, it will protect you very well. The moment you misuse it, it will mean your death. If you ever lose this gun, you have to die. If you protect it, it will protect you.'

Afterwards they gave me four full magazines, two grenades and the tools for cleaning the gun. We were all told that we had to memorise the number of the gun; the number meant that the gun was ours and that remembering the number created a bond between the soldier and his gun. To this day I still remember the nine-digit number of my gun, a figure that I will never forget.

When they gave me the gun, I liked it so much. I was always holding it proudly. Although I didn't fire it, I carried it everywhere and never left it behind. When I went for a long call, I would take it. When I went for a short call, I would also take it. My colleagues did not always do that. They would often just hang it in a tree or put it on top of a hut, but not me. From the day I received my gun till the day I was arrested, my gun was never further than a few metres away from me. Only much later did I ever consider that this gift I had received could eventually cause my own death.

My Life as a Soldier

The day after the ceremony was over, we were sent on our first military test. We were told that we were soldiers now, and the only way to test our abilities was in active combat. We were being sent to attack five Sudanese villages and come back with lots of food. The moment they announced the mission I was filled with excitement. Something had happened to me during the ceremony; I really felt like a soldier now. And although I had reluctantly killed before, this time I felt eager to do so. I told myself that I would be the first to kill an enemy.

Minutes after the mission was announced, we set out and walked for several hours. We were slowly descending from our higher altitude, and the landscape was becoming dryer. After many hours of walking, we were finally ordered to stop. The commander told us that we had several targets and that our group would be split up so that each group would attack a separate target. There were five Sudanese villages in this area, and we would be attacking all of them. My group was under the command of a lieutenant called Nyeko. We consisted of a few experienced soldiers and about fifty new recruits, many of us eagerly awaiting our first battle.

Some twenty minutes after we split up, we reached the perimeter of the village. The moment I saw the first villagers, the commander and several others in the front of our group started to shoot, and for half a minute the villagers' guns were firing back at us. I had been ordered to defend the rear of the group, so when the fighting started, I was the furthest away from the gun battle. Immediately I rushed to the front of our group, but by the time I got there the gunfight was already over. The villagers quickly realised that they were dealing with the LRA and knew all too well that we wouldn't be deterred that easily. Just the term LRA, or more precisely, Olum Olum, which was what the Acholis from Sudan called us, was enough to spread panic through the local communities that were within walking distance of Palutaka. Within seconds, the villagers made a run for it, leaving us with months of food supplies.

We were ordered to go into the village and take as much food as we could carry. I grabbed some cassavas, a bag full of sesame seeds and some eggs that were still warm from the hens. I don't know if the hens also fled or if someone else took them, but by the time I entered the hut they were already gone. After everything was fully loaded, we marched back to Palutaka. We completed the mission without sustaining a single injury.

After we came back from the test, my life started to improve a little. I was still under many restrictions and I was still hungry, as we received very little of all the food that we looted, but now I could at least move with the senior soldiers and converse and laugh with them. We were all soldiers now. In my first month in Palutaka, I had never conversed with anyone. I listened to the commands they gave and only replied with 'Yes, sir' or 'Yes, teacher' – *laphony* as we used to call our commanders – but I never had a real conversation. New recruits weren't allowed to talk too much. But now I had the freedom to speak and move around more freely, although I was never allowed to move too far, and always required a clear purpose as to why I was moving to a certain position.

I believe that it was during the ceremony that followed my training that my transformation into a soldier began. It was as if the civilian in me was dying, and in its place a guerrilla was awakened. I could feel that the Spirit had invoked something in me. I started to really believe in Kony's Friday prayers and I began to behave like a soldier. I became very aggressive, especially to other new recruits. Occasionally I witnessed a brutal execution of someone who had tried to escape, and I wasn't as horrified by it as I was when I witnessed my first killing. I started to see it as normal; I even started to believe my commander when he said that they deserved it. I also grew used to all the caning, and as time passed, I stopped caring about human lives altogether. I could kill someone in cold blood without giving a thought to the life that I had just terminated. The only life that was still sacred for me was my own.

I remember one day, not very long after the ceremony, that we went to collect bamboo to build a hut. We had to walk a long distance to collect this bamboo, as it didn't grow near our camp, and during this walk, there was a colleague who began disturbing me by making fun of my size.

'Look at this pathetic little soldier. Looking all tough and angry. Hey, you there, kadogo, I bet you are really struggling to carry that big gun of yours, aren't you, kiddo?'

He thought he could get away with it because he was older and bigger and a little bit more senior than me, but he was wrong. When he harassed me for a second time, I punched him to the ground with the butt of my gun and put the barrel against his head. I told him I would shoot him. I even started to remove his clothes and his gun. I would have killed this boy and walked away without even considering the human life at stake. The only reason I didn't was because another colleague intervened. I don't know what came over me and I certainly cannot explain it, but this is what happened to me in the LRA. Before, I would have ignored the insults, but not any more.

This is what the Spirit did to us. This is how a primary-school teacher became one of the most brutal commanders. This is how innocent young abductees returned to their families one day and executed them while smiling. The mind doesn't work in the same way any more. It was the Spirit now that was working in me. The Spirit made me become aggressive and ruthless. At a certain point I was angry all the time, even though I didn't know the reason for my anger.

I think this was why my commanders started to see potential in me. As months went by, I was increasingly given tasks to command and supervise others. Usually, these were new recruits who had just come in and lacked military training, but sometimes it was other, more senior soldiers. I always treated them badly, especially the new recruits. I caned them brutally for minor mistakes and I repeatedly threatened to kill them. I think that if those people were to see me today, they would still fear and hate me. But at that time, I didn't care. It felt good giving out orders. I really liked the power that I had over others.

'Do this, do that . . . if you refuse, I kill you.'

My section commander observed this change in me, and I think that he started to like me a little. Sometimes he would call me over and compliment me on my behaviour, explaining that with more effort I could even reach up to his rank one day. We actually started to converse quite often. It was during these conversations that he told me a bit about himself and the history of the LRA in Sudan. He too had been abducted by the LRA, but not as a child – when he was already a mature adult. Because of his age, we always called him Mzee, the respectful Swahili word for an older person.

Back in the days before he was abducted, he had been a teacher. He told me that the Ugandan government officials had constantly harassed him, and that the government had marginalised the people of the north, especially the Acholis. When he was abducted in 1991, he was so angry at the Ugandan government that he didn't even mind being in the LRA. He believed that the LRA was fighting a just war. I don't know how he turned from somebody who educated young people into somebody who tortured and killed them, but within four years he had advanced to the position of lieutenant major and was among the most ruthless commanders of the LRA. He told me that sometimes he felt sorry for what they did to young children, but that the end justified the means. In this case the end result would be a decent society in which the Acholis would reign supreme.

In addition to giving me advice on military matters, he also taught me about the ideology of the LRA. He told me stories about the early days of the war and how Joseph Kony came to Sudan.

'You know, this whole war started with the betrayal by Museveni against Tito Okello, the Acholi president of Uganda. Ever since Museveni won the presidency by a coup d'état, he has been out to destroy the Acholis. That is why the Ugandan National Liberation Army, the UNLA, a rebel movement made up out of former government soldiers and Alice Lakwena's Holy Spirit Movement, started the rebellion against this false government.'

I enjoyed listening to these stories at least as much as he liked telling them to me, so he continued.

'Do you know the story of Alice Lakwena and her journey to Paraa?'

'I heard my parents talk about it one day, sir, but I remember it only vaguely,' I replied.

At this answer, he slapped me in the face really hard, telling me that I should be ashamed of myself for not knowing the origins of the LRA insurgency now that I was completely embroiled in it.

'Then let me tell you the story, boy. It was in 1985 that an Acholi woman called Alice Auma became possessed with the spirit of an Italian soldier called Lakwena.'

He told me that it was this spirit that ordered Alice to go to Paraa in the national park to hold a court with the animals and ask who was responsible for all the bloodshed in Uganda. The Spirit Lakwena asked the animals if they were responsible, but they denied their role. Instead, the animals showed their wounds to Alice, wounds that were clearly inflicted by humans. Next the spirit ordered Alice to go to Murchison Falls, where she spoke to the water. The moment Lakwena started talking, the waterfall stopped flowing. Lakwena asked the waterfall who was responsible for the killings, and the waterfall replied that it was the two-legged animals who threw their brothers in the water. Next Lakwena ordered Alice to go to Mount Kilak in Opit. She told the mountains that God had sent her to ask who was responsible for all the theft in the world. The mountain replied by saying that he had gone nowhere and that he hadn't stolen anyone's children. Instead, the mountain blamed the people who came to him asking him to kill and steal from the people.

The Mzee went on, 'God gave Alice the Spirit Lakwena and bestowed his blessings on her to be victorious in her fight. When Alice was later defeated in Jinja, due to the unfaithfulness of her followers, the Spirit Lakwena passed from Alice to Joseph Kony, and now he is continuing the battle that she started.'

My commander told me more about the war that Alice Lakwena fought against the government, including how the UNLA betrayed the Acholis, and the early beginnings of the LRA. He told me about terrible massacres that the Acholi soldiers had executed in a region called the Luwero Triangle, causing the soldiers to rise against the new government. Although my parents had also told me bits about the history of my country, I understood very little of it. My commander probably noticed my confused expression, because he told me that I didn't need to know about the politics. I was a soldier and I was expected to execute orders.

Several weeks later, the commander called me over again and we started to converse. I asked the commander how the LRA came into Sudan and he told me the whole story.

'You have to know that Palutaka is a place that is also inhabited by Acholis, but by the Acholis of Sudan. They are the same tribe and they speak the same language as we do. The only difference is that they live in a different country,' he replied. He explained that in the early days of the Lord's Resistance Army, even before it was called the LRA, Joseph Kony operated only within Uganda. This was before the Acholi civilians started to collaborate with Museveni, betraying Kony. Before Kony entered Sudan, he collaborated with a small Sudanese militia called the Jess Commando. Mzee told me that the Jess Commando was made up of a small band of Acholis in Sudan who were at war with the Sudan People's Liberation Army (SPLA), a Sudanese rebel movement consisting mainly of Dinkas, which he described as a vicious tribe from the north.

For the SPLA, the Jess Commando was not a serious threat; it was more like a nuisance, since their real war was against the Arabic government of Sudan, with whom we shared our camp. In the late 1980s the Jess Commando asked the Sudanese government to help them in their fight against the SPLA and this help was willingly granted. But the Jess Commando wasn't a real army; they were more like a small civil defence unit and they didn't have the strength to fight the SPLA, which was the largest rebel movement in all of Africa at that time. That is why they invited the LRA to come to Sudan. They saw the LRA as fellow Acholis who could help them in their fight against the SPLA.

The Mzee really knew how to tell a story. I learned so much from him that day.

He told me how the Jess Commando established the first contacts between the LRA and the Sudanese government. As the Sudanese government was locked in a ferocious war with the SPLA, they gladly invited the LRA into their territory, on the condition that they would help the government defeat the SPLA. The Sudanese government was also happy to assist the LRA in their fight against the Ugandan government, as they were involved in a kind of proxy war against Uganda over their funding the SPLA.

It was not long after Kony established his base in Palutaka that relations between the LRA and Jess Commando soured. The leadership of the Jess Commando believed that they had brought into their territory a group of Acholi saviours who would rid them of the SPLA. But it soon turned out that we weren't the redeemers they had hoped for. Because of our overwhelming food shortages, we were forced to plunder the villages the Jess Commando was protecting. We also started to recruit their children into our army. That is why, at that point, we were also at war with the Sudanese villagers, including those of Acholi blood. Meanwhile, the Sudanese government couldn't care less. They had at their disposal a strong force that put considerable pressure on the SPLA from the south. They didn't care what the consequences were for the southerners who lived in the vicinity of the LRA, even though these southerners were their supporters. They even gave us the mandate and the weapons to overwhelm southern Sudan.

I always enjoyed these stories from my commander. Not only did I like storytelling, but it also allowed me time away from hard labour. However, despite the fact that he had become friendly towards me, outside of our conversations he continued to publicly degrade me so that I was always aware of my inferior position.

By the time that I arrived in Palutaka, the Jess Commando was no longer a threat. They were the armed civilians that I had encountered during my first military test, and it had already become very clear to me that they had no power whatsoever to resist the LRA.

The LRA, on the other hand, was strengthening. Almost weekly, battalions came back with new recruits and our force was rapidly expanding. To my mind it wouldn't be much longer before we were strong enough to overthrow the government. This was an idea that excited me because it meant that once that had happened, I could return home to my parents.

My talks with the commander had given me a greater awareness of the political dimensions of this war and I started to get a better understanding of our role. We had to eliminate the government of Uganda to make life better for the Acholi tribe, which had been marginalised by the West Uganda-led government. I began to feel a sense of duty and responsibility towards my tribe. I started to dream about how proud my parents would be once we had liberated them.

These talks also strengthened the relationship between Mzee and me. Not that he started to be overly kind to me; he was still a very brutal man. Increasingly, however, he gave me tasks that carried greater responsibility. In the first month after the training my main tasks were farming, fetching water and collecting wood for building huts, under the command of a sergeant or other low-ranking officer. But slowly I was assigned tasks of more importance.

Several weeks after my training, I got my first commanding task. I was to take several new recruits to the bush and make them collect wood for the new huts that we were constructing. It was rare in the LRA that a junior soldier without rank was given a task to lead others. I knew this and I did it proudly. I made sure that my group carried back as much wood as was humanly possible to further impress the commander. This meant that occasionally I had to cane some of the new recruits, but in the end they all obeyed my commands and carried as much wood as I ordered them to.

Although my commander never really showed his appreciation, a week later I was sent on an even more important assignment. I was to guard the road that goes from Palutaka to Uganda. I had to make sure that no one would cross our checkpoint without the main camp knowing who it was. I was sent to this position with another boy, who had been abducted from Sudan and who had served in the LRA longer than me. I was unfamiliar with this boy because he was from another section, but during those weeks we got to know each other a little bit.

The place that we had to guard was about one kilometre away from Palutaka. It was our task to monitor those using the road and then to alert others in Palutaka about any visitors. Although this task was quite important, it was also very boring, as we rarely saw anyone. The only people who ever used the road were Sudanese soldiers. When they came close, we would announce ourselves and then shoot once in the air to alert the people in Palutaka that friendly people were coming. In case of any enemies, we were to shoot our entire magazines and then the commanders would know that we were under attack. But we never saw any enemies. Sometimes an LRA patrol would pass our position to check if we were still there, but this only happened occasionally.

The other boy and I would remain on guard duty until the commanders sent replacements, and this could take either twelve hours or up to four days. If the patrol ever caught us sleeping, a heavy caning would follow. What was even worse was that sometimes they totally forgot about us. Then we wouldn't receive any food and water at all, leaving us hungry, sometimes for up to twenty-four hours. Another bad thing about guard duty was that it meant that I couldn't collect the vegetable peel any more, so I was slowly growing hungry again. But I did not complain. I knew that it was an honour to guard this important checkpoint and so I did it to the best of my abilities.

As months went by, both my character and my roles were changing. What always remained the same, however, were the hardships in Palutaka. Even though the training was over, we still had to do the compulsory morning marches. Even battle-hardened soldiers who had been in the LRA for more than three years had to do the morning marches. I think that our Mzee stayed up all night thinking about new ways to exhaust us.

What also continued was the famine. In Sudan, we were always hungry. With more recruits coming in almost weekly, food stocks dwindled even further. I missed opportunities to collect vegetable peel as often, and even when I did have the chance, I had to be very fast because by this time I wasn't the only one who knew about it, so there was always a silent competition to get it. I was starving most of the time. Food was the only thing on my mind every day. Every week people fell sick from hunger all around me. In the morning they would complain about severe stomach problems and headaches, and this usually resulted in their death later in the day. I knew that I had to do something in order to survive, and so I devised a plan.

During the guard missions, the boy from Sudan told me about a Sudanese village not far from our position. Together we fantasised about all the food they had. I started to dream about this village, even though I had never seen it. In my dreams I idealised the village to the extent that it started to look like my own home village that I had been forced to leave behind months earlier. However, it was not the memory of home that caused so much pain – it was purely the lack of food. Apart from killing myself, I was prepared to do almost anything for a decent meal.

I don't recall when this happened, but it must have been at least seven or eight months after I arrived in Palutaka. By this time, I understood my new context well enough to know I shouldn't ask permission to go to the village – it would never be granted. Even worse, I might be granted permission, but then I would not be allowed to keep the food. This had happened to me twice before. The first time was after we looted a village during our military test. The second time was when I was sent to hunt for some game. That time I managed to kill a sizable rat, but I never even got to taste a single bite of the animal. Instead I was just given some of the soup they had boiled it in. No, this time I was determined to keep the food for myself.

I decided to sneak out of the LRA camp to look for this village on a Friday, because Fridays were prayer days, when it was the easiest to slip away for a few hours without being noticed. Once I'd sneaked out of the camp, I came across the guards who were surrounding it, but I told them I was being sent out to guard the road again. They did not question me any further and let me go.

The directions the boy from Sudan had given me were pretty clear. He told me about an old trail that led to the village, but which was now overgrown with bush because it was rarely used after the war began. The reason the village had managed to last untouched for so long was probably because of its extreme isolation from any of the main roads. It took me a while to find the trail, but when I finally found it, it was easy to follow. Sometimes the path would be overgrown and then it would take me some time to find it again, but all in all it wasn't very difficult. After I'd followed the path for about three hours, I began to hear noises in the distance. I slowed my pace and trod carefully ahead, moving in complete silence. When I came to the end of the bush I crawled on the ground and I finally saw the village that I had been dreaming and fantasising about.

Although it was completely different from what I had imagined, it was a real pleasure for the eye. I was lying at the edge of a large garden where I saw that they had planted some cassava and sorghum. At the other side of the garden was the village. There were only about ten houses, but for me that was perfect. What made me even more excited was that I saw a few women peeling massive piles of groundnuts; clearly they had recently finished their harvest. In the middle of the village was the granary and I could only imagine all the good things inside. I also saw children playing various games outside and some men and women digging in the gardens. This whole site reminded me of home, how I used to play with my friends, and how my parents would go out to the garden to get us food.

These memories of home made me sad and this sadness transformed into rage. Not at the LRA who had abducted me and who denied me the type of life that I was seeing in front of my eyes, but at these people that I watched. I despised their happiness and I wanted to take it away from them as mine had been taken from me. But for the moment I couldn't do anything. The men were all armed with AK-47s and although they were not many, no doubt they could easily overpower and kill me in my attempt to get food. The only option available to me was to go back to the LRA camp and think of another idea. I managed to dig out a few cassava plants at the edge of the garden, and then I went back.

I cursed the whole way back. I felt angry and aggressive. I had just seen so much food less than 200 metres away, and yet it was so far out of reach. I went over everything I had seen, and I devised a plan. I didn't want to tell my commander about my findings because, first of all, he would seriously cane me if he found out that I had missed Mass. Second, he would never give me any credit for my role, and I would likely end up eating next to nothing from the loot. Instead I decided to let some others in on the plan and offer to share the food. I calculated that it would take four people.

Once I returned, I went to lie down in my hut. Even though my journey had taken about eight hours, nobody even noticed that I had been gone.

The next day I was ordered to lead a small group of people to collect some bamboo. Although I was one of the youngest in this group of people, and not the most senior soldier, they all obeyed my orders. I didn't know all of them because they came from different sections, but I decided that this would be the group that I would select. It was actually better that we came from different units, because this meant that our absence was less likely to be noticed. During this task I told three of the most hard-working boys about my plan and asked them for their help. At first I didn't mention that we would do this without official permission, but at the time it didn't seem as if anybody cared about that. They seemed very excited about the idea, and when I described all the food, they went crazy with desire. We were all starving and I realised that their extreme hunger would persuade them to take considerable risks. On our way back I informed them that they mustn't tell anyone about this because we didn't have permission, and everyone understood why.

We agreed to meet at the stream the next day after the morning march. It was also only two days after I saw the village, so this would mean that the piles of groundnuts would still be there. Plus it was a Sunday, which was favourable because every Sunday, just like on Fridays, we attended Mass instead of working. The Masses were huge affairs on the holy grounds of Control Altar, and thousands would sit together and listen to the preaching, so it would be hard to notice that we were missing. That night I dreamed about the village over and over again.

When I woke up the following morning I started with the daily routine. As usual, we were one of the first units to be up and we started our march very early. Afterwards I was told to clean our compound. I did this very quickly and then excused myself to go to the stream. When I got there two others were already waiting and after a short while the fourth person also came. We all had our jerrycans with us, and decided to hide them until we came back. And then the four of us set off.

We made sure to go around the camp to avoid the soldiers guarding the camp's perimeter, and initially we walked very carefully so we wouldn't run into the patrol. Once we were outside the camp, I led the rest to the trailhead and we started to follow it, this time more easily than my journey two days before. Because I knew the way and had organised this whole mission, I was the leader and the others followed my commands very carefully. It took me a bit less time to reach the village than it had previously. When we got close, I ordered everybody to remain behind while I went ahead to observe the village. I took the exact same route and when I came up to the edge of the garden, I saw an almost identical picture.

The piles of groundnuts were still the same size, a group of women was still peeling them, and the children were still playing their stupid games. But there were no men. I looked everywhere but I didn't see a single man. This both comforted and disturbed me at the same time. If the men weren't here, getting the food would be extremely easy. It was simply a matter of encircling the women, tying them up and grabbing all the food. Yet I had the concern that we might run into an ambush. To be sure that the men weren't there I circled the village, but still I didn't see any of them. I went back to my colleagues and told them that the whole plan should be executed as silently and quickly as possible. The men might have gone to the bush to hunt and they could be either far away or very close. I gave a briefing and then we all crawled up to the village. On my mark, we started running.

The women noticed us when we were halfway through the garden. Immediately they panicked and while some froze, others started to run. It all happened very fast. When we reached the end of the village I ordered another boy to assist me in herding all the women and children to the centre while the other two went after the ones who had escaped. We started to round up all the women and children, and it was then that I heard a few gunshots. About half a minute later, my two colleagues came back with some of the women and explained that they had shot one woman who was trying to run away. I took the rope that we had brought from Palutaka and gave one boy the order to tie up all the women, while another was to hold them at gunpoint. I told the third boy to start filling several bags up with the groundnuts while I went searching the huts. The first hut was empty, except for a bed and some other items. After a quick glimpse I left it and entered the second hut. Here a big surprise awaited me. This hut was filled with dried and smoked meat. The moment I entered the hut, I smelled the very enticing aroma and immediately started to indulge myself. I had to force myself not to take too much, because with the lack of nutrition I had been facing this could be very dangerous. Besides, we were in a great rush to get out before the men returned. This threat was especially eminent now that my colleague had fired his gun.

I put all the meat in a large bag and quickly left the hut. In the meantime, my colleagues had tied up all the women and children and they were now eating and filling up the bags at the same time. I ordered them to stop eating and to get ready to go. I think, all in all, this whole ordeal took maybe ten to fifteen minutes. Afterwards we loaded all the bags and quickly ran away.

In the rush of excitement, I forgot about the anger that I had felt so intensely two days before. When we reached the edge of the bush one of the boys put down his sack to eat some more, but I ordered him to continue moving because we had to get as far away from the village as possible very quickly. After we had walked more than an hour, I told everyone that we could take a short rest. We shared a few pieces of meat and I took some raw cassava and groundnuts. I don't think any food had ever tasted as good.

During the whole attack I was driven by an enormous amount of adrenaline, but now it started to fade away. I realised what I had just accomplished: I had single-handedly commanded a group and carried out a very successful mission to get food. Thanks to me, everything had gone well. The plan had succeeded. I can still feel the pride that I felt that day. We were all excited. The boy who had shot the woman bragged about how he had stopped her and how he managed to catch the others, and I boasted what a successful mission it was and that it was all my idea. After a very short break I told them to move on again, and for a while we continued to laugh and joke with each other in very high spirits.

As we made our way back, I began to worry about our return. How would we get all this stuff into the LRA camp without being noticed? It had taken us about the same length of time as my first trip, so this meant that it would still be light when we got to Palutaka. It would be easier to carry this stuff into Palutaka when it was dark, but the longer we waited the greater the chance that they would discover our absence. I decided to speed up our return to Palutaka and to hide most of the food somewhere close to the stream, in a place where nobody would be able to find it. This is exactly what we did. I think it was around eight hours after we had left Palutaka that morning that we came to the stream and we found a good hiding place in some really thick bush. Afterwards we went to our jerrycans, filled them up and returned to our respective units in Palutaka.

When I got close to my hut, I noticed that there was a problem. I saw my commander walking around, extremely stressed. When I was almost at my hut, he saw me and that is when my trouble began. He started yelling at me and he looked at me with the eyes of a devil.

'Where were you? Do you know I can kill you for missing Mass? We have sent out a search party to execute you, but now that you have come back, maybe I should execute you myself.'

My absence had been noticed and I immediately realised that I was in serious trouble. Whatever happened next, I told myself that I wouldn't tell the commander about the village or the food. I took immense pride in what I had done that day and I wouldn't allow my commander to take that away from me, even if he wanted to kill me. Minutes after the commander started yelling at me, he punched me in my stomach, and I found myself crawling on the ground. My commander immediately grabbed a stick and started to cane me ferociously.

'Where did you go? You know that any attempt to escape will cost you your life, don't you, boy? You are lucky that the search party hasn't found you yet because they will make you stay in Sudan for all of eternity. Now where did you go?'

The last time I received a beating as severe as this one was on the day that I was abducted. However I didn't tell the commander anything about the village. I told him that I was hungry and that I had been out looking for fruits and animals or anything edible. Initially the commander didn't believe me and continued beating me. He eventually grew tired of beating me and of my repetitive answers to his questions, and he threw me into the hut. Though the beating was terrible, at least he stopped short of killing me. As a silent act of defiance, I took a small piece of meat, which I had put in my pocket, and slid it in my mouth.

Half an hour later my commander came back. As he entered my hut, I could see that he was still furious and I wondered what he would do next. He started screaming at me again.

'I told you the rules very clearly when you came here, didn't I? Didn't I tell you never to undertake anything without asking me for permission? Everybody is hungry, but by disobeying me, you have risked your life.'

For a moment I thought he was going to kill me, and I told him that I was deeply sorry. At this point he slapped me in the face with all his might and told me that I wasn't sorry yet, but that soon I would be. Afterwards he sent me on guard duty without any food. This was very late in the afternoon. I could barely walk because of the beating, but he pushed me hard to walk faster and faster, with his gun poking me in the back. He picked someone to accompany me so that I wouldn't try to escape, and assured me again that he would kill me if I did anything stupid.

For four whole days he forced me to stand guard with an absolute minimum of food and water. There was always somebody who was guarding me, so I had no chance to get to the place where we had concealed the food. All the people who guarded me were instructed by my commander to beat the shit out of me should I fall asleep. Occasionally at night I would get away with closing my eyes for a little while, but whenever they caught me doing that I would be in trouble.

In the meantime, I was growing really angry with the commander. I hated the man. All I had done was look after myself, and now I couldn't even reach the place where I had stashed the food. Luckily, I had kept some meat and groundnuts in my pockets, so I had at least something to eat. After four days, I came back from guard duty and my commander immediately came to visit me.

'I hope that in the last few days you had time to consider what happens when you defy me. But if you think that it is over, you are wrong. From now on your task will be to stand guard all the time. From tomorrow onwards, you will have to stand guard for a full week. You will learn what it is to be sorry.'

I was so angry. The punishment he gave me was outrageous and I was determined not to undergo it. That day I went to the place where we had stashed our food and I took a smaller bag, which I completely filled with groundnuts and dried meat. With this I walked up to the headquarters of my brigade and asked to talk to the brigadier. Initially they wanted to know why and asked me some difficult questions, but after a few minutes I was allowed to see the overall commander of our brigade, Commander Raska Lukwiya, who had the rank of a colonel. I gave him the bag of food as a tribute, and afterwards told him the full story. I told him about the beatings that I had received and the tasks that my commander had given me. I think my story impressed him a little because after I had finished, he took me with him to question my commander.

'Why did you beat this boy?'

My commander answered the question and then they got into a short argument. The colonel ordered my commander to remove his shirt and to lie down.

'This is what you get for beating the shit out of good soldiers.'

The colonel started to brutally cane my commander. I don't know when I felt more pride: after I had looted all that food, or now, when my commander was being punished because he had abused me. Although the caning my commander received was nowhere near as vicious as his attack on me, it drew much attention and he was publicly humiliated. After the colonel stopped beating him, he ordered the commander to be put on guard duty for an entire week, subsisting on a minimum of food and water rations.

'That will teach you to treat *my* soldiers like that.'

Sometime that week, I was selected to go on a big mission to Uganda. This was the first time I had been selected for this type of mission, and I had a feeling it was so that I wouldn't have to face my commander for a while. Before the journey began, we were all guided to the gate, the assembly point of Control Altar, where we received a blessing and got our briefing on the mission. It was Joseph Kony himself who addressed us. As always, his lecture was very long and elaborate, but it did lift everyone's spirits.

'The Spirit has decided that we need more recruits for our final stand against the hordes of the corrupt government. It is your mission is to find us more recruits. We order you all to abduct at least five children, three for the movement and two for yourself.'

Although the speech went on for at least another hour, this is the only fragment that I can remember from it. I wasn't exactly sure what it meant to abduct two children for myself, but I was very happy to leave Sudan and be away from my commander.

This time I took an extra bottle of water with me and we started to cross Sudan to go into Uganda. Again, the march was long and hard, but I had eaten really well the previous couple of days and all the training had made me much stronger. This time I wasn't suffering as much as I had when I first arrived in Sudan. We crossed the river and sneaked into Kitgum unnoticed. It was good to be in Uganda again.

Part III
Losing My Humanity

The Person I Feared Becoming

After we crossed the border we came to a place called Limu. The area was uninhabited and here we followed a secret LRA trail. Somebody told me about the trail and the major problem with it – bees! Minutes later, the bees started attacking us viciously. I don't know what it was about this place that attracted bees, but there were millions of them! It appeared that they liked the oil we used to clean our guns with, and when we passed their nests, they came out, attacking us in the thousands. Like everybody else, I was stung several times and it didn't take long before we were all running, even the commanders. The area where the bees' nests were located stretched for little over a kilometre, but even after we had passed the nests the bees continued to follow us. In retrospect, it must have been funny to see all those dangerous and well-armed men running from some small insects, but at the time there was nothing funny about it. The stings of African bees really hurt and even after I stopped running, I felt a burning sensation all over my body. But, as always, there was no time to rest or sit down and remove the stings; we were in a hurry and had to continue.

From Limu we moved only a short distance until we reached the Padwat reserve,* where we stayed for some time. The landscape was somehow nice because of its familiarity, and to our delight, all the game in the reserve meant that we had enough to eat. Several hours after we passed the boundary, we saw a few edible rats, which we quickly shot, and we all enjoyed a little bit of the meat. Our commander allowed us a longer break than we had had in the last couple of days so that we could regain our strength. The long walk and our chronic famine in Palutaka had weakened us all, and I felt extremely relieved when I finally sat down and ate something. As I ate, I noticed that for the first time in several months I didn't feel so angry. I could even describe my feelings as being relaxed, at ease. Before I was abducted, I had never been outside of Uganda, and it felt good to be back again. For the first time since my abduction, I wasn't completely preoccupied with my struggle for survival. The familiarity of the landscape inspired me to reflect on my life as it was before, something I rarely did in those days.

The landscape reminded me of the plains where I used to herd the cows together with my father. I remembered how my father would put me on the back of the animals when I got tired from walking. At those times, I would feel as if I was the god of the plains, a feeling actually not that much different from what I felt now, holding my AK and with safety in numbers. My thoughts remained on my father. I wondered what he would be doing right now. And my mother – would she be digging in the garden? Or would she have gone to Gulu to sell some of our harvest with my younger siblings? As I wondered how the war and my absence affected them, I felt a strange detachment. I really cherished the

---

* The Padwat reserve is also called Tim Padwat Wildlife Area, located in present-day Lamwo District in Palabek Ogili sub county, adjacent to the South Sudan border.

memories of my family, but somehow, I didn't long to go back to them. I was a soldier now. I had lost my innocence when I killed that boy just before we departed for Sudan. It would only feel right now to return to my family after we had defeated all our enemies. Escaping did not cross my mind.

After I'd sat in the sun for maybe an hour and a half, we were ordered to move again. We walked in long lines and I was somewhere in the front. At night we set up camp and allowed ourselves some fires for cooking. I sat around the fire with a few other soldiers, laughing and talking. Although we discussed many different things, the topics that amused us the most were the people we had killed, battle stories and fantasies about the kids that we would soon recruit. One of my colleagues said that he would frighten them so much that they would piss in their pants. Another had bigger ambitions: he said he would force the children to kill their own parents, so that they would never be able to return to this 'unholy' world, which is how we referred to the world of the civilians. We were the holies, sacred warriors in the army of God, and the ones we would abduct were fortunate to have the honour of joining us. My colleagues were bragging about what was to come, and I joined in. At that point I didn't really care about the mission: I wanted to make an impression on the commander, to improve my own life. That was all I cared about.

As it was a clear and warm night in the middle of the dry season, we all slept under the open sky without putting up our little makeshift tents. When the morning came, I knew that it wouldn't be long now before we reached our first populated area. Our mission would soon begin.

Ironically enough, we were being commanded by the same man

who had been responsible for my own abduction, and who had instructed others to almost beat me to death. I don't think I will ever be able to forget this man, who at one point I had regarded as my personal nemesis. His name was Ojara. He was a short man, extremely dark of colour. We Acholis are dark by nature, but he took darkness to another level. He had a beard covering his face and his dreadlocks were longer than most of ours. For around two months I had been his personal assistant. I had carried his chair and even his gun when he went for a long call. I remembered how much I used to hate this man, who I had called 'teacher', but in retrospect I realised he had been quite good to me. I no longer cared enough to actually hate him. By now I regarded him with indifference, maybe even a little admiration. He had done his duty back then, just as I was about to during this mission.

We got to the edge of the game park and saw the first signs of civilisation. We didn't see any people, but at least there were signs that people had been here not long before. So far, as we walked through the bush, the only sign of humanity had been the occasional dust road or walking trail. But now we started to come across some overgrown plots and empty huts. It was clear that this land on the edge of the park, a favourite entry route of the LRA into Uganda, was now abandoned. But it also meant that we were getting closer to the populated areas of Kitgum. At the edge of the park, Ojara came up to me and called me by the name he had given me on an earlier occasion: 'Attiena, are you ready to fulfil your duty?'

It wasn't as much a question as a confirmation that he remembered me and, as my former teacher, would have high expectations of me.

'Yes, sir, I will catch many.'

It seemed that the commander was pleased with my answer and, in order to give me a head start, he ordered me to join the advance party. The advance party was the combat group that spearheaded any attack, so the order to join this elite group gave me the opportunity to make a first selection of recruits.

It was some days later that we carried out our first attack. I was still in the advance party, following a trail that was barely visible. The terrain we walked through was bushy and we couldn't see far ahead of ourselves. We marched in silence. The only sounds were our gumboots and the cracking of the branches we stepped on. We always moved fast, or with 'ninety-nine' speed, as we used to call it, and soon we stumbled upon our first inhabited village. Before reaching the village, we had seen some plots of land where crops were growing, so we already knew we were close to our target. We saw the first hut from a short distance away. Outside the hut we saw a woman grinding millet and children playing around her. The kids were still very young, not yet fit for recruitment. They were the very first humans we had sighted on this mission and we hoped that her hut marked the outer edge of a larger village. Once we had seen her, we all knelt down so that she wouldn't see us. No alarm had been raised and we wanted to keep it that way.

Our commander decided not to wait for the main body of our battalion, and he sent four soldiers out to arrest this woman as quickly and quietly as possible. In the meantime, he sent others, including myself, to go around the village, cutting off any escape routes. As we crawled through the bush, more huts started to become visible. The houses were scattered and far apart. In between the huts grew the bush, so it was impossible to see the whole village at once. At what we thought to be the other end of the village – there was no way to be completely sure – we stumbled on three huts built close to one another. Smoke was coming out of the huts, so it was clear that they were cooking something. A small group of men were playing cards outside and there were also children playing around – some of them the right age for recruitment. We decided to pull off a surprise attack with five of my colleagues, while others went further, to surround the village.

We waited for maybe two minutes while the others encircled the huts, and then we launched our attack. The five of us ran towards the huts at full speed. As we came close the men saw us and screamed to their children to run, but it was already too late. One of the men ran into a hut and I immediately followed him inside. There were three other people in there. The man tried to hide his son and daughter under a blanket, but it was too late; I had already seen them. As I pointed my gun at the family, I told the father and mother to step away from the blanket and to lie on the ground. At first the father refused, and I had to hit him with my gun, after which he did what he was told. I then pulled the blanket away and underneath were two kids, a boy of around my age and a much younger girl. As I looked the boy in the eye, I knew I had found my first recruit. Although he was a little bit bigger than me, he was very scared of me. I grabbed him by his T-shirt and started to pull him out of the hut while the family remained inside. The father started to beg for his son's life.

'Please don't take him – he is just a boy. If you have to take someone from my family, take me; I will do anything you ask of me.'

Although I understood the words this man was uttering, I couldn't give them any meaning. His pleas couldn't reach me any more. I was extremely aggressive back then and I didn't feel any sympathy for this family whatsoever. As the father got on his knees to beg for his son's life, I took my gun and smashed him in the face once more. The man fell to the ground, half unconscious, which caused the mother to rise up and make noise. I didn't care for her either. With the barrel of my gun in her face I told her that I would shoot her entire family if she would not lie down and be quiet. My words were very effective. As I took the boy outside, I saw that everybody was lying on the ground. By now our attack on the village had fully begun.

All around us we could hear a lot of screaming and occasionally a gunshot. We couldn't see what was going on in the rest of the village, but it was clear that we were not the only ones who had discovered civilians. Together with my five colleagues, we forced everybody to leave their huts and to lie on the ground. We separated the children who were old enough to be recruited from the adults. The ones who were too young were left with their parents. While some of us held the new recruits at gunpoint, others tied up all the adults. We then guided them to the first hut, the assembly point where our commander had told us to bring the civilians.

By the time we came back, the whole of our battalion had arrived in the village and there were hundreds of holies around. Ojara started to lecture the villagers at the assembly point. While he spoke, we could hear that at the other side of the village the attack was still ensuing. In the meantime, my colleagues started to scout the surrounding bushes, to see if they could find anybody still hiding. As I saw my commander, I started to hold on tight to the boy I had abducted, to make sure that my commander would notice that I'd captured someone. Strangely enough, our commander was very friendly towards the villagers. He told them that nobody would be shot and that they would all be treated with respect. As he was saying this, gunshots could still be heard at the other end of the village, making his words sound unreliable. As more civilians were being rounded up from all sides, my commander continued his speech. He told the people in the village that they should immediately stop supporting the government troops. We were fighting this war on their behalf and therefore they had to support us. Ojara took aside one woman and told her that we wouldn't steal her harvest. Instead we kindly requested her to give us a small share so that we could continue our struggle. She was too terrified to answer. Ojara continued to ask others for food, and one elder pointed out the granary, telling Ojara to take as much as he wanted. It was a strange thing to see. Ojara was friendly and asked very nicely if we could take some of their food. However, we just took their children without asking. Ojara told them that their children were in good hands.

'The Lord's Resistance Army will look after them now and they have an important role to play in releasing us all from tyranny.'

I couldn't hold on to the boy I had abducted, as my duty was in the advance party and all the abducted children were to be held captive in the main body, so I gave the boy to two of my colleagues, and told them very clearly that I would kill them if the boy escaped. Immediately after, I started to march away. The main body remained stationed for a few more minutes to check the surrounding bush for any more people still hiding. But then they also left soon after. It was dangerous to stay in one place too long, particularly if it was a village. When the Ugandan army got word of the attack, they would surely send helicopter gunships, and we lacked the proper weapons to fight these.

The next day we all assembled again and everybody who had

abducted someone was to write the name of the abductee. All the abductees were lined up and forced to lie down. I ordered several boys to collect some branches from the mango trees nearby. Once they came back, Ojara stepped up, and on his command, we started to beat the crap out of the twenty recruits with the branches we'd collected. For every abductee there were three or four rebels beating him. I hit the boy no softer than I had been caned myself, back when my own name had been written. After several minutes, when they were more dead than alive, Ojara told us that it was enough. We wanted soldiers, not zombies. Although it was my task to clean the wounds of the boy, I ordered someone else to do it. Being with the rebels for almost a year meant that there were many colleagues who had been there for less time than me and so I was in a position to bully them around a bit. We stayed in that place for the night, and early in the morning we were on the move again. I was still marching in the advance party, so I never knew how my abductee was managing to walk during the first few days. But every once in a while, I did see him, and he proved to be quite strong.

We continued to walk for several days. By now the Ugandan army would surely have got word that the village had been attacked and would no doubt attempt to follow us, to ambush us. But that attempt would be futile. Since the attack we had walked some hundred miles, zigzagging through the country, and there was no way of tracing us. Twice we had come across other settlements, where the main body undertook the attacks while we guarded the exit roads to the villages.

Maybe a week after I had abducted my first kid, I got the easiest opportunity to abduct my second. I was still in the advance party, walking in the front as the very first man in our 200-warrior-strong rebel army. We were walking on a small village road that was surrounded by tall grass and thick bush. The natural cover blocked our sight of what was happening around us, but it also meant that we were invisible to any enemy forces. Just as we passed a sharp turn in the road, a boy – who became my second abductee – bumped into me on a bicycle that was much too big for him. As we collided, he fell to the ground and started to crawl away, but my gumboots were already standing on his back, my gun touching the back of his head. As I was the first to catch him, he was mine. Although he was a little bit young for abduction, maybe around ten years or younger, there was no way I would let him go. I started to question the boy.

'Who are you? Where do you come from? Where is that village?'

As I questioned him, the boy cried and pissed his pants. I ordered him to stop crying and forced him to answer my questions. It turned out that the boy was going to his uncle in the next village, and that his home village was nearby. While I was questioning the boy, the commander of the advance party came up to me and ordered me to go to the main group and to report to Ojara. Together with a colleague I bound the arms of the boy and led him towards the main group. I found them maybe ten to fifteen minutes later and went straight up to Ojara. I was really happy to have the opportunity to show him that I had abducted another kid, and I told him about the two villages. Ojara started to question the boy about specific directions, and then decided to attack the two villages at once. He split the troops: one group was to join the advance party and attack the village where the boy came from, while the others went for the boy's uncle's village. Ojara gave me and several others the order to stay behind to guard our new recruits. Maybe half an hour later I heard, somewhere in the distance, attacks coming from two different directions.

As I remained behind, I started to question the first boy I had abducted. As he had now been with us for a week, he was no longer so fearful as when I first met him and gave straight answers to all my questions. His name was Otema. He told me that he was still at primary school. His family were farmers, and after school, and during weekends and holidays, he used to help with the farming. The family were growing the usual Acholi crops, such as cassava, millet and beans, and used to own cattle, but the Karamojong had stolen them a long time ago. As I questioned him, I couldn't help but see the similarities between him and me. So far I hadn't really considered any of the abducted children as human, but this was rapidly changing during our conversation. Before, I had only cared about improving my own position, and had no qualms regarding the boy as a trophy. But now I saw that he was no different from me. When he asked me what would happen to him, I hit him in the face and told him that I was the one doing the questioning. I didn't want to answer the question because it opened up a Pandora's box of my own questions. It didn't change my perception of my own role in this war, but it did change my perception of his. Did I really want him to suffer what I had suffered? A very strange feeling was creeping up on me, one that could jeopardise my life. At that moment I wanted to release the boy, but I also knew I couldn't. This was the main reason I hit him so hard in the face. Not because he had asked me a question, but because I was afraid of the answer.

Initially I had planned to question the 'bicycle boy' as well, but now I didn't want to talk to anybody any more. I went to the group of abductees, watching over them but at the same time unwilling to stop any of them from escaping. In the background I heard the noises from the attack receding, and within a few minutes the first group came back with maybe twenty new recruits. We waited another few minutes for the other group to congregate – who also had around the same number of recruits – before we continued.

From now on, I became assigned to the main body. Not long after the attack, we crossed the Achwa River into Gulu District, where I had grown up. The next few weeks we marched like only the LRA could. We walked for hundreds of miles, with no obvious direction in mind. Sometimes we would be in the west of Gulu District or cross into Adjumani in the West Nile sub-region, and at other times we were close to Kitgum again. We carried out many different attacks, always on small villages, and all the attacks were similar, starting with us surrounding the villages, rounding every-body up at a single assembly point, and separating the children from the parents. The attacks were never very brutal. We didn't carry out any great massacres. This was not to say that nobody got killed during the mission, but we never destroyed complete villages, setting everything ablaze and killing everyone.

It was somewhere during the fourth week of the mission that I abducted my third child, a girl this time. Again, I made sure that Ojara had seen me abducting her before I gave her away to the others to guard. I usually tried to stay away from the abductees, because I felt sorry for the ones I had abducted and didn't want to face them. Many things that occurred during these weeks are a bit blurred in my memory. I remember a few skirmishes with the Ugandan army, but it was always only a few Ugandan soldiers fighting our whole battalion and those cowards always fled the minute they had the opportunity. What I do remember is the time that Otema and the girl I abducted escaped.

We had stopped for the night close to a small river. I ordered Otema and the girl, whose name I don't know, to fetch water. I accompanied them to the water source and while they were filling jerrycans, I started to clean my gun. Tired from the endless walking and the very little sleep we got, I wasn't paying attention. So at one point I looked up, and I saw that Otema and the girl had slowly crossed the river, while pretending to fill the jerrycan, and had started running. At that point I knew I was in trouble. Since I was in the process of cleaning my gun, I couldn't shoot them. While I could have chased after them, I was carrying mortars and mines, and I was under very specific orders never to leave these behind. However, at that point in time, those were my two options: go after them and leave the artillery stuff, or let them go. At the same time a bout of sympathy ran through me. I had actually wanted to allow Otema to escape earlier, and now he had taken matters into his own hands. Once they were out of sight, however, my sympathy turned into anger. I knew that I had to tell Ojara, and who knew what he would do to me. Self-preservation got the better of me, and I swore that if Otema and the girl were ever found, I would be the one to kill them.

The first commander I met in the camp was Ojara himself, so I told them how they had escaped. As I was narrating the story, Ojara's eyes turned bloodshot, and I knew he was fuming with anger. When I finished my story, Ojara gave me a hard slap in the face, and with a very high-pitched but forceful voice, another sign of his anger, he told me that I must never let my guard down again. I was sure that worse was to come. Ojara ordered some soldiers to look for them, and he told me that if they were found, I would have to kill the boy, while the new recruits would take care of the girl. While I awaited further punishment, Ojara cooled down a bit.

In this mission, because of the sheer number of abductees, people escaped very often, and my case wasn't unique. He was actually proud of my decision not to leave the artillery components to chase after them.

'Attiena Mortar, let this be a lesson to you. The next time when people escape under your guard, there will be hell to pay. But you were far away, and you had the artillery to carry, so I will forgive you only this once.'

While Ojara was undoubtedly a brutal man in combat and against our enemies, to us he was like a father figure. Once a soldier was initiated into the LRA, he didn't like to cane them. Of course, sometimes he did cane people, but he usually liked to lead by setting the right example and giving encouragement. Also, as my captor, he was proud to see the progress I had made, like a father being proud of his son. I had built my reputation as a ferocious soldier in battle, and I think that this helped to prevent a serious caning. That night when I went to sleep, I felt good again. Because of the absence of real punishment, my anger towards Otema and the girl diminished, and by allowing them to escape, I had the feeling that I had done something good in this whole bloody mess.

When I woke up the next morning, I was assigned to the blocking force. I was given no reason why I had been transferred, but I guessed it had to do with the children's escape under my guard the previous day. Again it was business as usual: we marched long distances through the countryside and the advance and main body would often attack villages, while we in the blocking force kept guard, making sure nobody could attack us from behind. Because of this assignment, we were never involved in the skirmishes. Then one day, in a place that looked very familiar to me, we stopped and were told to prepare a big attack.

The attack that Commander Ojara referred to was on a place called Parongo, which lies somewhere between Karuma and Pakwach. The moment I heard the name Parongo, I stiffened. At once I realised why I knew this place. My mother had brothers who lived around this area, and I had visited several times as a young boy. I knew the place very well.

Apparently, we had been specifically given the mission of attacking Parongo's trading centre when we left Sudan. In Parongo the civilians were notorious for attacking the LRA with spears, bows and arrows, especially when we marched in small groups. This needed to end. Our instruction was to teach them a lesson they would never forget.

As Parongo was quite an important place, there were Ugandan army barracks there. On our march through Uganda, we had learned that our enemies no longer called themselves the National Resistance Army, but the Uganda People's Defence Force, or UPDF, and we were determined to put their new name to the test. Just before we started our attack, we all assembled by a mango tree, a few hundred metres away from the barracks. Our instructions were very clear: the UPDF camp had to be destroyed, the civilians were to be killed and the trading centre had to burn.

The advance party was instructed to move to the north of Parongo to make sure that nobody could escape, and the blocking force was to do the same for the south. The main body would then carry out the attack from the west. I was selected with about thirty others to attack the barracks. We were told that timing was important. The moment we started our attack on the barracks, the main body would start the attack on the trading centre. These things were to happen simultaneously. Several minutes after the advance party and the blocking force marched off, the main body also began to march. The barracks were a few hundred metres away from the trading centre, to the southwest of Parongo.

As we came close, we dropped to the ground and started crawling towards the barracks until we were within striking distance. It was a rather small barracks, consisting of maybe thirty soldiers. We started our attack by shooting off three rocket-propelled grenades (RPGs) to instil terror in our enemies and inflict serious damage. By the time I started firing my gun, the UPDF soldiers had already started to run away. So much for their name. We joked about how their previous name suited them better. Indeed, they were able to resist a little bit, but the defence of the people of Uganda needed real men, not these cowards who ran away after three shells were fired. In the RPG attack we had killed several and only managed to catch one UPDF soldier alive, who was badly injured. One of my colleagues immediately put a bullet in his head. We plundered the barracks for ammunition and weapons and afterwards we set all the huts on fire. We even burned the iron huts, using petrol that we found in the barracks. After we had finished, we headed to Parongo, where the attack had already begun. This was the worst massacre I had witnessed so far.

On the outer edges of Parongo I saw bodies lying everywhere. We walked in from the south, and there were already many houses burning. After a few minutes I came to the main road where the horror was at its worst. There was a large truck carrying thousands of bottles of Coca-Cola and I saw the driver lying beside the truck in a pool of his own blood. The whole road was scattered with the bodies of those who had tried to flee the initial onslaught. A little further there was a petrol truck. When I came close enough, I saw the driver being pulled out of the truck. He was then ordered to stand in front of a firing squad, which shot at his legs so that he could never drive a truck again. In the meantime, his petrol was being used to burn the trading centre. I feared that I could come across my uncles, but luckily, they were not there. I never told any of my colleagues that this was the place where my mother had relatives, out of fear that they would force me to kill all the civilians.

I also went north of the road and started to blast my gun at some houses, unaware if there were civilians inside or not. I never went in to check, so I will never know. Afterwards I threw some petrol from the truck over the huts and started to burn them. I burned four huts in total that day. How many civilians had I killed? Now I truly hope none, but back then I didn't care. I did not actively kill anyone, but I may have killed people when I was shooting and burning the huts. I will never know, and I actually don't even want to know. All around me people were being arrested and sent to the road, where everybody was assembling. Those who tried to run were executed on the spot. Those who surrendered would suffer the same fate, only a little later. The abducted civilians were all taken to Mount Onu, where they were all executed one by one. Only twelve women were released to continue their now miserable lives.

During the attack I managed to abduct one more child. I found him somewhere in the north of Parongo; he was walking around helplessly, lost and screaming for his mother. I was filled with so much anger and hate that I didn't care about anything, including that boy. Seeing all that death and suffering had a profound effect on me. The smell of burning bodies and the screams of those still living causes your emotions to freeze. At those moments you don't care about human life any more. Some people go into some kind of a dream mode, where your actions are separated from the bloody consequences. Others explode into a killing frenzy. I was somewhere in between. I felt so much anger and hate, but everything happened as if in some kind of a dream.

That was what happened when I set those huts on fire. I was somehow in a whirl of excitement whereby I had managed to separate my own actions from their potentially life-threatening consequences. I didn't kill anybody intentionally that day, but only because I didn't really have the opportunity to. Not because I was better than the others. In these situations, everyone can be a killer. The reason I didn't shoot any of the soldiers was because I was not qualified to shoot with RPGs and by the time I started shooting my gun the soldiers had already started to run away. When I entered Parongo, most of the people had either fled or already been arrested or killed. The huts I shot at and burned were probably empty, but if they weren't, I couldn't have cared less. Did I hear screams coming from those huts? I honestly cannot remember. There were screams everywhere, and if somebody did scream in those huts, I probably would not have known. But even if I had heard some, I would have still burned the huts down. Now I think differently, but during that attack I was indifferent to human suffering. The same with the boy I abducted. I could have taken pity on him, or I could have shot him, but I didn't do either because I didn't care. I saw these children as trophies, as objects that would improve my own standing with the commander and, eventually, my position in the LRA. I remember that I kicked the boy and that I dragged him violently to the assembly point, where I made sure that people noticed I had abducted another one, before I gave him to the others who were guarding the new recruits. Afterwards I didn't see him any more because he was put under the guard of a different unit from my own.

Once the attack was over, we headed westwards, taking the arrested civilians with us towards a place we called Mount Onu, near Pakwach, where most of them were executed. By the time we arrived I was getting back to my senses, and the anger and the hate I felt was receding. I was standing guard somewhere at the foot of the mountain when the civilians were killed, and I was happy that I didn't witness any of that. Killing people in a battle frenzy is one thing, but marching them for fifty miles with the express purpose of killing them in cold blood is something entirely different. We then marched back in the direction of Parongo again. Occasionally we attacked a small village, but never destroyed them. When we had moved some distance away from Parongo, we released some women we had abducted to help us carry some of the looted goods, and quickly went on. Why did we release those women? Maybe to spread the word that no one should ever attack us again, maybe because we no longer needed the stuff that they carried, maybe out of sympathy? I will never know the true reason. The LRA was very erratic like that. Sometimes we abducted and killed, other times we released people and let them live. You could never know beforehand what the intention was, or what a victim's fate would be. It depended on the mood swings of the commanders, which were very unpredictable.

About fifty miles further to the east, somewhere at the edge of Murchison Falls National Park, we attacked a camp of park rangers. We captured maybe twenty or so of them, and they were all executed in a little shed close to their camp. I was standing outside the hut when I heard them being executed one by one. What amazed me most was their silence. They knew they were going to die and yet they didn't scream. Not a single one of them. The one doing the killing was a boy who would always volunteer whenever someone had to be killed. He was young, not much older than me, but he had been with the rebels for a while. He was abducted when he was nine years old and somewhere along the way something had snapped in him. He liked the killing too much. The strange thing was that he was a funny guy who was actually very nice when he was not killing. But whenever somebody needed to be killed, he was the first in line.

As we continued going east, our excitement grew with every step we took. We all knew that we were getting close to Karuma Falls, where the River Nile narrows to about twenty to thirty metres while making a steep descent. Since the early days of the insurgency, the Nile had always been the natural boundary that stopped our march to Kampala. Alice Lakwena was defeated close to the Nile, in Jinja, and we had also been unable to penetrate this natural border. The Nile was a formidable boundary, and swimming from one side to the other was nothing short of committing suicide. The only way to cross it was by using a bridge, and the few bridges crossing it were heavily guarded by the enemy troops. So with every step closer to the bridge, rumours started spreading that this time we would cross. In our minds, the bridge was the last step before taking Kampala; after that, there were no natural boundaries that would prevent us from overthrowing Museveni. By crossing Karuma we would show that Museveni wasn't invulnerable, and it might even cause him to flee. As we came closer, our excitement started to mount. Crossing Karuma was not an instruction given to us by Kony, but when our commander noticed our high morale, he decided that we would show Museveni the power of the Spirit. In my head I already saw myself returning to my parents, loaded with medals, as a highly decorated commander who was given the rank of captain for his bravery at Karuma Bridge.

When we came to the bridge at five in the morning, we immediately started to launch our assault, using every single combatant that we had. We all lined up as close to the bridge as possible without being noticed. We could see some soldiers patrolling the bridge, but there were only a few, less than ten. Their barracks were in the village of Karuma, some 300 metres away from the bridge. Usually there was one battalion stationed there, with some brigades further from Karuma, who could be called in at any given moment. By now we had abducted more than 200 children, maybe even more than 300. The modest battalion with which we had left Sudan had now almost turned into a brigade. Although most of the newly abducted had not received weapons training, and most of them were unarmed, we looked like a formidable force. The soldiers guarding the bridge were taken completely by surprise. UPDF soldiers had been guarding this bridge every day for ten years and nothing had ever happened. Every night they had probably heaved a sigh of relief that they were guarding the bridge and not fighting at the frontline. But now the frontline had suddenly sprung upon them at ninety-nine speed. The moment the soldiers saw us they threw away their guns and they started to flee. They were at the end of the bridge with a head start of at least 400 metres. By the time we crossed the bridge, the soldiers had already reached Karuma village, where they alerted the barracks. But none of them stayed around to put up a fight. All of them ran away like frightened chickens. We tried hard to capture at least one soldier, but those cowards never gave us the chance.

When we entered the little village of Karuma, two civilians were arrested. My commander said that they were intelligence, working for the government, so they had to be questioned. In the meantime, the majority of us went up to the barracks, which we plundered. We took everything that there was to be found, which was a lot. B-10s, AK-47s, AK-49s, hand grenades, mortars, mines and much more. It was actually more than we could carry, and the newly abducted were forced to carry the heaviest load. All this took us maybe half an hour. I still remember how excited I was. At that time, I really thought that we had defeated the last battalion that stood between Kampala and us. Actually, the vast majority of us thought the same, but our commanders knew better. They knew very well that it wouldn't be long before this place was swarming with government tanks, gunships, aeroplanes and at least a 1,000-soldier-strong brigade. So the moment we came down from the barracks we got the order to cross the bridge again and to go back into Gulu District. I felt so disappointed. I had really thought that this would be the day we would march into Kampala, but the order to go back definitely saved my life.

By the time I reached Gulu District, the first government forces had already started to cross the bridge. The two civilians we had captured were both killed, shot in the head. But we vanished in the thick bush again, leaving as little trail as possible.

By now we had attained most of our chief objectives. Parongo was burning and we had abducted many new recruits. The group of abductees was so large that it was getting difficult to manage and guard them all at the same time, so the time had come to move back to Sudan. Initially, when we had just entered Uganda, I thought that life here as a rebel was much more comfortable. In Uganda there was always plenty of food to plunder, but there was rarely a moment to relax. We were always on the move, often walking for more than eighteen hours a day. Staying at one place for more than a day was dangerous, because there was always the threat that the UPDF would amass all their forces, including mobile units and air-craft, to destroy us. In Palutaka, we never had to worry about this. But then, in Palutaka we were always hungry. By now I had grown strong and battle-hardened. Although we were only kids, we were all very muscular because of the heavy loads that we had to carry and all the walking. The marching had become especially tough after the raid on Karuma. As I was still in the artillery department, I had to carry my gun, two landmines, an RPG, hand grenades and, of course, lots of ammunition. The further we got, the heavier the load became. Once in a while we found a good place to stash weapons and ammunition, but then we plundered another village and were loaded with bags of millet flour or some other goods.

Although we were slowly going back to Sudan, our mission wasn't over. Whenever we passed a village, we would always attack it and abduct even more children. At least they could help us carry the load. A couple of days after Karuma, I was again selected for an attack on a small village, where I managed to abduct two more children. There was no escaping the abductions. If you were chosen to be in the advance party and were the first to enter a vil-lage, you were expected to abduct some children. Five was the target. As always, I made sure that the commanding people were aware of my 'trophies', and then I handed them over to the guards in the main body.

As the days passed, we were getting closer to the border of Sudan. About one week after our attack on Karuma we crossed the Achwa River again and here we were ordered to rest for a bit. I was assigned to assist in guarding the abductees. By now we had abducted very many, maybe even up to 600, while we were only 200, so guarding them became a difficult task. If they wanted to flee, they only had to do it simultaneously so that there was no way that we could catch them all. But our methods to prevent them from escaping were also very effective.

Fear was our main tool. Whenever we caught one who tried to escape, all the new abductees were forced to execute him, the same way I had been forced to kill that boy ten months earlier. We always wrote the name of everyone we abducted. Before the writing of the name they would be tied up with ropes, and afterwards, at least in the first few weeks after writing their name, they would be too wounded to even attempt an escape. Ojara and the captains also told all the new abductees that the Spirit protected us and that the Spirit saw everything, even thoughts, so most were too afraid to even think about escaping. Then there was the last method we used, which was a sort of 'divide and rule' strategy. Abductees were encouraged to report anything suspicious about their fellow abductees. If they reported any rumour about someone attempting to escape, they would receive better treatment and receive extra food rations, while those who were planning to escape would be seriously caned. In this way it became very hard for abductees to trust each other. The attempt was to break down any group solidarity, and so whenever someone wanted to escape, they had to do it on their own.

By the time we reached the border of Sudan, we had been successful in abducting many children. About two dozen of them had escaped, but the rest were still with us. If every single combatant that had set out from Sudan had indeed abducted five, we would have recruited around a thousand new soldiers, but I doubt if it was really this many. Anyway, Ojara appeared to be happy. We had burned Parongo and had helped swell the ranks of the LRA considerably, but the biggest challenge of our mission was yet to come – crossing the semi-desert of Sudan to reach Palutaka in the warmest season of the year.

Just like the first time, as I had when I had to cross it as a new abductee, this time too I suffered. The heat and the thirst don't spare anyone. Every time is a risk, no matter how often you have done it. But, much like the first time, I did manage to make it and so did the vast majority of others. As I was walking at the front, I didn't see any people dying of thirst and exhaustion, but I am sure that lives were lost during what we called the 'death march'. When we arrived in Palutaka, we, the combatants, were welcomed as proud warriors and a special speech was made in our honour.

The Attack on Palutaka

After I came back from my mission, life in Palutaka hadn't changed all that much, with a few exceptions. Ojara had put in a good word for me, describing how well I had performed, and for this reason my status improved a bit. My plundering of the Sudanese village months before had gained me some respect among the higher officers, and my direct commander seemed to have forgiven me – at least, he didn't mention my treacherous act any more. Only once did he tell me very clearly that if I ever again went to a higher commander to complain about him behind his back, he would personally kill me. I was careful enough to take his words very seriously.

The famine in the area continued. In the weeks following our return I started to lose weight and every day was a struggle to find enough food.

After several weeks, rumours began that there was an increasing rate of enemy activity in our area and that troops were massing together to plan our destruction. It was unclear where these rumours originated, as ordinary privates were never informed about the strategic issues, but somehow these stories spread. I thought that our Arab allies, who were usually more talkative and less disciplined, were the source of this talk.

One morning, I woke up before sunrise, expecting the day to begin with the usual routine of a morning march. In the darkness of pre-dawn, I went to the stream to fill a jerrycan of water. Upon my return I passed the gate of Control Altar and I saw that a very large group was amassing there, ready to march out. Although this wasn't an unusual sight, as battle groups departed all the time towards Uganda, there seemed to be something different about this group. Their equipment was light, for fast movement rather than endurance. Normally when groups went to Uganda, they carried extra guns, artillery and ammunition, all to be stashed somewhere in the bush to avoid having to return to Sudan for more supplies. However, this group was carrying only a few provisions for a short march and not enough ammunition for an extended campaign.

Without asking what was going on, I passed the group and I went to the gate at Stockree to deliver the jerrycan of water to my commander. He told me that one of the artillery boys from the battle group had fallen sick and that I was needed to replace him. He told me to hurry, as the group was all set to leave. My AK-47 was already over my shoulder, so I only took the time to collect some extra ammunition and grenades, and then hurried back to Control Altar. I didn't mind that I had been selected. In fact, I had become a little bored with the daily routine in Palutaka and was glad to have the opportunity to escape it.

It was still very early morning when we set out. Because we were armed very lightly, we moved with great speed. We were not told where we were going, or the nature of the mission. The only thing I knew was that we were in a great hurry and that we were heading in the direction of the Ugandan border. My colleagues and I didn't discuss it since many of us believed it was bad luck to talk about a mission beforehand.

The speed with which we were marching was somewhere between running and walking, which gave me a clue about the destination. A slower pace would be used for a long-distance journey, running was reserved for short distances, so it had to be something mid-range. We quickly crossed a tremendous distance as we steadily descended downhill. We were not far from the route that I had taken two and a half months earlier when I returned to Uganda for the first time. Morning turned into noon and then into afternoon, and still we continued our march. Finally, around four in the afternoon, we were allowed a break. Our commander instructed us to eat all the food we had brought with us, and then ordered us to remain there as he went on ahead.

Initially it was quiet around us. To pass the time there was a lot of joking between us. The humour was very dark, as we joked about the naming of some of my colleagues or the things that our victims had said before they were killed. After about half an hour, the atmosphere changed a little. Although our commander still hadn't returned, we started to hear gunfire from a far distance. It was clear that this was why we had been sent here. The moment we heard the sounds of battle, all joking stopped and our loaded guns were pointed in the direction of the gunfire. This almost proved fatal to our commander when he finally returned to explain the mission to us.

He explained that we had arrived at a place called Pajok, where a full battalion of the Sudanese army was under severe attack by a combined force of Ugandan soldiers, Sudanese rebels and a new force he called 'mercenaries'. This was an unfamiliar English word, but I would soon find out its meaning. He told us that we were fighting a well-armed enemy of at least a brigade in strength, which meant at least 2,000 soldiers. In comparison, we had only one full battalion, less than 500 people, which was strengthened by a battalion or two from our Arab allies. We were ordered to march out again and soon we came to a fast-flowing river. We crossed it in the usual way and headed towards the action. Our progress slowed significantly as we entered the battle zone. When we got closer, the gunfire slowly died out, which indicated that one episode of the battle had ended. At a certain point our commander told us to line up and to let nobody pass. He left us to defend this line, returning shortly with around 100 or 200 additional Arab fighters.

For a long while we stood there in the bush, waiting for our enemies to approach. We were not allowed to sit or lie down. Instead we were told to face our enemy while standing and we were given the firm order that whatever happened, we were not to retreat. We spent at least an hour this way in tense silence. Eventually the Arabs who were with us began to complain about the heat of the sun and some of them even requested to go back to their position. Our commander was very tough on them. As always, we proved to be the more disciplined soldiers. Another half hour passed. Then all around us hell broke loose.

The RPG that flew towards us caught us by surprise. It hit a small group of Arabs about twenty metres to the left of where I stood. The initial RPG round killed two of them and wounded several others. I saw their bodies fly, but immediately my attention shifted in front of me. A few seconds passed and I still didn't see anything. Suddenly we were hit by all kinds of artillery. Mortar shells were exploding all around us. Through the explosions I heard a tank rolling in our direction. This was when it became clear that this would be a very heavy battle, unlike any I had experienced before.

Among the wounded was a guy who was standing next to me when the whole attack began. As we advanced, he was only three metres away from me when he was shot and badly hurt. A bomb splinter had hit his leg and shattered his bone, and he was screaming in pain. For a split second, I realised that it could have been me lying there, but I immediately suppressed this thought. In battle you shouldn't think about these things. Our commander put a stick in his mouth, and he told him to hold on and to be quiet.

The bombardment continued for several minutes and then, as suddenly as it started, it stopped. At that moment I saw the first foot soldiers marching towards us, from approximately a hundred metres away. This is when the battle really began. I targeted my gun on the first soldier and for this first shot I aimed really well. A fraction of a second later he lay dead on the ground. All around me my colleagues unloaded their guns on our enemies while we slowly moved forward. After the tank shot its first few rounds, it was destroyed by several of our RPGs. There were only a few vehicles that attacked us and soon they were rendered useless.

We held the high ground, and as we slowly advanced downwards, our enemies fell in the hundreds. The enemies that advanced on us moved in a very long column, three to four men deep. They tried to advance strategically, which meant that the first line would take cover, then shoot at us while the next line advanced. Initially this tactic worked, causing many deaths on our side, but we eventually proved to be superior and soon our enemies had no choice but to retreat.

I have no clue as to how many soldiers I shot or who I was

actually fighting, but it was clear that they had underestimated us. The heaviest fighting took place about a hundred metres away from me, towards the position where the tanks were disabled. Here the Arabs were fighting alongside my colleagues. This group had destroyed the tanks and they also had the majority of the RPGs. The attacking forces did not expect that between attacks the Arabs had been reinforced with a full battalion of LRA soldiers. The battalion they sent towards us was not enough. I have no way of recalling how long it took us to force them to retreat, but it was still light when they started running away. We ran after them and I managed to shoot one more soldier in his back, when I heard my commander scream that we were to return to our initial position.

When we were back, our commander reported the damage. I was reminded of my belief that success in battle depends on the breasts that the soldiers suckled when they were babies. Our Acholi mothers had strong breasts and because we had suckled from them as babies, we were much stronger soldiers. Many of the Arabs had fled during the battle and it was our soldiers who had secured the victory. I wouldn't say that in battle I was untouched by fear, but with me, fear caused an intense focus and a stronger determination to kill, rather than a blackout or urge to flee.

But no matter how strong the breast or how much holy shea oil we had smeared on our bodies, bullets did harm us. Among the LRA soldiers were at least thirty deaths and more wounded. The Arabs who hadn't fled had been hit badly. Our commander sent an Arab lieutenant to see where his forces had run to and order them back. Some other Arabs and Acholis were ordered to bring the wounded to the Arab sickbay.

In the meantime, we held our position and our focus was entirely directed to the bush in front of us. My eyes scouted the bush and except for some dead bodies, mainly of our enemies, I didn't see anything of concern. Our commander congratulated us for our performance, but he told us firmly that the battle had just begun, and we were to expect more.

As dusk began to fall, the second wave began. This time our enemies did not make the mistake of underestimating us. As with the first attack, the battle began with significant artillery fire from the mortars and tanks. Explosions all around me ripped my eardrums and beneath this sound I heard many tanks and armoured personnel carriers (APCs) rolling in our direction. When the bombardment stopped, we saw the first ground forces approaching. These ground forces were not Africans: they were the mercenaries that our commander had warned us about. In fighting them I did notice two differences. Their aim was much better and whenever they shot at us, they rarely missed. But their light skin compromised them. Especially in the dusk, they stood out, which offered us very clear targets. It soon became clear to us that these white men were just as vulnerable to bullets as our black enemies, and many of them died.

Then the tanks arrived. Because we were equipped only lightly, we had no means of fighting these tanks. We only had a few remaining RPGs but not enough to destroy all that was rolling in our direction. Furthermore, the foot soldiers were not only better trained, but there were also more of them. I knew for sure that I had killed at least one so-called mercenary, but they shot many more of us. Instead of advancing, we were forced to shoot while we walked backwards. As always, the first to retreat were the Arabs, but the moment our commander saw them fleeing, he followed them. When I saw my commander running off, I quickly went too.

Soon we all retreated and there was nothing glorious about it. We sustained many more casualties than in the first attack and this time we left our wounded where they fell. While we ran away, the mercenaries pursued us, but soon we had lost them. We all gathered at the river, and crossed it before even performing our body count. I think that we lost at least forty people during the first few minutes of the second attack, and all in all I estimate that out of the 300 people who set out, only 200 returned.

On the other side of the river our commander told us that the brigade that had defeated us was only a small fraction of the army. This massive enemy force was rolling towards Palutaka for a major attack. We were ordered to rush back to assist in the defence of Palutaka with all the speed that we could muster. To move more quickly, we left the few lightly wounded to return at their own pace.

Our return was even faster than the speed we used to reach Pajok, despite the fact that it was dark but for a half-moon. We encountered only one road that we had to pass: the road to Winkibui, about two hours from Palutaka. After our commander determined the road to be free from enemies, we crossed it with extreme speed. The road was at least three metres wide but we used only one step to cross it. Eventually we had to slow a bit because even the commander himself couldn't keep up, but still we marched faster than any normal army would.

When we were around two kilometres from the camp, our commander called in to inform them that we were coming. We arrived in Palutaka at around one or two in the morning, finding the camp in the highest state of alert. We first encountered the patrolling units. They weren't there to stop an attack, but rather to take away the element of surprise in case the enemy attempted an attack in the middle of the night.

But we were not worried about an immediate attack. Although the main forces of our enemy had a head start, none of us believed that they had marched so fast that they had already reached Palutaka. Furthermore, they were equipped with tanks, Katyusha rocket launchers* and APCs, and considering the extremely bad conditions of the roads in Sudan, it would still take them at least ten to twelve hours to reach Palutaka. For the moment we were safe.

When we arrived, Joseph Kony himself was awaiting us. He told us how proud he was of our victory, but that we had to be aware of the visitors who were coming. He started a small speech about what type of welcome we would give our visitors, but I was unable to focus. The only thing I wanted was to lie down and to rest after a gruelling day and the fastest march that I had ever done. Kony told us that we had to be alert and that we could not sleep in our huts that night. Instead, we were all ordered to go to the trenches, where we were allowed some good hours of sleep before the battle was to begin. Despite the discomfort of the location, it took me only seconds before I was gone.

The next morning, I woke up very early. An eerie atmosphere lay over Palutaka; it was unusually quiet, and everybody was tense. We believed that it was here that we would take a final stand against our enemy. The terrible battle of Pajok would only be a foretaste of what awaited us this day.

Strategically, we were in a very good position. Although not really on a hill, we did hold the high ground, and the encampment was surrounded by deep trenches. We were also very heavily equipped with RPGs, one B-10, mortars and enough ammunition

---

* Russian-made weapon systems mounted on trucks that can fire dozens of missiles in quick succession.

to hold out for several days at least. To our north were the Arabs, who were equipped with tanks, heavy artillery and APCs.

In the morning, at around eight o'clock, some porters brought us a large tin filled to the top with bullets. We were given extra magazines to fill so that we would not lose precious time in the middle of an attacking wave. We expected our visitors to come from the east, from the river, which was our water supply, and it was there that our heaviest and most experienced forces were concentrated. I was among them. No one else was allowed to go to the stream that morning because of the concern that our enemies had lined up at the other side of it. Throughout the night, colleagues had collected enough water to last for some days, and all the jerrycans were filled and distributed among the trenches. Early in the morning all the young mothers and pregnant girls were marched out of the camp, towards the northwest. All others who were capable of fighting were either in the camp, or in the trenches surrounding it. We were prepared and ready for the upcoming battle.

Hours passed. I had been up since dawn, but by ten o'clock there was still an eerie silence. I remained alert. The area in front of me was not very bushy, and for a stretch of 200 metres our enemy would have little to hide behind. The field was mainly covered by grass before the thick bush at the banks of the stream. Behind the stream was the mountain that loomed over Palutaka. I knew our enemy was out there, somewhere in the mountains at the other side of the riverbank, yet I didn't see anything. At a certain point, the silent tension became so unbearable that I actually wished the battle would begin, so that we could be over it sooner. It was clear that I had no idea what I was to encounter.

At around eleven, it finally began. What I witnessed was the heaviest bombardment that I had ever seen in my life and truly hope never to see again. It started from the other side of the mountain, where Katyusha rocket launchers, howitzers* and other heavy artillery equipment started to unload bombs and heavy rockets onto Palutaka. The first explosions fell in the middle of the camp, which was still full of people carrying items and equipment from one side of the camp to the other. Only once did I glance back, and what I saw was utter devastation. Several rockets also landed on our side of the camp, setting almost everything ablaze. The air heated up, directing wind towards the flames. Breathing became difficult. Our order was to remain standing and to await the enemy, but I am sure that the only thing people wanted to do was to crawl as deep as possible into the trenches. Whenever there were a few seconds in which no explosion hit our side of the camp, we could hear them falling on the other side. The Arabs were also under heavy assault. Between the sounds of the bombardment were the cries of those whose limbs had been blasted off their bodies. It was so terrible.

While the bombardment continued, we heard many tanks rolling towards the north of the camp. Before we saw our first enemy, the battle broke loose in the Arab side of the camp. This is where the main action would take place, a battle including tanks and other heavy equipment.

As this battle began, we started to see our first 'visitors' coming from the east. Line after line of them appeared from the bush some 200 metres away. The lines were extremely wide, covering the whole length of the eastern trenches, and they were made up out of

---

* A type of artillery piece characterised by a relatively short barrel and the use of comparatively small propellant charges to propel projectiles over relatively high trajectories, with a steep angle of descent.

thousands of soldiers. As they drew closer, their first line started to fire at us with massive firepower. The heavy artillery attack stopped, and the mortar fire began. The front line was equipped with RPGs and bazookas, and all around me people were dying.

I wanted to start firing, but our commander was very clear that we should not start shooting until they were very near, so that we wouldn't spill too many bullets. This decision cost us a tremendous number of lives. When the first enemy line reached the halfway point of the open field, we were in clear firing range of them and although only parts of our bodies were revealed to them, we offered clear targets. Still our commander refused to give the order. It was only when they were about seventy or eighty metres away from us that we got the order to shoot.

Complete chaos broke loose. All around me I saw people dying as my colleagues were hit, but the majority fell in front of us. As we got the order to fire, our enemies started to charge us. Because of the trenches, our visitors had a much harder time hitting us than we did them. Running towards us, they offered very clear and easy targets. In less than a minute I shot at least ten of them, but the waves just kept coming. Those who actually reached the trenches were welcomed by sharpened bayonets, but most never made it that far.

Another few lines advanced towards us and as I changed my magazine, the soldier next to me, a kid barely my age, covered me by shooting two soldiers ten metres away from our position. By the time he had emptied his magazine I had reloaded my gun and then I covered for him. A few metres away from me a visitor had managed to reach the trench. I was focused on the action in front of me, but I heard his screams as my colleague drove a bayonet through him. The problem was that whenever someone reached the trench, two soldiers had to deal with this person. This meant less firepower to hold the other lines off. But our enemy was running out of soldiers and after a ferocious first attempt, they gave up their attack and were ordered to withdraw.

At this point I heard our commander scream from the top of his lungs for us to charge. As ordered, we crawled from the trenches and ran after the enemy. We followed them for at least a hundred metres, shooting many in their backs before our commander told us to return to our trenches. This was just in time, for while we ran back a heavy mortar bombardment began in the field above our trenches. The bombardment started even before I reached my trench – as I dived in mortars were falling all around us. Several of my colleagues didn't manage to reach the trench in time and were showered by the mortar splinters.

We heard our commander contacting the commanders of the southern and western trenches, requesting reinforcements. When the battle on our side ceased, we could hear it continuing on the Arab side of the camp. Very heavy explosions set almost all of Palutaka on fire.

For a moment I sat down in my trench, crying and despairing. I had survived the first wave, but I knew that this wouldn't be the end of it. The enemy forces were massive, and they wouldn't give up easily. Furthermore, our safety also relied heavily on what happened on the Arab side of the camp. If their camp was breached, the enemy would be able to outflank us and then we would all be shot.

Suddenly, a captain kicked me in the stomach, and he told me to stand. At that moment the second wave of attack began. This was even more ferocious than the first, but again we managed to repel them. Their attacks kept on coming, wave after wave. In the third wave both my neighbours in the trench were shot dead, which meant that I became very vulnerable. There were at least eight metres of trench to defend on my own, but somehow I managed. Whenever the enemy retreated, we were ordered to follow. Then we would run back to the trench while their mortar bombardment began. This happened several times. There was always someone who made the return too late and who was caught by the bombardment. A few times the enemy came very close, but then we shot many of them and they had to withdraw. In the meantime, the battle on the northern side of the camp continued heavily and we started to hear rumours that the Arabs were losing.

It was already late in the day when the decisive moment came. We were under severe attack by ground forces coming from the east. After they had retreated several times, they revised their tactics. It felt as though they threw in all their reserves, beginning with a heavy mortar bombardment aimed at our trenches. Then ground forces appeared slowly from the bush near the stream, and this time they took better cover, making it harder for us to hit them. The previous mortar bombardments had created so many craters that the troops had much more opportunity to seek cover. Yet the closer the enemy came, the easier it got to hit them. We were in a standoff with our enemies and for the moment we managed to hold our ground.

What we didn't know was that the battle in the northern section had come to an end and the Arabs were in retreat. I was extremely lucky to be one of the first to notice this. As I hadn't heard any instruction from my commander for almost a minute, I allowed myself to take a quick glimpse behind, and this is when I saw our commander in the distance, running for his life like a cowardly cheetah. Behind him were several Arabs also on the run. I shifted my attention to the north and saw the first enemy tanks rolling in my direction. They were still far off, but close enough to start bombarding the hell out of us. A fraction of a second later, I crawled out of the trench and made a run for it.

In a fast and unpredictable zigzag, I started to run away from this horrible scene of destruction. I had no time to warn any of my colleagues, many of whom were still completely occupied with the battle up front and had no idea of what was happening behind their backs. It was because of their cover fire that I actually stood a chance. Seconds after me, several of my colleagues also noticed what had happened and they also started to run. The battle we left behind died out quickly; it didn't take long for my colleagues to notice what was going on, but by then it was already too late for them. Without anybody left to offer covering fire, they proved easy targets for the thousands of foot soldiers who chased them down. The tanks soon started to open fire on the area to the east of the road that runs through the middle of Palutaka. By this time, I had already reached the road and I was in relative safety.

There was nothing graceful or tactical about our retreat. We just ran for our lives, using a slight zigzag motion to make it difficult for the enemy to get a clear shot. Without looking back, I just continued to run through what I had come to consider home. By now all the grass huts were on fire and visibility was very low because of all the thick black smoke. What I could see was utter chaos and destruction. Here and there were body parts of those who had perished in the first wave of bombardment. All around me my colleagues ran for their lives through the thick smoke. As I passed the gate of Stockree, I saw that my former hut was also ablaze; in fact, nothing from our brigade was still standing. Seconds later I reached the western trenches of our camp, which had just been abandoned minutes before. In a giant leap I jumped over the trenches and left the camp. I kept on moving towards the west. My commander was already far out of sight, but there were hundreds of LRA soldiers fleeing and I just kept following them. After running at top speed for more than fifteen minutes we looked around and we noticed that we were no longer being followed. We slowed our pace and began to assemble all the people we could find.

The entire force of the LRA was scattered into dozens or maybe even hundreds of smaller groups. The group that I had followed was commanded by a major and, luckily, he was in the possession of a walkie-talkie so that we could reach the main group. For many other scattered groups, it took days, sometimes even weeks, before they found the main group.

Kony had taken a large group of combatants, including thirty of his bodyguards – who were regarded as some of the best fighters in the LRA – to join up with all the mothers, children and pregnant women somewhere to the northwest of Palutaka. We headed there as well, and it took us several hours to catch up with them. There were thousands of us marching. As we proceeded, other groups managed to find us and join our ranks. It wasn't until after midnight that we could finally rest and reflect for the first time on what had happened that day.

Although the vast majority of the LRA had survived the attack, hundreds of our best combatants had lost their lives. Only once before, during the attack on Parongo, had I seen so much death and destruction, yet this time we were the victims of the onslaught. All around me there were wounded and many of us were crying. Never had I killed so many people in one single day, nor had I seen so many of my colleagues die in one day. Visions of the battle ran through my head and I was completely traumatised. When I closed my eyes, I saw how my fellow soldiers were shot dead when they stood just metres away from me. A very loud high-pitched sound rang in my ears, but through it I still heard the agonised cries of those young porters who had lost their limbs during the initial attack. It was the newest recruits who were selected to carry messages and supplies, those with no battle experience and often without military training. The limbs I saw could have belonged to any of the three remaining kids that I had abducted and taken to Sudan.

In my mind I saw some of the people I had killed that day. The first few kills of the day especially stuck into my mind. In my dreams they were alive again and they were very vengeful against me. I opened my eyes, preferring to lie awake and suffer the consequences of restlessness the next day than to see all this human suffering replayed in my mind. But even with my eyes open I was unable to escape the images: the tanks, the burning huts, the screaming soldiers, that young porter whose lower body had become separated from his chest.

That night we spent under the open skies, making do with the very little that we had taken with us from Palutaka. I was actually happy that our break was very short. After only half an hour we were ordered to march on again through the night.

We had lost Palutaka and our future was insecure. Nobody knew where we were going or where we would sleep the next day. Although we always suffered from a lack of food in Palutaka, it would be worse in other places. Palutaka was extremely fertile and there was always enough water. It was an ideal area for an army to settle, but this was something that our Dinka enemy also realised, and they had mustered their full fighting force, combined with their Ugandan allies and hired guns, to defeat us. Only God knew where we would end up now.

It was for the first time in almost a year since the indoctrination had begun that I started to doubt our connection to God. If we were His army, how could He abandon us like this? I also started to question how He, in all His wisdom, could have given us such cowardly allies as the Arabs, who were the object of my worst anger. I felt that we would have won our battle if they hadn't lost theirs. I cursed the breasts from which the Arabs suckled. They were not strong breasts. They were breasts that made the children grow up to be cowards. Even all their expensive equipment, tanks, APCs and artillery couldn't cover up for their cowardly nature. I was so angry that evening that if an Arab had walked into our camp, I might have shot him. But the Arabs were also in the retreat and they had a different destination.

The whole future of the LRA was unsure at this point. When we saw the first sunlight the next morning, we took our second rest. My exhaustion finally took over and I fell asleep, unsure what would happen when I woke up, but delighted that I didn't have to think about it for a few hours.

The Deserts of Sudan

I had a very restless sleep that morning. I was haunted by terrible nightmares and every half hour I woke up bathed in sweat. Whenever I closed my eyes, even when I was still awake, the horrible images of the previous two days would come back to me.

I awoke around noon to an atmosphere of defeat and despair. Most of my colleagues were silent and I couldn't hear any sounds of laughter. We had lost Palutaka and it was clear that we would not try to recapture it. We had to look for a new home. We all knew that the next few months would be very tough. It would be only a few days before all the provisions that we had taken from Palutaka would run out and then what would we eat? Although we were always hungry in Palutaka, at least we had had our gardens there and we had grown all kinds of crops. The crops hadn't been enough to feed the whole army, but they went quite far. Now we had nothing. For the next few months we would be forced to rely solely on the goodwill of the Arabs to feed us, and on plundering, hunting and gathering.

We also knew that it wouldn't be long before our enemies would start to pursue us, so it was critical that we find a place that would give us a strategic advantage in case of attack. Our military morale hadn't wholly died out. We were severely weakened but far from defeated. Although hundreds of our finest soldiers had been either wounded or killed, thousands had survived, and these survivors were bitter, angry and vengeful. Our commanders had already promised that we would strike back, and we were all anxious for our fine day of vengeance.

I saw that the first groups had already started to march off in a northwestern direction, and the rest of us soon joined them. Throughout our march we reconnected with many scattered groups of LRA fighters and our numbers grew. I was amazed by the number of survivors. The main group continued to walk further away from Palutaka, while dozens of scouting groups were sent in different directions to find a new location for our camp. Two days later, we were ordered to march south again, and at the end of the third day we reached the ideal spot, a place called Kit One. Kit One was also in a green hilly area, not all that far away from Palutaka. We eventually set up camp there on a hill, which proved to be very difficult for building grass huts, but it gave us a very strategic defensive position.

We arrived at Kit One late in the evening, at around eleven. Although there was a bit of moonlight, it was too dark to start collecting grass and to make up camp, so instead we slept under the open sky again. I had another restless night. This time I was not only haunted by all the images of war, but also by countless insects. I changed positions many times, but it appeared that the insects were everywhere.

The next morning, I was awakened by our Mzee, the commander of the artillery unit, who told me that he had a special mission for me. I think this was his strategy of getting back at me. Whenever he was ordered to select someone for a dangerous mission, he always picked me: first when I was sent with the battle group to assist the Arabs, and now again. Our unit consisted of at least fifty guys and he could have chosen any of them, but it was always me. I was wondering what kind of suicidal thing I had to do now.

The Mzee took me to Control Altar Brigade's assembly point. On the way he told me that I had been selected because of my excellent performance in combat and because of my courage, but I was sure that his personal vendetta with me also played a role in my selection. When we got to the location, there was a group of about 300 of the best-trained guerrillas, commanded by a major. The major explained that we had a dangerous mission in front of us that would lead us through the heartland of our enemies. He told us that in the last few hours of the battle, hundreds of soldiers had carried our armouries out of Palutaka. Most of the weaponry would stay in Kit One in case of another attack, but we also needed to stash some weapons and armour in Uganda. In the future we would strike back at our enemies, and would then need our weapon supply to be close by.

To deliver all the weaponry, we had to slip through hostile territory unnoticed. It was essential that our weapons didn't fall into enemy hands, so we had to avoid any enemy contact. We were given enough water and food supplies as well as all the weaponry that we could carry, and then we set off. I was carrying hundreds of bullets packed into two bullet belts, five bomb fuses tied together with ropes, and, of course, my own AK-47. The strongest soldiers had to carry one full tin of bullets all by themselves, and these tins were extremely heavy. The top commanders didn't carry anything. Because of all the weight we were carrying and because we were marching through hostile territory, our movement was really slow. The trip to Uganda was the hardest so far, but this time there was no rush. Our commander gave us enough time to rest and we had enough provisions to take our time.

After a couple of days, we reached the river that separates Sudan from Uganda. Crossing the river itself took almost half a day, as we couldn't transfer all our ammunition across the river at once; instead we had to go back and forth many times. Drained by exhaustion, I nearly lost my grip on the rope at one point, but a colleague managed to help me. This was the only serious trouble that I ran into during the entire mission. After crossing the river, we walked for several more miles until we finally found some good places to hide our ammunition. The first spot we selected was a very high termite hill. We needed to protect the weapons before they were stashed. The bullets were put into a jerrycan and the bigger weapons were wrapped in a plastic cover, so that everything would remain waterproof. My colleagues who had carried shovels were selected to dig the hill out. After they were done and the weapons were stashed, we set several landmines around the termite hill so that nobody but ourselves could gain access to the weapons. Afterwards we chose two additional places to hide the remaining weaponry. All of the locations were in the Padwat game reserve, which we chose because there would be no people to interfere with the weapons or accidentally step on the landmines and thus reveal the hiding place.

After all this was over, we safely returned to Sudan without meeting a single Ugandan civilian. We hadn't hidden the weapons far from the river separating Uganda from Sudan, so going back didn't take us long, and without the heavy burdens we made good time.

When we were well into Sudan, we received a message that Kit

One was under attack and that we were needed quickly to aid with its defence. We quickened our pace, but it was already too late. Kit One was more than two days' march from where we were, and even by running, we wouldn't reach it within a day. Hours after the first message, we got a revised message telling us not to go to Kit One, as it was completely overrun by the SPLA, our Sudanese enemies.

We continued marching and after two days we came very close to Kit One. We didn't dare to go straight into the camp, since we suspected that a whole division of enemy forces were occupying it. Instead we went around it. Once we passed Kit One it didn't take us very long to find the trail that the army of thousands of LRA had left behind in their retreat, so we just followed this trail. As usual, the advance party was in the lead, scanning for enemy activity, while the blocking force made sure that the enemy couldn't attack us from the back. It took us about five to six hours after passing Kit One before we reached the second camp, a place conveniently called Kit Two. Kit Two was nothing more than a place in the bush. When we arrived, I saw thousands of people trying to dig trenches so that we could defend ourselves, but there was little effort being taken to actually construct a military camp. No huts had been built and even the headquarters was nothing more than a small depression in the ground. It looked as if we were preparing for another attack.

Sure enough, this attack came only one day after we arrived in Kit Two. As with the first attack on Palutaka, it started in the morning with a very heavy bombardment. The trenches were not dug as deep as the ones in Palutaka and quite a number of people died in the initial bombardment. Afterwards the ground forces came with thousands of combatants and there was no way that we could hold them for long with our poor defences. Throughout the battle I was again in the frontline, where there was the most death and suffering.

When the first wave of attack came, we managed to hold our enemies off, but with every subsequent wave it became more difficult.

One of the problems was that we weren't allowed to sit or to lie down. In the LRA, we had to face our enemy standing and bare-chested, and it was this military tradition that cost us many lives that day. Again, the majority of casualties were the more experienced fighters, as they were sent to the most dangerous spots. The trenches weren't deep enough, and when we stood, half our bodies were in clear sight, which made it easy for our enemies to injure us. We managed to hold them off for maybe one or two hours, but by this time we had suffered hundreds of casualties. A grenade exploded very close to my position and I saw that several of my colleagues were blasted away. On my other side a boy was hit in the lung by a bullet.

When the third assault came, I saw the commander making a run for it, and I immediately followed. Once again, I was one of the first to follow the commander in his retreat and I had the bullet fire of thousands of my colleagues for protection. Those who stopped firing last had a real problem, trying to escape without being hit in the back. Again, in retreat I saw the bodies that had been torn apart from the initial bombardment.

It seemed that we left a couple of hundred dead behind us, and this time there was no one to blame for our defeat but our own poor defences. We realised then that the enemy forces were too numerous and we were constantly outnumbered and outgunned, so we had to find another way to defeat them.

As we sounded the retreat, we began to march with incredible speed. The mothers and children had a head start of several hours, but it only took us half a day to catch up with them. When night fell, we continued to march, and by first light the next day we were still on the move. By now I could see that the landscape had changed.

We were coming into terrain dominated by yellowish grassland. The further we marched, the dryer it got. After we had walked for almost twenty-four hours, we passed some very large barracks of our Sudanese allies. Here we finally got the order to rest a little while our commanders went to negotiate with the Arabs. I don't know what they were talking about, but to our relief we soon saw the Arabs starting to unload some of their food provisions for us. Of course it wasn't much. The Arabs told us that it should be enough to last for more than two weeks, but after only two days all the food was gone. However, the little they gave us was better than nothing, and the minimum of food in our stomachs gave us the strength to march on.

This time we could follow the main road. We were now in land occupied by the Sudanese government and there we had nothing to worry about. We passed four Sudanese army barracks and kept on walking, following the road. After several days we finally came to the place that would be the LRA's new home for many years to come: Aru Junction. Aru was located in between Nimule at the border of Uganda and Juba, the largest town in southern Sudan. The landscape in Aru was very arid and inhospitable. The only plants that grew there were dry grasses, thorny bushes and trees that could go without water for months on end. When we were given the order to set up camp in this desolate place, we all knew that our lives would become even more difficult.

We arrived in Aru early in the morning and were given the order to start building our camp. Hundreds of us were instructed to collect bundles of tall grass, while others were ordered to dig trenches or to fetch water from a river that was supposed to be somewhere nearby. Many were sent to collect bamboo from a bamboo forest that we had passed on the way, maybe half a day's march from there.

On the second day after our arrival the first huts were constructed and within a very short time this desolate place was transformed into a military camp. The activity was intense. I was instructed to lead several new recruits to hack down some of the trees that grew in the area so that the new command centres could be constructed. As I was hacking into a tree, I saw long rows of people coming back with jerrycans, a clear sign that there was indeed water somewhere near this dry place. All around us thousands of people were constructing a camp all at the same time. It was quite a stunning sight. Hundreds were digging trenches for the camp's defence. In other areas, people were digging the land and planting all kinds of seeds that would feed us one day. At least a thousand people were cutting the long dry grass from which we made our huts, and hundreds of huts were already under construction. As soon as we delivered the timber, people were immediately instructed to start the construction of the new headquarters of the various brigades, starting with Control Altar.

Kony's hut had already been built. Surrounding it, the huts of all his wives were under construction. I was ordered to go to my commander for further instructions. Close to where Stockree headquarters would be built, I found the place where our artillery unit would be stationed. I immediately found the Mzee. He instructed me to help some of my unit members with the construction of the huts, so that for the first time in many nights, we wouldn't have to sleep under the open sky.

The next morning, we started our first parade and afterwards the construction continued. I was selected to cut more timber, this time for the construction of Stockree headquarters. By now the last of the food given to us by the Arabs was gone. The next night all of us went to bed with no food in our stomachs whatsoever.

The next day early in the morning, the commander started parading us again, but it was clear that morale was very low. Everyone was hungry. Ever since the start of the exodus from Palutaka, food had been a serious problem. Thanks to our Arab allies we had been fed during our march, but they wouldn't continue to supply us. It was not their problem that we were hungry. Again, we worked the whole day on the construction of our new camp and at night we went to bed again without eating anything. By now I was getting really hungry.

When we woke up the next morning, we were forced to parade again, and afterwards we were sent out to cut some tall grass for the construction of even more huts. Throughout this activity there was only one thing on our minds – food. Hunger made everything difficult. To cut the grass we had to walk a small distance, because we had used all the grass in the immediate area around the camp. While we walked, I picked some grass and put it in my mouth. I thought that if cows and goats could eat it, so could I. I didn't like the taste of it, but at least it filled my stomach.

Very close to this place I noticed a tree with very large leaves that was heavy with fruit. It didn't grow in Uganda or in Palutaka, so I had never seen it before. I wasn't the only one to see the tree, but since no one recognised this type of tree, people were concerned about eating the strange yellowish fruit. I picked one of the fruits and I started to eat it. It tasted very bitter.

As I picked a second fruit, two boys came up to me and told me to immediately stop eating. For a moment I was scared that they were warning me that it was poisonous, but then I saw that they just wanted all the fruit for themselves. They grabbed the fruit that I was about to put in my mouth and ate it themselves. When I tried to reach for my gun, I got a terrible blow in my face. I knew these boys very well and so I also knew better than to resist. They had been in the LRA for a long time, in the same unit as me, and our commander respected them. The tallest of the two, who we called Aguam, was trained in artillery and he knew how to set landmines and mortars. The other, Arob, was never sent for the artillery training, but he was a very good soldier. Both of them came from the Kitgum region.

I didn't like either of the two. Both had given me a hard time in the first few weeks when I was in Palutaka. They were always bullying me and sometimes they even stole my food. Arob was especially cruel. The moment they had seen me eating the fruit from the tree, they presumed that the fruit was safe to eat. They kicked me away from the tree to have it entirely to themselves. I was extremely angry with them, but I couldn't do anything. I sat just a few metres away from them, watching. After only two minutes they sent me back to my task of cutting the grass, and threatened to report me for disobedience.

I walked away and when I was about twenty metres from the tree I started to cut the grass. However, I soon started to feel a strange sensation in my stomach. At first I thought that the pain was caused by hunger, but I quickly realised that it was more serious. I had only eaten one fruit, but within ten minutes a terrible pain went through my stomach and then I started to throw up. The world was spinning around my head and little white bubbles of foam started to come out of my mouth. It felt like my stomach was actually on fire, burning me from the inside out. At the same time my vision started to blur a little, and I saw everything double.

In the meantime, Aguam and Arob had continued to eat the strange fruit. It wasn't long before they began to feel the same pains that I did. I hadn't yet realised that my former bullies had just saved my life until I saw them crawling on the ground. From where I was, I could see that their mouths were covered with the same white foam that was coming out of my mouth. One of them said something to me and he tried to get up to come towards me, but he immediately fell down from the pain in his stomach. In the meantime, my own pain was getting much worse. As I was squealing on the ground, some of my colleagues lifted me up and carried me back to my division. I remember very little after this.

When I woke up the next morning the pain in my stomach had diminished and I was feeling a lot better. I was given some soup to eat with a little bit of bread, and this helped immensely. As I finished the bread, my commander told me that Arob and Aguam had died. The poisonous fruit had caused them a horrible and painful death. They had survived for several hours in terrible agony after the poisoning began, but there was nothing that could be done for them. They had simply eaten way too much of the killer fruit.

I stayed in the hut for another two days, recovering. I was still not feeling well and I had a fever. During those two days I was given soup to drink and a handful of bread to eat, which helped me to get back on my feet. By the third day I came out of the hut with enough strength to work again.

I was surprised to see that the barren, desolate grassland had turned into a fully functioning camp. The majority of huts had been constructed and gardens were beginning to be cultivated. Although Aru was a very dry place, water was being collected from a nearby river. It was used both to quench our thirst and to sprinkle the gardens. The surrounding environment of Aru was hostile to a group as large as the LRA, but somehow Kony seemed to have made it work.

Although the camp appeared to be functioning on the surface, Aru still wasn't a good place for us. Few things grew there, and the area was sparsely populated, which meant that there were only a few settlements around for us to plunder. Within only a few weeks all the plundering that was possible was done. Sometimes our groups would revisit a settlement that had already been robbed, but that was like plucking the feathers from a featherless chicken. When our commanders told us that there was no food, there really wasn't any food – nothing. Often days went by without eating, and then when we finally were able to eat something, it was only a handful. This meant that we had to actively seek other ways to get any kind of nutrition. We would try eating anything that looked slightly edible in the area. Some of these things were poisonous, like the yellowish fruit that I had tried, others just made us sick. Some things had no nutritional value and other things were utterly disgusting, but at least they filled our stomachs.

In the search for food many more kids died eating poisonous fruit. People started to eat grass, as I had done, but we soon realised that the grass had no nutrients and that it eventually made us sick. We ate the leaves of a tree that in Acholi is called *ugali*. The leaves of this tree were a little bit sour, but they did fill our stomachs. We tried roots and tubers that grew underground. There was one thing that looked a little bit like a potato, although it was extremely bitter. We soon stopped tasting its bitterness, since the severe hunger we felt made everything taste OK. Whenever somebody discovered something new that was edible, they tried to keep it a secret as long as possible. But it didn't take long for everyone to know about all the edible things that could be found in the area surrounding Aru.

Yet somehow the commanders always appeared to have enough to eat. Every evening they threw away potato peel. One day when I saw them doing it, my hunger drove me to run towards it the moment the commander had turned his back. By the time he started to walk away I had already put a few handfuls in my mouth. When the commander turned around and saw me, I got a terrible punishment, because it was still forbidden to eat the peel. In full view of many others who also wanted to go for the peel, he lay me down and brought over the device that was used to clean the insides of our gun barrels. He hit my neck with it over and over. In total I got twenty strokes, and for what? My only crime was trying to save myself from starvation. For the next few days I could barely move my head without feeling an excruciating pain. It was really horrible, but it had been worth it. At least I had some food in my stomach again.

Once in a while, a battle group would return with plundered food and then we would be eating again for a couple of days, but afterwards we had to depend on our own resourcefulness. Although the famine was horrible, most of us usually had just enough food to prevent starvation. Many still died of hunger and diseases related to malnutrition, but the vast majority survived on the bare minimum.

Unfortunately, hunger wasn't the only problem in Aru. Getting water there was like getting water in the desert. Only a few days after I recovered from my food poisoning, I was ordered to fetch some water from the river. I set out with a group of around fifteen people, because we were warned that there might be Sudanese villagers there who were always armed and who would try to fight us over the only water source in the area. We had to travel in groups of at least ten people and we each had to carry our weapons in addition to a twenty-litre jerrycan. Initially, I thought that the river would be very close by, but after we'd walked for over an hour, we still hadn't reached it. When we finally got there, I was in shock. It was nothing more than a dried-up riverbed covered with green grass and mud. It appeared that there had not been a river there for a very long time. We climbed down the riverbank looking for Sudanese civilians, but we didn't see any.

To get the water from the riverbed we had to dig holes in the mud. At a depth of about thirty centimetres, muddy water would appear. We used the palms of our hands to catch this water and put it in a jerrycan that had been cut in half. Then we had to wait a few seconds for the hole to fill up again. Once the split jerrycan was full, we transferred the water into a jerrycan that was still in one piece. We put our T-shirts over the top of the intact jerrycan in order to filter the water, but the result was still a little bit muddy. It was a painstakingly slow process. Since this was the only water source for an army of thousands, not to mention all the civilian settlements in the area, it was very important to scout for other armed civilians while we slowly filled our jerrycans.

The first time we went out to collect water, it took us maybe six hours all in all to go back and forth from Aru, but over time it took us even longer. Not only did we have to fight with armed civilians on many occasions, fights we always won, but the places where we could find water became further and further from the camp. As thousands of people collected water every day from the same spot, these areas would dry out very quickly. If you were able to collect water at a certain spot on one day, the next day you would have to collect it ten metres or so further downstream. This meant that after half a year, the fresh water source had moved several kilometres further away from the camp than its initial point. Eventually, this nearly doubled the time it took us to collect the water.

The lack of water meant that we could only use it to drink and to water our crops. There was rarely any water for bathing and as a result we were always dusty and dirty. Once in a while, we were allowed to use the water to bathe, because our leaders still wanted us to be clean. Even then, it was difficult to clean ourselves properly using the dirty water. It didn't take long before the first combatants had lice and soon everyone was affected. After several weeks we all felt extremely dirty, but this simply became our reality. Everybody was always scratching at the lice, but only a good bath could solve the problem; scratching didn't help a single bit.

Only when we were ordered to collect the water did we have the opportunity to drink as much as we could at the river, but even then, we had to be careful not to be spotted by a higher commander.

Because of the lack of water and food, various diseases began to affect us. It started with diarrhoea. As so many of us tried to eat poisonous food, diarrhoea was one of the most common diseases among our ranks. Already in the first few weeks I saw a few people who died from it, and it only grew worse over time. I remember one boy from my unit who died in the first week, shortly after I had barely recovered myself. He told me in the morning that he had a terrible headache and that he was suffering from diarrhoea. This was the same day that I was first sent out to fetch the water. By the time I came back, a few older boys were carrying his body out of the camp. Only six or seven hours had passed since I had talked to him, but his pain had already become lethal. His dead body was immediately taken out of the camp and thrown away to rot.

This boy was lucky enough to die in his hut, because he became ill so fast. Normally, when it was noticed that a person was mortally ill, they had to walk out of the camp with the last energy still in them. They would be walked out for a long distance of at least eight to ten kilometres, and when it was clear that they couldn't walk back, due to the severity of their illness, they were left there to die a lonely death.

Apart from diarrhoea there were many other diseases affecting us, some of which were lethal and others that were just a nuisance. Fever could be very dangerous in our state of malnutrition. Several times I saw people get fever around me, and it was usually a fifty-fifty chance whether or not they would survive. There were skin infections, as well as all kinds of coughing diseases and swelling diseases. I didn't know all the names, but what I did know was that it was of crucial importance to remain healthy. This meant whenever I saw a sick person, I would stay away from them. I always tried to drink as much water as I possibly could. Even with food, I had to be very resourceful to at least try to eat enough so that I would preserve some energy.

But all these precautions didn't prevent me from getting sick. There was one day, maybe a month or so after I had arrived in Aru, that I woke up with a swollen leg. I had no idea how it got like this. I checked for signs of a wound or bite-mark but there were none. There was no explanation for the swelling. When I tried to walk, I fell to the ground again. The pain was really bad, and I was completely immobilised, which was dangerous in the LRA. What worried me the most was the slight fever that came with the leg infection. The fever wasn't all that bad, but I knew my odds. When my commander examined my leg, he sent me to the medical ward of Control Altar, where I was given some medicine. I stayed there for a couple of days to recover. I never told them about the fever, as I was really afraid that they would march me off. I was very lucky that after a few days the swelling went down by itself and also that the fever never affected me much. Perhaps it was because of the medicine and the food I received there that I was able to strengthen up again. Whatever it was, those few days really helped.

Aru was set up in the same way as Palutaka, with the main difference being that we didn't have an Arab camp neighbouring ours. In the middle of the camp was the headquarters of Control Altar, and surrounding it were the sub-camps of the four different divisions. Stockree was located north of Control Altar. Within a few weeks, thousands of huts had been constructed and it looked as though we had been there for ever. We established a daily routine that, apart from our worsened hunger, bad hygiene and chronic thirst, was not much different from our routine in Palutaka.

The prayer sessions on every Friday and Sunday continued. The LRA was a deeply religious movement, so skipping prayers was only allowed when there was a very good reason. I actually never wanted to skip them. The prayers always filled me with energy and motivation. After the prayer sessions, I always wanted to go back to Uganda to deliver our people from the tyranny of Museveni.

Aru was always full of life. Among the boys there were also thousands of girls and young women, many of whom had children at very early ages. It is a mistake, however, to think that the women were only there for getting pregnant and delivering babies. Many of them were also warriors who had to fight just like we did.

For women there were some special regulations. Upon abduction, we would all be massed together, boys and girls, but the girls would always be under the command of a female commander, while the boys would fall under the male commander. Then later, when we reached the assembly points, the women and boys would be separated. The women would be assigned to different commanders, while the boys would be assigned to units.

Again, with the women there would be a difference depending on age. The really young women, those of twelve and below, would be called *ting tings*, and they were given various domestic tasks, which included babysitting, cleaning the compound, cooking food, etc. Slightly older girls, sometimes as young as twelve, but more commonly fourteen to fifteen, were given to commanders as wives. Only after the marriage ritual was a commander allowed to sleep with them.

Most commanders, especially the higher-ranking ones, had many wives, and it was often the first wife that was commanding the rest, all the way down to the *ting tings*. However, the ultimate control of a family unit fell to the commander himself, and he was allowed to do with them what he wanted. When a commander died, his wives were divided and given to other commanders. Consequently, some commanders had very many wives, even more than ten or twenty. This meant that some wives were only a wife in name, and didn't have to perform sexual duties. Also, some wives were unable to have children, so they were given additional fighting tasks. However, infertile or not, every single woman was married out. This was inescapable. While I understood much later that the women in the camps suffered a lot of sexual violence, at the time I thought that the women were given preferential treatment, and that life was generally better for them. This was mostly because of their close proximity to the commanders, which meant that they were fed much better than we were.

There were some very specific rules for girls. For example, when they were menstruating, they were not allowed to cook food for any men, nor were they allowed to touch any military hardware or take part in armed battles. This was because we considered menstruation a bad omen that would bring disaster in battle. Women who were menstruating were allowed to cook for one another, but not for men or for other women who weren't having their period.

A second rule was that pregnant women should not go into battle. Sometimes, during extended missions, women got pregnant while in Uganda. In those cases, the woman would have to deliver while on the move. She would be placed on a stretcher while the march continued, but would not be allowed to make any sound. However, usually, if a woman was a few months pregnant, she would not be selected for a mission.

Also, women were not trained in artillery. Artillery was considered purely a man's job, both because of the weight of the artillery compartments, for example the mortar, but also because women weren't trusted with that much firepower.

Apart from this, women were given the same military training, and they were as deadly as the men. In the various battles that I fought, I saw young mothers firing their AK-47s at our enemies with their babies strapped on their backs. Some women were even given ranks, like sergeant, lieutenant and captain.

In my section of twelve people, there were four women. Anying was married to Mzee, my commander. She was the one in charge of all the women in our brigade. Among these women were the second and third wives to the Mzee, so Anying was commanding all of them. Actually, quite often she would command us as well, and Anying was better than Mzee at commanding. She was the one who forced us to parade and do push-ups very early in the morning. She was tall, dark and slender. A very beautiful woman. Mzee's second wife was called Ayaa. She was also extremely tough. She had not had any children, so she was sent into armed combat often. She was a very fierce warrior. Everybody in Stockree knew about Anying and Ayaa. Mzee's third wife was named Christine, and she was still very young at the time, either fifteen or sixteen. Then after her there was a *ting ting* whose name I forget.

We regarded these young women and girls as we would our sisters. We never fancied them as potential girlfriends. We were not allowed to talk to them without a good reason. We only talked to them when the husband sent us to call them, or if we were given an order to give to them. If anyone was found conversing with a woman without a proper reason, they could be killed in front of a firing squad. This was a very strict rule.

We were certainly not allowed to date any women, also under penalty of execution. Being with the women was only allowed if one was actually married. But, at least for me, the threat of execution was never necessary. Because of the initiation rites that had been done, I never got an erection or had sexual feelings of any kind. They told us very clearly that if we were to have sex or even fantasise about sex, a bullet would stray during battle and hit us in our private parts. In addition to these threats, they smeared special shea oil on us that prevented erections. It was only when a person got married that the leaders would perform a special ritual that would allow him to become erect again. So, because of this fear, the rituals and the ointment, I never had any feelings for any of the women apart from a feeling of brother/sisterhood.

My relation with the other boys was different. With them I was allowed to talk and, on many occasions, we sat together just to converse and laugh. Although life was harsh in Aru, we were always joking and laughing with each other, mostly about battle-field experiences or massacres, but sometimes also about other things, for example we fantasised about the future, when we would have defeated the government and would be generals in our victorious army.

While I got on quite well with some of the boys, I never befriended or trusted anyone. I never shared my secrets, such as when I had found a new thing to eat or a new place where the commanders threw away vegetable peel. Nor would I share any stories about my former home and family. None of us really thought about our previous lives any more, and even when we did, we would keep it to ourselves out of the fear of repercussions. So the conversations were always about past or future battles, and the people we had killed. These were the kind of conversations that were also encouraged and stimulated by our commanders.

Ever since I had been abducted, the LRA continued to be very active in raising new recruits. With one year of service, I was actually more senior than many of my fellow combatants. In Aru, battalions of the LRA would go out on almost a weekly basis, and they always came back with many new recruits. While I didn't hate the new recruits, I did hate the fact that they represented hundreds of new mouths to feed, thereby adding to my own hunger. Because I was more senior than the new recruits, my role shifted from being bullied to becoming a bully. Whenever I got the chance, I would try to steal food from them. The younger ones especially had a difficult time with me. I would push them around and always let them perform the heaviest duties. For example, if we went to fetch water, I ordered them to do the digging while I would stand on guard. If we collected bamboo, they would carry the heaviest bundles. The new recruits suffered greatly, and many of them never made it past their first few weeks in camp. The ones who survived were hardened by the experience, which would benefit them in the long run.

The weather conditions in Aru continued to be very dry. This wasn't to say that it never rained at all. In the first six weeks it drizzled only once, as it was the dry season. The moment that it started to drizzle we all tried to collect as much water as possible. The frustrating thing was that we very often saw heavy rain clouds in the distance, over the mountains, but they always remained there, raining on places that we couldn't reach. The rainclouds could usually be seen hanging over the mountains of Magwi and Palutaka, a very frustrating reminder of our former home, and the inglorious battle that had ended our life of relative luxury. In the rainy season it drizzled more often, but we never got any real showers.

The conditions in Aru camp in these early days after arriving were very difficult, but I survived, and after I had been there for maybe one and a half or two months, a new chapter began in my story as a combatant for the LRA. I was made a commander.

Part IV
The Birth of a Monster

Exorcism of the Civilian Mind

I was growing frustrated with the harsh life in Aru. I prayed to get out of the camp, even if it meant that I had to go back to Uganda and participate in more awful massacres. After about a month and a half, my prayers were answered.

One evening a large truck entered our camp. The moment it stopped at the gate of Control Altar, I was selected, together with six other boys in my artillery unit, to go to the truck and wait for instructions. We had no idea what was about to happen, but we shared a feeling of excitement. At the truck we joined a group of fourteen others. I recognised most of them and I knew that they were all experienced combatants like the six of us. The moment we arrived, we were all lined up and a high-ranking commander, a colonel, gave us our instructions. It was explained that we were to go and pick enough bamboo to fill the entire truck. Because of the potential risk of ambush, we had to be well armed and focused on the bushes surrounding the road as we travelled.

We all felt that there was some deception in this story. Using a truck to collect bamboo was a good idea, but why would some of the most experienced warriors be sent out in the evening to collect bamboo on a truck that probably came from our Arab allies? It didn't really make sense. Despite this, in the LRA we never questioned an order, and anyway I was happy that I could escape the boring life in Aru for at least one evening.

Just before we left, we each received an extra magazine of bullets and we set off in the truck. We were going in a northerly direction, away from a perfectly good bamboo forest that was only a half-day walk southeast from Aru. The road was very bumpy and after we had travelled for several hours, I was convinced that the bamboo mission was a cover story. We remained alert in case of an ambush, as instructed, but nothing happened on the journey. In the middle of the night, the truck finally came to a standstill and we were told to get out.

By this time we were very close to Juba and we could see that many people still lived in the area, although, like northern Uganda, it was in the middle of a war zone. We were sent into a big stone building where there were many beds lined up and we were allowed a few hours of sleep. In the morning we were given some food. It was not as much as we'd hoped for, but much more than we were used to eating in Aru. During the breakfast we talked among ourselves, each of us wondering what we were doing there. We were in some kind of military barracks, sharing breakfast with Arab soldiers, so it was clear that we were not there to collect bamboo.

It was clear that this was an Arab barracks, but there were also some commanders of the LRA present as well, including a colonel. After the breakfast we were given an orientation to our new surroundings. They showed us the way to the showers, the toilet and other areas to find things we needed. But they didn't inform us of the purpose of our mission.

I assumed that we had merely been shifted to another location and I didn't worry about it. The conditions in this camp were far better than the conditions in Aru. Here we could wash ourselves, there were decent toilets, real beds to sleep in, and most importantly, there was adequate food. After a tour of the facilities they ordered us to sit under a large tree. The LRA colonel came to us and began to explain to us why we were really there.

'You boys might think that you are tough and dangerous. Do you think that you are a tough soldier?'

He was talking directly to me.

'Sir, yes, sir'

The commander looked at me and then his gaze went to the rest of the group.

'We will teach you what it is to be a tough soldier. What I see in all of you is that you still have the mind of the civilian and because of that you are all weaker than me. This will change soon. In this place we will take the civilian mind away from you and you shall receive the training that will make you elite in our ranks. We will start today with the exorcism of your civilian spirit!'

We were taken to the woods surrounding the camp where we were ordered to remove our shirts. We were forced to sing songs while clapping. We were ordered to sing louder and louder and to clap faster. We could sing any song that we liked the most. Those who wanted a Christian song sang a Christian song, those who wanted to sing a traditional song sang a traditional song; it didn't matter to our leaders. I chose the latter, an Acholi song that accompanies the warrior dance. Others sang their own favourites. We did this for the entire day, and well into the night. Whenever our voices weakened, they would slap our faces and we would sing much louder again. At night, fires were lit, and we continued singing and singing.

Initially, the singing didn't make much sense to me, but after a while I entered a trance. It was as if we were dreaming. We were clapping and singing in the here and now, but our spirits were somewhere else. I felt myself becoming enraged as the last remaining bits of my civilian spirit were fighting against a force that was much stronger. I could sense when my civilian spirit was finally driven away, and the remaining humanity was squeezed out of my body. Slowly the spirit of the soldier was instilled in its place.

This was their way to force out the civilian mind, and it worked. For three nights in a row we did this continuously, from eight in the evening to six in the morning. Bare-chested, we clapped and danced and sang our songs. They didn't allow us a single minute of rest or sleep, nor could we show any signs of fatigue. The end of a thick rope was kept in the ashes of the raging fire. Whenever someone yawned or dozed off, the burning end of this rope was pressed against their chest. But most of us never felt any fatigue. We were becoming too angry and aggressive to feel tired, as our spirits were transformed. I was one of them. In the three nights, I was not even burned once.

By the end of the first night, my spirit was already transformed. I was angry and aggressive, without even knowing why. The others seemed to be angry as well. It was well into the morning before the clapping and singing stopped.

Then we started to march. In this infuriated state of mind, we all marched much faster than we were supposed to. Everyone was marching on their own, not minding the rest of the group. This sloppiness was quickly beaten out of us. The language in which they spoke to us was a mixture between English, Kiswahili and Acholi.

'Left-right, left-right, left-right . . . STOP . . . turn around . . . left-right, left-right, left-right.'

We each marched with a club to represent our guns. Our real guns were stored in the armoury. During the marching there was a lot of caning. Anyone who joked, marched out of line with the others or didn't lift their legs high enough would be caned. Anyone who was caned would then have to perform hot exercise, a punishment that always entailed heavy exercise and lots of caning. None of us escaped these punishments. For three days non-stop we marched, and clapped and sang the whole night through. By the second day many of us were getting tired, but we were allowed no excuses to dodge the training. The worse we performed during the marching, the more punishment we received; there was no escaping it. By the end of the third day we had all received such a severe mental and physical battering that surely the civilian inside us was dead.

After several days of only marching and singing, advanced weapons were added to the training package. We always marched in the morning upon arising and afterwards we ate something. When the sun was very hot we would march some more while the commander just sat in the shade of a tree. After the second march we received arms training. It started with the small guns, like AK-47s and AK-49s, as well as PKMs (machine guns), SMGs (sub-machine guns) and M4s (assault rifles) among others. We learned how to take all the guns apart, reassemble them, clean them and shoot. I always liked target practice the most.

This training went on for a very long time, and we learned all that we had to know about almost every light gun in the world. We were constantly tested on how fast we could assemble the AK, and we continued to improve. We learned the different sounds of the gun and the range that each gun had. We learned that every type of gun has strong points and weaknesses. Some would jam easily, others were not very precise or didn't have a long range, and others were difficult to clean and needed much more attention and care. The simplest and the best gun remained the AK-47 and the AK-49.

At times we were woken up in the middle of the night for a long march, other nights they allowed us to sleep. We would sometimes be woken up by gunfire nearby and then our instructors would come in and ask us what type of gun had just been fired. Anyone who didn't know received heavy caning or was forced to do push-ups the whole night through.

During this time the twenty of us in training really got to know each other. Whenever we had spare time we joked together and bragged that we were now the best soldiers in the LRA, since we had received this training, and it was probably true. This was elite training, and very few of our colleagues would ever learn more about military affairs than we did in those months with the Arabs.

After gun training for almost a month, we moved forward another step with artillery training. This was the main reason we were sent there. The marching still continued – that never stopped – but instead of gun training in the afternoon, we now received bomb training. It started very simply with the hand grenade. We learned all that we could know about different types of grenades. One grenade is stuck with a little bit of timber. On the timber there is a cap that you can screw off and then a cord to pull. After pulling the cord there is a delay of several seconds to throw it away before it explodes. There was another type of grenade with a pin to pull out and a handle to press. The moment it is pressed there is a hissing of air, and pressing it three times arms it, and it must be thrown quickly. Another type of grenade only has to be pressed once before it is armed and must be tossed. They showed us a grenade that was designed especially for ambush. The fuse is connected to a taut rope that can be placed where someone could accidentally step on it, activating it, and making it explode immediately.

They showed us pictures of the insides of hand grenades and what exactly happens once the pin is pulled. Then we learned how to throw the various grenades, and with every type the procedure was a little bit different. We had to see how they rolled and how to make sure that the target was destroyed with one throw. The training in hand grenades alone took us almost a full week.

After the hand-grenade week, we continued with landmines. There were many different manufacturers and brands. These landmines, however, could all be categorised into two main types. There were those intended for people, the personnel landmines, and those intended for vehicles. This wasn't a size thing. Some of the really small mines were actually meant to blow up big trucks, while some of the really big ones were meant for people.

All the mines had two components that were essential to make them dangerous: the mine itself and the fuse. Without the fuse the landmine was harmless, and we could actually dance on it, but the moment the fuse was installed it could not be stepped on without exploding. The top of the mine could be removed, and with most mines there was a hole in the middle. This is where the fuse was put to complete the explosive device.

We also learned the best places to plant them, how to dig a hole in the ground, and how to disguise them so that no one would see them until they said bang. We learned how to arm and disarm them, even when there was somebody already standing on them. It was essential that we knew each type of mine, especially when arming or disarming them, because they all worked a little bit differently. This training was critical, since disarming landmines was very dangerous work.

After landmines we received training for rocket-propelled grenades. The RPGs are very simple weapons to assemble and fire, so the training was completed in less than a week. There were short-range and long-range, anti-tank and anti-personnel grenades. The anti-personnel grenade made a very big explosion with lots of bomb splinters, so that it could kill many people at once. Anti-tank and anti-personnel grenades were armed in the same way. They had three parts: the booster, the sustainer motor and the warhead, which is what we called the 'bomb' of the RPG. It was very easy to arm them. The most difficult aspect about firing the RPG was the strong backfire. Younger soldiers like me had to be especially careful, because the backfire could easily push us over. We had to make sure that we knew how to sit or stand correctly before firing.

After this, we moved on to other weapons. First, we got to know everything about the B-10, a type of bazooka that could easily destroy a helicopter. It required a tripod to fire it with precision. In the LRA we had only one B-10, which was located in Control Altar. We were also trained on something we called a 'Silencer'. This was a very short gun that could shoot ten small bombs in a row. This weapon wasn't very precise, as it had no targeting device, but it was very effective if the enemy was packed together. After the first day of training with the Silencer, I regretted that we hadn't possessed such weapons during the assault on Palutaka.

The next training, in mortars, turned out to be important because in the year to come I would use the mortar many times.

The mortar was a very common weapon in the LRA, as we had many of them. It was also very deadly. For more than two weeks we were trained in the use of mortars, as they were much more complicated than the RPG.

With mortars, there were three different types: 60 mm, 81 mm and 82 mm. The 60 mm mortar was the most common one and it was portable. With each mortar there were also three main parts: the support, the barrel and the base plate. We learned how to adjust the barrel and how to aim. We learned to assemble the mortar in a manner of seconds, fire two shots and then disassemble it, move a couple of hundred metres, and do the whole thing over again. This was essential, because in battle you never leave a mortar in the same place for too long as it releases smoke after it's fired, which the enemy can use to learn your exact position.

After mortar training, we moved on to something called 'Fourteen', a very big artillery piece. It had a range of several kilometres and was the type of weapon used against us during the assault on Palutaka, so I had experienced first-hand how dangerous it was. The Fourteen had four barrels and a wheel to adjust the aim. We were trained in this weapon for almost a week, even though the LRA didn't possess one. A few more big artillery pieces followed, but this training was a bit irrelevant because the LRA didn't own all these big arms. Our colonel told us that as we were a guerilla army, we didn't use those very heavy guns because they compromised mobility.

Throughout the artillery training, which took several months, we continued our daily marching, gradually using heavier loads. After we were very proficient in marching, we moved on to running; even for running there were standard, prescribed ways of doing it. Every day between ten in the morning and four in the afternoon, we had to either march or run. We were well fed, so were able to muster the energy to do all the marching and the running, but it was really tough. There were also frequent night exercises. We could never expect a full night's sleep because they could wake us up at any time for more training.

Twice a week we were allowed to take a shower, which was a big improvement when compared to Aru. In the training camp there were only the few Acholi selected from the various brigades, plus a few commanders. Everyone else who received the training was Arab. We were also by far the youngest, but that didn't mean that we were weaker than the rest. Among ourselves we established good relations. Whenever we were not training and praying, we would joke around, laughing about things that had happened during the training and bragging about who was the best soldier. Although the training was very, very heavy, I did prefer it to the life of hunger in Aru.

For the last two months we had guerilla training: how to command and how to ensure the obedience of those we commanded. Then came tactics of war. For this we learned to use the alphabet for communication. Whenever we found ourselves in an ambush and we were surrounded from all sides, we had to use the O. Within the O formation, all the normal privates would be at the outskirts of the O, defending, while the artillery and the command centre would be in the middle. When we were conducting ambushes ourselves, we would move in a C formation, which was perfect for surrounding enemy barracks. The tips of the C would move around the barracks, blocking the escape routes, while the main body would be in the middle of the C, starting the assault. I realised that this was exactly how we had attacked Parongo, leaving only one very dangerous exit route for the enemy, between the tips of the C. In open battles, when we were operating in open fields with the enemy in sight, we were to either use the I, L or V formations. With V the artillery was in the tip of the V, making it almost impossible for the enemy to target, while in the I and the L formations the artillery would be mobile.

After all the alphabet strategies, we learned how to recognise the strategies of our enemy and how to respond to each of them. They taught us how best to defend ourselves against mobile units and even against helicopters and fighting jets. With every new lesson – with the exception of very dangerous manoeuvres like disarming a landmine – they always explained things to us twice before we had to do it ourselves. If we failed the test, we would be caned. If we passed the test well, we would get additional food rations. This is the way they trained us, using the cassava and the stick.

Although it was impossible to keep exact track of the time, my estimate is that the training lasted about six months. Every Friday and Sunday we had our usual prayer sessions and these days we rarely trained. On all other days we were trained for at least twelve hours. We developed great confidence that the LRA could not be defeated. We could sustain attacks and we might get temporarily weakened, but by following 'the way of the guerilla' we could never be wiped out. We were now well-trained combatants invigorated with the spirit of a soldier.

The training ended as abruptly as it had started. They had succeeded in their goal of killing the civilian spirit in us. By the time the training was over I had little in common with a normal civilian. I felt aggressive, ready to kill almost anyone, and very eager to put my new training to the test. I was ready. Towards the end of the training I began to yearn for some action. I had had enough of the training: I got the picture. I was actually looking forward to going back to Aru, because I knew that my new skills would not be wasted fetching water or collecting bamboo.

The Birth of a Monster

The day that the training ended came without warning. Nobody informed us what was happening when we were ordered to enter the truck once more, but it soon became clear to all of us that we were back on the road to Aru.

The camp had grown considerably since I had left. The potato and cassava gardens were now flourishing and deep trenches had been dug all around the camp. We were taken immediately to the gate of Control Altar, where a whole battalion had already been assembled. As we jumped off the truck, we were told to join it. The battalion consisted of many new recruits who had just finished their first training. The twenty of us were now the most experienced soldiers within this battalion, with the exception of the commander leading it. Although we had not yet been given a rank, our superior training meant that we were now in commanding positions. I was assigned several dozen new recruits. We were quickly introduced and even before I was informed myself, they told all the new kids that I would be their commander. The one speaking to us at the gate of Control Altar was Kony himself.

He told us that today our skills would be put to the test. We had all survived the training and this already made us tough soldiers, but the real soldiers' spirit could only be tested in battle. He told us that the enemy we would face in the coming few days was battle-hardened and superior in numbers. But he reminded us that those infidels fought without the Lord's support, and that was why we would win the battle. God would protect the holiest of us and those who did not survive this campaign were not worthy to fight for the Lord's army in the first place. Today, we were going to conquer our enemies, and as proof of our victory, he wanted us to bring back at least one enemy's testicle. 'Those who have the nerve to come back without a testicle will suffer the consequences. Go now and conquer!'

These were the words that I had waited to hear for many days. In those last few weeks of our military training in Juba we noticed that we received bigger food rations and that the training days were much shorter. Although no one told us anything about an upcoming battle, we sensed that something was about to happen. Like most of my colleagues who had been selected for the Juba training, I had grown sick and tired of the training because I now considered myself to be the best soldier in the world. I didn't need any more training; I needed to go out there and kill.

In the months of my training I had become very angry. Most of the time I didn't even know what it was that made me so angry, but I felt a constant urge to kill and destroy. I was so aggressive. If I had possessed a mirror, I would probably have seen the same destruction in my eyes that I had seen in those dreaded eyes that I looked at on the day of my abduction. I was slowly turning into the demon that I had promised myself I would never become.

It was clear that we were all ready to slaughter, so when we finally got the word that we would go to kill some Dinkas, as we used to call the SPLA, we were all very excited and very happy. Finally, we had our chance to get back at them and make them pay for what they had done to us in Palutaka.

After Kony's speech, we started to prepare for our mission. All the new recruits were given a gun and we packed enough ammunition to last through one very heavy battle. For the first time I had dozens of soldiers under my command. I carried an RPG launcher and I instructed my recruits to carry the grenades. We marched back in the direction of Palutaka, which our enemies had driven us out of approximately seven months earlier. Leading us was a lieutenant colonel who had been abducted many years before me and who had worked himself up the ranks. We also had a doctor with us, and I was in charge of the artillery for the northern flank. During the march I was filled with excitement and anger. I had been with the LRA now for about a year and a half and finally all my training would be put to the test.

The Dinka camp was a long way from Aru. We walked for two days before we finally came close, but we didn't rush. We all wanted to be fit for the battle, so we had several breaks every day for cooking, and at night we would sleep well. I was having wild dreams about killing the Dinkas and slitting open their balls to remove the testicles. Never in my life had I expected that I would be so eager to kill.

When we took our break on the second evening, we were very close to the enemy barracks, but I didn't realise it. The commander knew, but he didn't tell us anything. That night we cooked our food and afterwards we took up defensive positions so that we could sleep at ease. Before we went to sleep the commander instructed us to sharpen our knives. Tomorrow we would be cutting Dinka balls.

We woke up very early in the morning when it was still dark. The enemy barracks was an hour's walk away from us. We proceeded in absolute silence, making sure not to step on any branches or anything that could make a noise. Our attack required surprise. By the first light in the eastern sky, we were very close to our target. The Dinka camp was surrounded by thick bush, which gave us the perfect cover to make our approach unnoticed. I was still very excited and happy. As we came close, I whispered to the boy nearest to me that I would be the first to cut the Dinka balls.

The enemy camp was much smaller than ours at Aru, but still big enough to harbour a formidable fighting force. Kony had said something about overwhelming numbers, but I had no idea that we would face several full battalions that outnumbered us three to one. Our battalion consisted of just over 200 men, while our enemies numbered anywhere up to 600 or 700 experienced soldiers. However, surprise and a reputation for absolute brutality were our advantage, and that would make their numbers count for nothing.

Their huts were also grass huts, but very different from the ones we built. The Dinka huts were much pointier and not as round. The granaries where they stored their food and weapons were higher off the ground and much smaller. The camp was surrounded by shallow trenches with sandbags up the sides. I recognised that our main task would be to ensure that the enemy never reached those trenches, because from there they could establish a strong defence. There was only one road that led out of the camp and it was directly on the other side of the camp from our approach. Once we made it past the trenches, there were few objects that we or the enemy could hide behind, with the exception of the huts and some trees. The strategy was to overwhelm the enemy as quickly as possible while we had the advantage of surprise. We also needed to avoid letting them know our true numbers. Fear was our ally and if they were to realise that they outnumbered us, their dread would quickly evaporate.

We approached the camp in a C formation, with the artillery department in the middle and the tips of the C blocking the enemy's escape routes. I had a clear target ahead of me and I proceeded as cautiously as possible. I commanded the C tip at the northern flank and along with the commander of the southern flank, my friend from Juba, we got into position about ten metres away from the camp, at the very edge of the bush. There we were ordered to hide and await the sign to attack. The order was given by the commander and everyone then whispered it to their neighbour until it reached the tips of the C.

Nearby I saw a woman going for a short call in the tall grass. Although I had never seen this woman before and she hadn't done anything to harm me, I hated her, and I wanted to shoot her right in the face. However, my assignment bore much more importance, and shooting this woman wasn't my task. Our commander had scouted the camp on the previous day, and my task was to blow up their armoury before any of the soldiers could get to it. I had the armoury in clear sight and my RPG was ready. I waited for the sign. In the meantime, the woman was only five metres away from me, but she didn't seem to have realised that we were there.

I was briefly reminded of my earlier hunting experiences and it caused me to smile. This was not a smile of happiness, but a smile of anticipation before a successful kill. I thought about the good old days when I was a young boy hunting birds. Now the game I was hunting had grown bigger and tougher, as had the weaponry I used to kill it.

As a small boy I began hunting for birds and edible rats using just my slinger and my catapult. Then, as now, the approach was very important. If the birds realised I was there, they would fly away and I would never catch one. So I had to approach them very carefully. When I was eight years old, I started hunting much bigger game using a deadlier weapon. In 1993 my mother and I took the train to visit my uncle, the one who lived near Parongo trading centre, very close to Murchison Falls National Park. This uncle gave me a spear because we were going to hunt for buffalo. That was the first time that I had a true lethal weapon and I was supposed to use it to pierce the heart of a buffalo. Together with many of my uncle's village-mates we started our hunt. We didn't go very far, because in this game park the animals were never very far away.

The night before our hunt some of the villagers set a wire to trap a buffalo, so first we went to check whether we had caught anything. When we came close to the trap, we heard the roar of a lion. We saw that there was indeed a buffalo in the wire, but it had already been killed and partially devoured by lions. Everyone in Africa knows that a single man without a gun should never face a lion alone, but we were in a big group and all armed with spears and machetes, and we were not about to give up that tasty buffalo flesh without a fight. So we proceeded. When we were very close to the buffalo, a female lion suddenly appeared from out of nowhere. We never saw her coming. The lion jumped on my uncle, who immediately passed out. This was the first time I had seen a lion, and it was only a few metres away from me. Before I even realised what I was doing, I threw away my spear and ran for my life. But one of my uncle's village-mates quickly grabbed me and warned me never to run away from a lion. Instead it is best to make a lot of noise and try to appear to be as big as possible. We all did this, and started advancing towards the lions again. The lions gave up their meal and quietly left the area. We immediately went to my uncle, and he was lucky enough to survive with only a mild concussion and some deep scratches. That night the whole village celebrated that we had chased away the lion, and everybody told me that I was a warrior.

Now, several years later, I waited there in the thick bush of our Sudanese enemies as a true warrior, eager to kill a prey that was much more dangerous than those lions. In my personal arsenal were the three kinds of weapons that had killed more people in the last fifty years than any other weapon ever made: the AK-47, the 60 mm mortar and the long RPG armed with anti-personnel warheads.

Suddenly something unexpected happened and I cursed myself for letting my attention slip for this brief moment. The woman who had gone for the short call had returned to the camp and had started to scream like a madwoman in her stupid Dinka language. If I had been more focused, I would have realised that she had noticed us and now she was warning the whole camp about our presence. I didn't need to understand the language to know what she was screaming.

Seconds after her screams the camp was fully alerted and I knew we needed to take action right away or we didn't stand a chance of winning this battle. I aimed my RPG at the armoury and without waiting for the signal of my commander I blasted it into pieces. A very large explosion followed, which was a clear sign that I had hit the right target. The screaming bitch had been very close to the armoury when I shot, and I was only hoping that I had killed her. What happened next was chaos. My colleague from the south flank fired his RPG at another target and every single LRA soldier opened fire on the camp simultaneously. Complete hell broke loose.

SPLA soldiers had appeared from their ugly huts as soon as the woman started screaming, and the moment the armoury blew up they all knew that they were under attack. Some of them ran towards the defensive trenches in front of the barracks, which was where our main fire was concentrated. They could not reach the trenches without crossing open terrain, giving us a perfect opportunity to shoot them. All the killers – what we called our fighters near the centre of the C – started shooting. A very silent morning had suddenly turned into an ear-shattering slaughterhouse. None of the SPLA soldiers made it to the trenches. I had given my RPG to someone to reload, and in the meantime I was firing the mortar. As we were very close to the trenches, I ordered my soldiers to focus all their fire on anyone trying to reach those trenches, while I kept bombarding the middle of the camp. The moment the RPG was ready I took it and destroyed another set of huts that were close together. On the other flank I could hear that my colleague had also reloaded his RPG and destroyed other targets.

The Dinkas were still trying to reach the trenches but were having great difficulty. As my RPG was being reloaded, I had a well-armed man in my sight. When he was within two metres of the trench, my bullet hit him in the leg. As he fell to the ground, I looked him in the eye and a second bullet pierced his face.

The Dinkas were totally overwhelmed by our attack. In the first ten minutes we killed very many of them. I shot another two people who tried to reach the trenches and in the meantime my RPG was reloaded again. I quickly lost count of how many I had killed. The Dinkas soon realised that it was impossible for them to reach the trenches. They set up defensive positions in the middle of the barracks, while they tried another way to cut us off. By this time the area between the huts and the trenches was covered by the bloody bodies of our enemies. I put my gun to the side and bombarded the area with my mortar, switching position after every two shots. By this time our enemy had grown smarter. Instead of running to the trenches directly, they approached the trenches to the east of the camp and from there ran towards the frontline while they ducked for cover. The east end was out of our range and the moment that the first of them came around to the trench in front of us the battle became more difficult for us.

As I was in a commanding position in artillery, I had two body-guards and two helpers. The helpers had received training in how to reload weapons like RPGs and mortars and they helped me with that. My bodyguards were supposed to make sure that nobody could take a clear shot at me. But at a certain point our enemies managed to set up a machine gun in the trench nearby, and then we were in trouble. As they started to blast away at us, I dived for cover. Seconds later my two bodyguards lay dead while the machine gunner was shooting his way towards the middle of the C formation. I had a brief moment of eye contact with the one who operated the machine gun. As he moved it back to take aim at me, my hand grenade was already flying towards his trench. Just when he had the chance to hit me, my grenade killed him and his helper.

More soldiers were entering the trenches, and all around me my colleagues were getting shot. We had failed in the most important objective: to keep the enemy from reaching the trenches. To avoid further loss of terrain, the main body was ordered to advance and take back the trenches, while the cutting forces, including the northern flank in my command, were ordered to provide crossfire.

I saw the main body stand up from their positions and run towards the trenches. Our crossfire and mortar bombardment made it difficult for our enemies to take a clear aim. Nevertheless, many of my colleagues were shot in that attack. The new recruits had been poorly trained and many of them suffered the consequences. Yet very few of the enemy forces had managed to reach the trench on the west side of the camp, and with a hundred of our soldiers running towards them, they were completely overwhelmed. A large group of Dinkas tried to flee the scene of battle, and they ran right into our position. They were out in the open, offering us clear targets, and none of them survived that day. Only seconds after the commander gave the order to take the trench we succeeded, but this did not mean that we had won the battle – far from it.

The Dinkas realised that they had been outflanked, but they were nowhere near defeated. They still had an overwhelming force and we stopped our advance at the trenches. This was exactly what our commander had warned us about the day before. The objective of our mission was to take the camp in a matter of minutes, because if they stopped our advance their numerical superiority would be a real problem for us, which is what happened.

Although we had conquered the trenches on the western side, enemy forces were still holding the trenches to the north, the south and the east, and most of their combatants were concentrated near the headquarters in the middle of the camp. After the main body had taken the western trenches, I ordered my men to take the northern trenches, but many of my subordinates were killed in this attack. In the end we managed to conquer a small section of the northern trenches, where we connected again with the main body. But by now they had driven us into a bottleneck and every few minutes we lost another soul.

I saw some new recruits who were guarding me being shot very near me. It was so terrible. Several times people right beside me were shot. When I saw them crawling on the ground in pain, I thought only about myself: *It could have been me lying there.*

Again, it was clear that the holy shea oil did not have the power to prevent bullets penetrating, as Kony had told us so often. But I continued fighting without any fear because I believed that the moment I became afraid would be the moment I would be shot. I was keenly focused on killing and slaughtering. My goal was to kill as many people as possible and not for one single moment did I lose faith in our victory.

During the intensity one of my better friends from Juba was shot in his belly. This boy had been in the LRA a year longer than me and he had been promoted to second-in-command of this battle. He was shot the moment that he tried to crawl out of the trench to command our troops to advance. Seeing that he had been shot, none of the other soldiers followed his example. The moment I saw him fall I ordered the new recruits to provide cover fire while I lifted him up and carried him back to our headquarters. The headquarters was some thirty metres outside of the SPLA camp, so I had to crawl out of the trench to bring him back. The moment I crawled out, bullets were flying all around me, but none of them hit me. At the headquarters I went straight to the doctor. My friend was still very much alive, but badly injured. The doctor was swamped by all the other wounded that he had to attend to, but considering the importance of my friend, he quickly shifted his attention to him.

By now we had lost about thirty young boys and girls, most of whom had fallen the moment we advanced to take the trench. However, the majority of our fighting force was still in good shape, and it was clear that our enemy had endured much higher losses, as we had killed hundreds of them in the first few minutes of the battle. Once I delivered my friend to the doctor, the lieutenant colonel came up to me with new instructions. He promoted me to second-in-command and he told me that I was to lead our advance on the enemy headquarters. With these orders I returned to the trenches, while my colleagues from Juba, who were stationed around the command centre, covered me with their mortars.

I was one of the few people running in the open, so I was a clear target for my enemy, but in Juba I had learned how to run in an uncontrolled zigzag. Bullets were flying all around me, but none of them even shredded my clothes. I went to the middle of the C formation and announced that I was now in charge and that we had to advance, or we would all be dead meat. I let the new recruits spread the word: the moment they heard my grenade explode, everyone was to rush forward. Seconds later I took my last grenade, pulled out the pin, armed it and threw it towards our enemies. As it exploded, I left the trench and 150 soldiers followed my lead. I took cover behind the first hut, while many of the recruits advanced even further. For a few moments our enemies put up a fierce resistance, but as we all advanced at the same time, the most cowardly of our enemies started to run away, weakening their defences. After several minutes I screamed to advance once more. We left the cover of the huts and granaries and ran towards our enemy's headquarters. At that moment our enemy lost heart and one after another they fled their defensive positions. This was lucky for us, because if they had stayed where they were, they could easily have slaughtered us.

Our enemy never realised that we were only a small battalion. Normally attacks happen in waves. You send your front troops and leave the reserves for the second wave of attack. So when we appeared from the trenches all at once, it created the impression that we still had a reserve force standing by somewhere in the bush, where the mortar fire was coming from. We were fortunate that our enemy was so weak-hearted. The few hundred that remained, including the fighters as well as the women and children, started running for their lives.

With their backs turned it felt like a feast for my aggressive mind. We shot as many in the back as possible. The enemies that still occupied the southern, northern and eastern trenches could easily have caused severe damage to us from their positions, but instead the majority of them decided to run. The few that did hold on were quickly overrun. Dozens of soldiers were shot in the back as they tried to flee. We slaughtered everyone who hadn't managed to escape. Women, children, the wounded and crippled, even babies were killed as we bashed in their small heads with the butts of our guns. I felt no remorse for anyone that I killed that day. They were the enemy. They had taken Palutaka and showed us no mercy, so no mercy would be given to them now. The Dinka bombs did not spare our small children when they attacked Palutaka, so why should we spare theirs? Above all, we killed the children because they were a risk. Some of our soldiers were not much older than eight, and even a four-year-old could throw a grenade.

Within minutes of the enemy sounding their retreat, every Dinka left behind was dead. I had just unzipped the trousers of one of our fallen enemies to cut out some Dinka balls, when my commander patted me on the shoulder and told me that I had done well, but that this battle wasn't over.

'We've lost more than fifty people and a big group of the enemy has escaped our wrath. We've killed their wounded, their women and their children. Don't drop your guard yet. They will be back.'

The commander ordered some to take our mortally wounded back to sickbay while the rest of us, including the lightly wounded, set up defensive positions. With so many wounded, the effectiveness of our fighting force was almost cut in half. That is why we needed anyone who could still put up a fight. Some of those who had been hit in the legs were ordered to lie down with their guns and prepare for the next attack. Everyone that was still able to fight entered the trenches that our enemies had nicely dug out for us, anxious to see whether the Dinkas would truly return.

The colonel was right. Out of the reach of our guns, the enemy had regrouped. From their new position they learned that we had killed all their women and children and they were filled with anger and revenge, which made them more determined than any enemy I had encountered before. The gun battle that followed was even worse than our conquering of their camp. In their trenches we had a strategic advantage, but they still outnumbered us two to one.

They started their attack from the bushes east of the road. Our defensive line was spread thin, as we didn't know which side they would come from. When I heard the battle start, I was still some distance away from where the actual fighting was happening. I was eager to go there, but I was under clear instructions to remain where I was. Later I heard that it was only because of our superior strategic position that they didn't immediately conquer us. In the first wave of attack, dozens of Dinkas ran towards us in an uncontrolled lust for revenge. Their rage made them disorganised and that was the only reason that they were stopped before they could retake the eastern trenches.

The second wave of attack started very near my position, where our defence was particularly thin. A group of at least fifty men ran towards us. We managed to shoot many of them, but we were unable to stop their advance. As they came closer, I realised that we couldn't hold them back. Without telling anyone, I crawled out of my trench to retreat. Many of my soldiers followed my example, but not everybody noticed. By the time they realised that they had been left behind, it was already too late for them. We moved back to the centre of the barracks, where earlier that day our enemy had held their ground. As our enemies advanced towards us in the centre, they were completely oblivious to our colleagues who were lining up on their eastern flank.

By now we had killed so many of them that our numbers were nearly equal. The fight continued for another hour, during which we finally defeated them for good. We killed every single last one of them, over 700 people.

All of our wounded lined up at the northeastern trenches had been killed and we had lost at least another twenty of our young recruits in the second battle. Only one hundred of us remained alive and many of these survivors were badly wounded. This filled my heart with even more anger and hatred than before the battle began. In my rage I was eager to kill, but there was nobody left to murder. I could barely process all the brutality that I had just witnessed. From the tops of my lungs I screamed out, 'WHERE ARE YOU COWARDLY DINKA FUCKS? WHERE THE FUCK ARE YOU? I AM NOT DONE KILLING YOU . . .'

I cursed every single one of the Dinkas, kicking their dead bodies as hard as I could. At that moment I cursed the whole world around me. I cursed Kony and the LRA. I even cursed God. How had they turned me into this monster? A year and a half ago, I was only a child. I was innocent. Now I was a killer of women, children and battle-hardened men.

After several minutes the lieutenant colonel came over to calm me down. He told me that it was time for me to collect my reward. I went to the Dinka whose trousers I had already unzipped and with a strange joy I cut his testicle, as if this final act would make the world a better place. All around me small boy soldiers were pulling the trousers off of slaughtered grown-ups to cut off their balls. Even the badly wounded were participating, and if they couldn't, they had somebody else do it for them.

Afterwards, we collected all of our enemy's guns as well as the guns of our own dead. We carried all the weapons we could manage, and we hid the rest near the Dinka camp in several hiding places. We would retrieve them another day. We left the critically wounded behind, the ones that were unable to make it to Aru. To us they were already dead, even though some would survive for many days. My friend from Juba was among those who were left behind, but he had only hours to live, as he was bleeding badly and the doctor had been unable to stitch him up.

With the extra weapons and the wounded, our march back was painstakingly slow. Even the slightly injured had to carry the more badly wounded as there was no other option to get them home. It is difficult to remember how many days it took to return, but it was at least two days longer than the journey out. Most of the time I was numb, not even feeling the pain of the heavy loot that I carried.

Invoking the Spirit of Vengeance

After days of marching, we returned to Aru a ragged-looking bunch. Almost half our force had either died during the battle or were too wounded to make it back, while dozens of soldiers with lighter wounds had to be supported by others. Except for the lieutenant colonel in command, this military campaign had been a test for all of us. For the new recruits it was their first battle and for those of us from the Juba training, it was the first time that we had commanded artillery units.

Despite our appearance, we were all greeted as heroes. We were told to go to Control Altar, where they quickly assembled hundreds and hundreds of people. We were standing in front of these people when Kony came to give us a speech. First, each one of us showed Kony the testicles we had taken from our victims. By now they had become grotesque, as the heat had caused them to rot. After Kony had seen them, we were allowed to throw them away.

Kony began speaking about how well we had done in battle. He praised us for being victorious against an army of superior numbers and experience. Even the most badly wounded forgot their pain during his speech and all of us felt so proud. Kony announced that from now on, all the new recruits who had participated in the battle would no longer be seen as unholies. They had proved their valour in battle and they had to be treated accordingly. At a certain point the new recruits were taken away. Those who were badly wounded were taken to the medical centre, while the rest began their final initiation rite into the LRA. The only ones still left standing in front of the camp were the nineteen survivors from the Juba training.

Now Kony continued his speech, but this time it was directed at us. He told everyone how the Spirit had seen our extraordinary valour and how the Spirit had uncovered the mind of the soldier deep within us. He told the hundreds of people assembled about our elite training and about our courage. Whenever he stopped talking, the crowd started clapping for us. That was the first moment since the battle had begun that I relaxed and smiled. Until that time I had been filled with aggression and not willing to talk to anyone. I felt a strong urge to destroy, even on our march back to Aru. But now, with all the applause, I finally regained some human feeling, even pride and a little bit of happiness.

When Kony ended his speech, he told everyone present that we had been promoted to the rank of sergeant and we each received a medal. I realised that this was the first time since I had joined the LRA that I had got any recognition for the countless times I had put my life on the line. The longer the speech lasted, the happier I became. When the ceremony was over, hundreds upon hundreds of people knew how courageous I had been in battle and afterwards I was often recognised by people I had never seen before. It was a nice moment, but otherwise life in Aru had changed very little.

The rank of sergeant was the second-lowest rank within the LRA, and it actually didn't mean all that much. It meant that from now on, whenever an assignment had to be carried out, like fetching water, collecting grass, or tasks like that, I would command others to do it. But this wasn't a big change, because even before I had been given a rank, I already commanded others. The new rank also did not mean that I received extra food rations. Hunger continued to be part of our everyday lives. The difference that it did make, however, was that sometimes we were selected for special occasions and ceremonies, because we could march so much better than the rest of the soldiers surrounding us.

On one occasion following this event, I remember being truly happy. That was the day that an important visitor came to Aru. Rebel leaders arrived from the West Nile Bank Front, a rebel movement that was also engaged in war with the Ugandan government. WNBF rebels fought in the West Nile sub-region, which borders Congo and Sudan. Among these rebels was Juma Oris, leader of the WNBF.

Because of my superior training and marching skills, I was chosen to be in the welcoming parade. Only those commanders or privates who had been in the LRA for a long time were selected, depending on our size and on how well we could march. We were told to make our guns as shiny as possible and, an hour or so before Juma Oris arrived, we were given uniforms that were attractive and of good quality.

This day was a special day. It started with Oris's arrival around noon, when we held the parade for him. Then there were speeches. After the speeches, the church choir started to sing and to play *boabs*, *adungko* and other traditional instruments. Afterwards we again started to demonstrate our skills in parading and assembling guns. A cow was slaughtered for this special occasion and those who participated in the parade were all allowed to taste the soup from the cow, with the remnants of beef in it. On this day I was filled with pride and happiness. I forgot my anger and I became human again.

Of course, we were never told the reason for this visit, but I think that Oris was there to discuss a plan to unite. Both our forces were waging an insurgency against Museveni and his army, so it made sense for us to combine our strength. I think Oris had come to review how the LRA operated, and for the most part he seemed to like what he saw. He gave a long speech in which he had only one critical comment, which was that he found us to be too young to be soldiers. He mentioned our negative international reputation and that the use of children could harm our standing with other governments. He quickly realised that he had to change topic, as this part of the speech did not make him popular with the crowd. Instead he began to describe how the government soldiers were weak and that they were all drunkards, and with these words we all started cheering. He continued by saying that the government forces were no match for our forces.

That day my heart was filled with emotion. We looked so beautiful in our uniforms. Anyone who had seen us would have been in awe with admiration. We didn't have to fetch water or do any of the other duties, and we all felt a little bit free. When we were not parading or listening to the speech, we were allowed to relax.

I think that this day was somewhere in early September 1996, because we were drawing close to Independence Day, another day that I clearly remember. Oris's visit came a week or so before we went back to Uganda for my second major mission there. When the day came to an end, we all regretted it a little bit. Upon his departure, we all shot three rounds in the air, as a way to honour him.

The following day we were still very excited. By now I felt completely at home and at ease in the LRA. I couldn't even think of my other life any more. For the first time I felt thoroughly appreciated and although my rank as sergeant didn't change my situation that much, it did make me feel important. I now had the opportunity to show my valour over and over, and I knew that as a sergeant, I could easily work my way up in the ranks. I often dreamed about my future. My image of the future was to have a high rank, commanding entire brigades in the final attack on Kampala. I couldn't imagine any other life than the life in the LRA. I didn't hate or detest it. It just felt natural. But in the week following the visit of Juma Oris, this feeling changed dramatically.

During that week there was a mission to get food from a village in Sudan. I was not the one in command; there were several people with a higher rank than me. One of them was a major, and there was also a first lieutenant. The team was selected in the morning at around eleven, when we were parading before the headquarters of Stockree Brigade. They chose a large group of us: everybody was to come back with a sack full of food, and the sack should be filled to the height of one's hip. If you didn't collect that amount, you would suffer the consequences. I was selected based on my strength and my capabilities as a fighter. We needed good fighters because taking food from Sudanese villages never happened without a fight. In those days all the villagers in Sudan were armed. We needed our guns and at least three or four loaded magazines. We did not carry any artillery with us, because that would only interfere with our ability to carry food back to Aru.

We started moving that morning, back in the direction of Uganda. After several hours, we passed the first barracks of the Sudanese army and several hours later we passed another one. But we kept on moving and moving. The village that we intended to plunder was very far away. At that time, we travelled only with water and a kind of cassava that was very bitter. It was shortly after we passed the second barracks of the Sudanese army that I started to feel sick. I don't know what the illness was, but it came on after I ate some of the cassava. The sickness drained all the power from my body. I drank a lot of water but the more I drank, the worse it became. There was pain in my joints, as if they were slowly stiffening and refusing to move. I was moving in the advance party, but at a certain point I lost the power to keep up with their pace. It felt like the energy was pouring out of me.

The commander of the advance party was Lieutenant Nyeko. I knew him quite well because he was in the same unit as me, but we were not friends. He had been with the rebels since the late 1980s and he was somewhere in his thirties, while I was no older than thirteen. We did not like each other at all. I don't know when this bad relationship started or what the reason was for it, but it was just one of those facts of life, and so far, I had never really cared about it. He used to bully me in my early days with the LRA, but as I grew in rank and prestige, we simply ignored each other. But this day he was leading the advance party and because of my illness I wasn't able to keep up with them, so he punished me. By now I was used to punishment, and even though I didn't like him, I realised that I was slowing everybody down. If I were in his position, I would have also punished the one stalling, but his punishment was really severe.

When he saw that I was fatigued, he pushed me to the ground and ordered me to take off my shirt. He began to hit me with the flat side of his panga. Normally you would give someone maybe ten or twenty strokes at the most, but he just kept on going. When he had hit me at least thirty times with all his strength, someone came up to stop him. This person screamed, 'NYEKO! WHY ARE YOU HITTING THIS BOY?'

But Nyeko's only reply was that if he objected, he would get the same treatment. Others also started to object to Nyeko.

'Nyeko, you are killing this sergeant. Stop this immediately, or I will report it to the higher commanders.'

But Nyeko was the highest-ranking officer nearby, and he threatened to beat up this guy, too. All this time he kept on beating me to the point that I was nearly dead. Finally, the main body caught up with us. Somehow, I was still conscious. When Brigade Major Oyet, who was commanding the battalion, saw what was happening, he exploded in anger, and this saved my life. While Nyeko was beating me, the major hit him in his back with the butt of a gun as hard as he could. Nyeko turned around and the major kicked him in the face and then started to scream, 'NYEKO, WHAT THE FUCK DO YOU THINK YOU ARE DOING? Are you killing this sergeant just for your fun? Do you think that we have spent so many of our resources in his training that you can go out and kill him? Take off your shirt. NOW!'

The commander grabbed the panga away from him. The whole blade was bent because Nyeko had hit me so hard and so many times. Then the major started hitting Nyeko with the same blade and he gave him at least thirty strokes. When the major had finished hitting him, Nyeko was ordered to stand and was given one last stroke with the flat side of the machete, right in his face. The commander told him that this would most probably cost him his rank. By this time Nyeko was trying to plead his way out of it.

Very humbly, he said, 'Sorry, sir, I was beating this boy who couldn't move, and I wanted him to move faster. I only wanted to teach him some discipline; I never wanted to kill him. Please forgive me.'

The major replied by saying that he didn't care about his apologies; he had seen what he had seen, and he would report it to the highest commanders in the LRA. Afterwards he told Nyeko that at least for this mission he had lost the privilege to command and that from now on he would always remain in his sight, so that he couldn't beat anyone else to death.

Afterwards the major came up to me to examine my wounds. By now I was bleeding all over my back and I was in terrible pain. He asked me if I could still walk, and somehow I did manage, but my illness combined with my injuries caused me to move very slowly. He told me to go back to the advance party, where one of the bigger guys was ordered to help me move. The rest of the trip was a living hell for me. Every step hurt, but I refused to give up. Not long after the incident we were allowed to rest and even sleep for several hours.

There was no way I could sleep that night with all the pain. While everyone else slept, I was awake thinking. Something profound was happening in me. Never in my entire life had I been this angry. My thoughts were focused on killing Nyeko. He was in the same unit as I was, which gave me hope. I realised without a single doubt that if I were to kill him in cold blood, I would surely be executed. So I had to think of another solution. The only way I knew that I could kill him and get away with it was in battle. I could shoot him in the back when we were engaged in fighting and nobody would ever suspect. Everyone would be too busy fighting and when my gun fired, they would assume that I was shooting at the enemy. This was it. This was my new goal in the LRA, and it became my obsession.

When everyone woke up, I had not closed my eyes for a single moment and my body was still hurting, but at least the illness was a little better. For some distance I managed to walk on my own, after which the commander ordered somebody to carry me again. By the evening of the second day we came to our destination. As expected, a terrible fight broke loose in the village we had come to plunder, but I was much too wounded to participate. When the fighting ended, someone gave me a sack and told me to go into the village and make sure that I plundered something. The village was at the foot of a very large hill and there had been very many people living there. As I walked through the village there were dead bodies everywhere, but by now I was used to these sights and they no longer affected me.

What did impress me was the abundance of food and animals. I didn't see the village before the fighting started, but it must have been market day, so we really got everything. There were many goats, chickens, ducks and even cows and pigs. Except for the pigs, we took all the animals. The pigs we just slaughtered and left to rot, because we were not allowed to eat them. Pigs were considered to be impure animals and eating them would dirty the soul, according to Joseph Kony and the Spirit, but all the other animals were good for eating. We also had groundnuts, simsim (sesame), sorghum, millet, maize, cassava and all kinds of other food. It was more than we could actually carry.

I filled my sack with many things, but while I was plundering the major came up to me and took away my sack. He filled it with some other heavy things and took it to Nyeko. He told Nyeko that he had to carry two bags now, his own and mine. For a single moment Nyeko and I had eye contact and we both understood each other clearly: either he would kill me, or I would kill him. We just had to wait for the right opportunity. When the commander saw the look in Nyeko's eyes, he slapped him in the face, and he told him not to even think about it. Then they both left, and I was assigned to the advance group. This time I had to walk on my own, as everyone else was fully loaded. The two-day trip back was again hell, but I made it.

Upon our return to camp both Nyeko and I were brought in front of some higher commanders. The major also assembled eye-witnesses to the beating. We retold our stories and they examined my wounds. Nyeko was forced to lie down and receive a hundred strokes as a punishment. I was also punished because I hadn't carried anything back from the village, but they only gave me twenty strokes with a thin branch, and they made sure that they didn't strike me on my old wounds. It was obvious that they were somewhat sympathetic towards me.

For the following week, Nyeko and I ignored each other. Any confrontation between us in the middle of Aru would have had bad consequences for both of us. Something changed inside me and in my attitude towards the LRA. I started to wonder whether I would be continuously beaten whenever a higher-ranking commander felt like it. I started to hate this life in the LRA.

For the first time since I had come to Sudan, I started to think a lot about my parents again. Although they had sometimes corrected me when I had done something wrong, they had never beaten me to the point of death, not even close to that. I tried to remember the faces of my siblings, but I noticed that this was difficult. I even started to dream about my parents again. I dreamed that I was digging with my father and herding cows again, although we had lost our cows a long time ago. I had other very funny dreams involving my family as well.

I couldn't share these dreams with anyone. They would have said that I had plans of escaping, but this wasn't the case at all. On the contrary, I had only one plan in my mind, and that was killing Nyeko. This was my secret.

The Girls of Aboke

I continued to recover for days after our return to Aru. They applied some kind of cream to my wounds and as a result they healed very quickly. Within four days I could move again with ease and after six days I didn't feel any more pain. I don't know if it was my young age, if it was the cream or if it was just me, but I always seemed to recover from injuries very quickly, no matter how serious they were. Nyeko and I were still in the same unit. The commanders realised that something had to be done to separate us for a while so that we could both cool off. But in my mind, I had only one thing left to do in my life and that was to execute this son of a whore. Several weeks of cooling off wouldn't help to take this desire away.

By now it was later in September and the LRA was stronger than ever. We had continued abducting people and had been reinforced with a constant flow of new arms from the Sudanese government. We now had a formidable force, much stronger than the army that had been defeated at Palutaka. Our leaders felt that they needed to demonstrate this renewed power to the Ugandan government.

The day that was planned for this show of strength was to be 9 October, Uganda's Independence Day.

A selection began for yet another mission to Uganda. At first it seemed like an ordinary mission, but there were clues that indicated the commanders were very excited about this one. The first thing I noticed that set this mission apart from many others was that only the very best soldiers were chosen from all the different brigades. Nyeko was still under punishment, so they selected me instead of him. Once the selection was over, we had to report at Control Altar, where we got our briefing. Again, it was Kony who gave us a speech. He told us that our new mission would let the Ugandan army know that they were no match for us, and that we could do anything we wanted in northern Uganda. More than half a year had passed since our defeat at Palutaka and we had fully recovered. Kony explained the goals of the mission. He stated that the people of northern Uganda were breaking our laws and that this had to stop. We had to show them an example that they would never forget. Kony believed that the laws of the Ugandan government didn't apply to the citizens of northern Uganda, so they had no reason to follow them. The only laws that were sacred were our own, and we had to make sure that the people of northern Uganda understood them very well. They would learn that breaking our laws was a crime and criminals had to be dealt with. In addition to being an army, we were also a police force.

However, this was not the main objective of the mission; it was clear that teaching people about our laws would not invoke a high level of enthusiasm from our commanders. The main objective of our mission would put the LRA in the spotlight of many international news agencies for the first time. Our main objective was to target St Mary's College, a girls' boarding school in Aboke. This was the most likely reason for the excitement among the commanders. Within a short time they would have many new females to choose as their wives. We were told that the preparation for this mission would take three days, which was very unusual.

We spent the time on the sacred grounds near the gate of Control Altar. The preparation included weapons training, resting, eating and a lot of target practice. They also gave us training on the one B-10 that the LRA possessed. We learned how to use it to shoot down aeroplanes and helicopters. Of course, there was little that they could add to my previous training with the B-10, but for the vast majority this type of elite artillery training was new, and they watched it with great interest. The most exciting part of the preparation for most of us was the eating. Every night we each received a very large roasted sweet potato, and we were allowed to eat it entirely by ourselves. It was because of this extra nourishment that the three days went by in a flash. On the morning of the fourth day we set out.

As always when we set out for Uganda, everyone was overloaded with extra ammunition. I was carrying a heavy load of several fuses, one bullet belt, my AK-47 and the barrel of the 60 mm mortar. Most of this stuff would be buried soon after arriving in Uganda, and after a few hours of marching we already looked forward to this.

The march through Sudan went without any major incidents. It was in the middle of September and this was in the rainy season, a fine season for marching since it wasn't too hot. Still, it took us at least four or five days to reach the Ugandan border.

When we arrived in the area that was occupied by the SPLA, we stopped moving in the daylight and continued marching only during the night. Close to Owiny Ki-Bul we had to cross the main road, which we did moving with ninety-nine speed because of the danger of being in the open. In the early hours of the following morning we passed Pajok, where we had fought that horrible battle against the white mercenaries. Over half a year had passed since that battle and now it was little more than a vague memory. The trauma that I still carried with me from the final battle in Palutaka overwhelmed all my other memories of battle. Not far from Pajok we took cover during daylight and at night we moved on again. When we reached Uganda we continued our march deep into the Padwat reserve, where we hid the extra arms we had been carrying. Although nobody said so out loud, it was apparent that this was a relief to everyone. We could now focus on the mission at hand.

We had several weeks to reach Aboke, so we could take our time. By now it was around 20 September and our mission at the Aboke Girls' School would happen on 9 October. Between these two dates we had a lot of distance to cover and many laws to teach.

In Uganda we moved during the daylight hours again. We never walked in a straight line. Instead we zigzagged cross-country, so that it appeared we had no clear destination. Whenever we came across civilians, we would tell them about our laws. Those we found that didn't break any of the laws were sometimes left alive. We told them what the laws were and then we let them go. But those who we found to be breaking our laws, whether unwittingly or not, were in deep trouble.

Some of our laws concerned animals that were not supposed to be kept or eaten. These included dogs, pigs and sheep. Whenever we saw any of those animals, we would kill them, and if we found their owners, we would deal with them too. Sometimes we would just beat them severely, and in other cases we killed them. The people who were savagely beaten must still hate us, but what they didn't realise was that they were extremely lucky that their lives were spared.

For most of us it didn't matter whether we killed someone or if we beat them up. Beating and killing had become routine. Some of my colleagues actually preferred shooting people instead of beating them up, as it involved less physical effort. Other colleagues were just cruel, and they preferred to kill for the fun of it. These few liked all the killing, especially when the process was very slow and there was a lot of torturing and bullying involved.

The majority of us didn't enjoy the killing, but we also didn't hate it. I was usually indifferent when I saw someone being executed, but it depended on my mood. Sometimes I didn't like the killing and could feel sorry for a victim when he was killed in an extremely brutal way. Most of the time I simply didn't care. It was only when I was in a battle rage that I was ever eager to do the killing myself. That was not to say that I would refuse to kill if I was given the strict order to do so. When ordered, I would kill without remorse or second thoughts. Luckily, I was never given those orders during this mission. There were always enough psychopaths in our group who would gladly line up to do this nasty work.

When we had been in Uganda for several days we carried out the first small massacre. We came across several people cultivating their fields on a Friday. This constituted their first crime: working on Fridays. That was enough for us to execute them. What made it even worse for them was that they had come to the fields on bicycles. Bicycles were absolutely forbidden because they allowed the civilians to report our whereabouts much faster to the Ugandan army.

When I think back, I can still see how those people were lined up and executed one after another. Some were begging for mercy while others met their fate in silence without any objection whatsoever. I always found this intriguing. How could people who knew that they were about to be executed submit without any distress? They didn't show any signs of extreme anger or even fear. It seemed like their minds were dead already and they only waited for their bodies to follow.

We didn't actually kill all that many people during this mission, but the deaths of those we did kill were especially horrific. In the first massacre the people were simply shot, but as the days passed our methods became increasingly cruel. We devised punishments that were in line with the crime that he or she had committed. If we found somebody on a bicycle, we would hack off his legs and cut off his buttocks. If we found a local leader, we would cut out his tongue that he used to report, his hands that he used for writing, and his ears that he used for listening. If we discovered somebody had been talking to government forces, we would cut off their lips so that they could never speak again. In this manner we set very clear examples as to what our laws contained.

We were a relatively small group in the region, compared to the Ugandan army and the SPLA. But because of our very effective strategy of fear and terror, we were able to control almost the entire north of Uganda and a large chunk of southern Sudan with an army of several thousand fighters. We didn't need a police force to enforce our laws. One brutal murder was often enough to broadcast the message; 'Radio Kabi', the rumour mill, would do the rest of the work. Within one week the story of a gruesome murder could travel from Pader all the way to Atiak and back. With every kilometre the story travelled, the details of the murder would get worse. In this way each of our murders had their intended effect. A murder was not about the person we had killed, it was about setting an example so that the rest of the country knew that we meant business when we told them to follow our laws.

In general, our killings were not personal, but on rare occasions they did have a personal element. Sometimes killings were motivated by revenge, and the examples we intended to teach were not for the people outside the LRA, but more for the people within it. We had such a mission when we moved into Gulu District, around 1 October, just over a week before Independence Day.

Near the trading centre of Awach, some thirty kilometres north of Gulu, we were told that we had to carry out another assignment. A few months earlier one of our more experienced soldiers, a boy called Otieno, had managed to escape. This crime alone carried the death penalty, but to make things worse, Otieno had also taken several guns and loads of ammunition belts with him when he escaped. Losing a human asset was one thing in the LRA, but losing weapons and armour was another. Otieno had been in the LRA for several years and he had made the fatal mistake of letting people know where he came from – Awach – and who his family was.

Awach was a 'protected' village, referred to this way because there was a small army barracks nearby. But these barracks never had more than fifty soldiers, and often the soldiers were based in the middle of the population centre, rather than around it, which in reality meant that it was the civilians who were protecting the soldiers rather than the other way around. We expected the soldiers to flee without a fight the moment we attacked them. Our mission was to enter Awach, find Otieno – who had been the protégé of our commander, who was now very angry with him –

make him disclose where the weapons were, and then kill the boy and his entire family – and families in Uganda are very large.

As we approached Awach it was already getting dark. We shot one RPG into the army base and this was enough to immobilise the whole barracks. It seemed that very few soldiers were actually present; we saw only two, who ran away. We managed to catch one of them because he fell, and we quickly executed him. The other kept on running straight through the bush, and we were unable to get a clear shot at him. Because it was getting dark, we soon lost him as he ran away in the direction of Patiko Ajulu, near Baker's Fort. We knew that we had only a few hours before he would come back with massive reinforcements, so we had to be long gone by then.

The advance and blocking forces had already surrounded Awach so that no one could escape. The main body entered Awach and all the civilians were just silent. Some of them tried to hide, but there was nowhere to go. Some tried to escape through the bush and were shot. Those who remained were arrested. We kicked in all the doors of the huts, and we arrested all the civilians and brought them to the middle of the village, where they were all tied up. Then the questioning and the caning started. Our commander beat up people randomly, asking everyone where Otieno was. In the meantime, we searched all the huts to see if Otieno was there, hiding from us. But we didn't find anyone hiding. Everyone was in the middle, where the questioning and the caning were taking place.

It didn't take long before a woman confessed after we threatened to kill her child. She told us that Otieno had been here, but that he had been taken away to Gulu, to the rehabilitation centre. Then she pointed out his family. Otieno's mother glared at her in hatred, but we had given this lady no option. If she hadn't told us what we wanted to hear, we would have killed her boy. When Otieno's family was revealed, our commander walked up to them and caned his mother and father with a very thick stick. He went completely mad: all his rage against Otieno was directed at this family. He beat them until there were no signs of life, and then he ordered some soldiers to spear them with bayonets. Every one of us was ordered to watch, so that we would learn never to escape. Any of us who contemplated escaping but still loved our families learned a valuable lesson.

After the family was executed, we got the order to plunder Awach. When we had finished, we had to patrol the village to make sure that the UPDF reinforcements didn't catch us by surprise. From the outer edges of Awach I saw that the rest of the civilians were beaten when the commander had finished with Otieno's family. He had no mercy, not even towards the children we were going to abduct.

During this whole time the reinforcements we thought the escaped soldier would get never came. By nightfall all the civilians were beaten half to death, and we got the order to move out. Only the soldiers with bayonets on their guns were ordered to stay. Although I didn't witness or hear the end of the massacre, I believe that all the civilians in Awach were killed that day. There was no other reason to keep the bayonets behind. When we crossed the valley and looked back, we saw the village was ablaze. I don't think anybody or anything in Awach could have survived that fire.

Although we never found Otieno, he would surely feel the consequences of his escape. Because of his actions, his family was now dead. Because he had taken guns with him, the village had been torched and its population massacred. After the Awach massacre we stayed in the vicinity of Gulu town for another week. Sometimes we even entered the town, which was the stronghold of the

UPDF. We never stayed in town for long, because we didn't want to get into a fight with the Fourth Division, but we did demonstrate to them that we had the ability to penetrate the town. First, we attacked the prestigious boys' school, Sir Samuel Baker Secondary School, where we abducted around twenty boys. The school was in the outskirts of Gulu town and the attack lasted only fifteen minutes. We were gone well before the Ugandan army could ever respond. We conducted these hit-and-run campaigns for almost a week. By the time we were near Aboke, our numbers had increased, with 200 fresh recruits.

Out of necessity we trained the new recruits while we were on the move. When we were cooking and stretching our legs, they had to march. If they didn't march properly, we would cane them. When we got the order to move out, their training continued during the next break. They never got any rest. We taught them how to disassemble and reassemble the parts of a gun. I introduced the recruits nearest to me to artillery training. We had the 60 mm mortar, the landmine, the RPG and the KPM. Although it wasn't professional artillery training, at least they were taught the basics.

During that week we came very near to my home village. We passed my former school, which was deserted because of the rumours that we were around. I could even see huts belonging to my distant relatives. We walked over the land that I used to cultivate with my dad, and we passed the little pool near the papyrus where I swam and played with my friend. The hut where I was born was less than one kilometre away from this place. The soil where we walked was drenched with memories of my youth.

I felt a deep pain in my chest. Although I had been indoctrinated by the LRA, I was getting tired of all the killing and the suffering. I longed to be back with my parents, especially now that I was only a few minutes' walk away from their hut. I wondered if they were at home. I knew that the chances of them being there were slim, as the rumours of our presence had probably reached this place long before our arrival, but I still felt a strong urge to check. I wasn't thinking of escaping. I just wanted to go home and say hello to my mum and dad, and drink a cup of tea with them before returning to my group. But I knew very well that I couldn't risk it. A visit like that would put my family in serious danger, so I quickly put this idea out of my head.

Our point commander, Agira, came up to me while we were walking along. He knew that I had been born somewhere in this area, although he didn't know exactly which village. He asked me if I wanted to show him my village, and I felt some panic. Luckily another soldier approached us at that same moment to report rumours of UPDF soldiers in the area. This took Agira's focus away from me and my family. We continued moving and the further we went, the more the memories faded away.

We kept travelling south, in the direction of Lalogi, near Aboke, never moving in a straight line to obscure our destination. Despite this it appeared that this entire region had heard of our arrival in the area. We occasionally ran into some civilians, but the places we passed through were mostly deserted.

On 8 October we reached the parish of Lalogi and started moving indirectly towards Aboke. During the day we moved deeper into the bush to avoid being noticed. At night we set up our camp in what is now known as Oyam District, hidden deep in the bush so nobody was aware that we were in the area. We used this to our advantage. In a surprise tactic we entered a small trading centre where they had lots of chickens and goats. The people there fled in all directions when they saw us. We killed anyone we could catch, but we were too hungry to bother chasing the rest. Most of us were more interested in boiling chickens and goats, even though the fleeing villagers were probably on their way to get the army. The moment that we conquered this trading centre we started boiling water and slaughtering animals for our Independence Day meal.

This was one advantage to being in Uganda. Although I didn't like the people's suffering, I did like all the extra food, which we never enjoyed in this abundance in Sudan. We didn't rush our meal, but there was a sense that we had to keep moving to stay ahead of the army.

After the feast we continued south. Our doctor, a lieutenant named Michael, went ahead of the advance party on a bicycle. He probably had some other business to attend to, because the commander, who trusted the doctor, fully expected him to return. I heard our head commander Agira tell him that they would meet up a little later, and so they did. Not even an hour after we had left the trading centre we found the doctor again, lying dead on the ground, shot down by arrows.

This is how we realised that we had walked into an ambush by a Local Defence Unit (LDU). They usually used bows and arrows to kill our scouts silently, and these were the weapons that they handled best. The LDUs included mainly farmers and young boys who had been given guns by the government to fight us. Their mandate was to protect civilians, but in my mind they did exactly the opposite. They were rarely strong enough to defeat us and the only thing they did was to anger us.

This was how the suffering in the north had started. In the late eighties, the LRA was very good to the citizens of northern Uganda. But when these citizens turned against the LRA in the early nineties, it caused the LRA to react harshly. Once the civilians started to kill rebels, the rebels had to teach them a valuable lesson: it is not wise to attack a rebel. It was the same thing with the killing of our doctor.

The moment we saw the doctor, we took up defensive positions against the ambush. The LDU militia opened fire at us. Some of them had guns, while others just had bows and arrows. The militia was strong in numbers, but it wasn't organised or trained the way our army was. Some of the boys didn't even know how to reload their guns. It didn't take us very long to win the battle, maybe twenty to thirty minutes. We killed all of the LDUs. On our side, only three received minor injuries – all flesh wounds, nothing really serious. One boy was hit in the buttocks, a girl was hit in the leg and another boy was hit in the shoulder. And then of course there was the doctor.

We took away all their weapons and we were surprised to find that they were well equipped. Some of the weapons were given to the fresh recruits. I saw that some of the Samuel Baker boys were now armed.

Suddenly a plane flew over and started to shoot at us with its machine gun. The LDU had called in the army and it was clear that they intended to fight us with heavy equipment. The B-10 was the only weapon we had to defend ourselves from an air attack, but actually hitting an aeroplane with a B-10 was almost impossible. So the best strategy was to hide in the bush, where the fighter plane had no way of finding us. We scattered into the bush and moved southeast in small groups. In this manner it didn't take us long to lose the plane.

Without our doctor we couldn't take care of the wounded. They had to be taken to our sickbay near Gulu, where we had another doctor who could attend to them. When the wounded were marched off, we continued our way south. It was around noon and our commander was still red hot over the death of our doctor. It was clear that he wanted more revenge. Eventually we entered Lira District, an area inhabited by the Langi tribe, who are related to the Acholi. We speak almost the same language, but because of the war, they really hated us. The LRA had always run into trouble when they were in the Lango region. In fact, the people from the LDU militia had been Langis. So our commander was determined to teach these civilians a lesson. We would give them an Independence Day that they would never forget.

It started with one civilian, who appeared to be following us but may have been completely oblivious to our presence. The commander thought that this man had to be intelligence, so we ambushed him and began questioning him. The man repeatedly claimed that he was only a farmer, but his words had no effect. He was brutally beaten by Oket Achelam, who was the second-in-command during this mission. We left the man behind half dead, probably so that the blocking force would kill him.

We continued marching straight into a large swampy area that was covered with papyrus. This was difficult terrain for marching, so the enemy would never suspect that we would come from this direction. Sometimes we would sink so deep in the muck that the water came up to our chests. Everything was soaking wet and cold. We entered the papyrus swamp at dusk and by the time we cleared it, it was already dark.

As the night was falling, we heard the beginnings of the celebrations. Independence Day is one of the most important public holidays and feast days in Uganda and everybody around was celebrating. In the Lango region this holiday bore special significance, because Uganda's independence was achieved by one of their leaders, Apollo Milton Obote. Everywhere we saw bonfires and heard the cheering and songs of joy. These people didn't realise that we were closing in on them and that their evening would end in terror. We slaughtered a lot of people on the roadside that night, and brutally ended the festivities. Commander Ojet actually cut out the heart of one civilian and placed it in the dead man's mouth.

Around midnight we stopped our massacres. By now it had started to drizzle, and dark clouds were covering the sky. I could see only as far as the colleague walking in front of me, but that was it. Many of us were equipped with flashlights, but we were not allowed to turn them on until we reached Aboke, for reasons of secrecy. We kept on moving until around three in the morning, when we finally entered Aboke. At this time everyone was in a deep sleep. Except for some barking dogs, there were no noises whatsoever. Before we entered the village our roles for the mission were assigned. I was selected to be a standby, which meant that I would take part in the attack. Only the most experienced soldiers were selected for this assignment. At least 50 per cent of those who had set out from Sudan were assigned roles in this mission. The rest stayed behind to guard the new recruits.

We approached our objective, St Mary's College, to find that the only thing keeping us out was a weak wire fence. It took us only a few seconds to get in. Some of our soldiers quickly stormed the church and the seminary, while others went straight for the girls. I ran into the schoolyard, but I was selected with two others to guard the main entry gate.

From where I stood, I couldn't see too much of the raid, but I could hear it very well. Within seconds the tranquillity of the school had turned into total chaos as hundreds of my colleagues tried to get into the heavily reinforced buildings. The entry doors to the buildings were made of steel and the windows were protected with iron bars, so it was very difficult to get in. I heard my colleagues screaming that they would blow up the building if the girls wouldn't open the door. These threats were effective: a girl in the first building opened the door and all the girls, most of them younger than I was, were forced to march out. Soon afterwards, our soldiers blasted a gaping hole in another of the buildings, and the girls inside were also forced out. These girls were clearly from higher up in the school and appeared to be older than me. In the meantime, I watched some of my colleagues pour petrol over the only vehicle around and set it ablaze. It was very chaotic and frightening for the girls.

Throughout the raid, which took several hours, I remained guarding the gate. When all the girls were bound with ropes and cloths, my colleagues marched them out of the schoolyard. This entire procession had to pass me at the gate. The girls all wore dark blue clothes and they all had decent shoes. I was somewhat envious of their nice clothes – they looked so beautiful, like they were going out dancing. Yet they wore expressions of complete terror. Many of the girls were crying. As they passed me, I tried to count them, but when more than a hundred had walked past, I lost count. When we had all cleared the gate we quickly marched as far away from Aboke as we could. It was still dark.

At dawn we came to a river, which was deep enough for the water to come up to my chest. Although the girls didn't like it, they were all forced to cross the river and they became dirty and soaked. It was still very early in the morning, so we were all cold. The girls were shivering, but it was difficult to tell if that was their fear or the chill.

We soon came to a village, which we attacked. A man there warned us that if we kept the girls, the army would be on our back, so he was immediately executed. We found some more children in the village, and we abducted them before moving out. We kept on moving until well into the morning, when we reached a second village. This village was deserted, so we had a couple of minutes' rest. When we set out again, a friend from the Juba training took over my position in support and I was reassigned to the blocking force. The main body now had over 400 people with all the fresh abductees.

The blocking force had about fifty warriors and it was led by the man responsible for my abduction, Major Ojara. While Ojara stayed in the middle, I was in command of the rear of our battalion, so out of the 300 experienced soldiers, I was the last in the group. Because of the Aboke girls and all the other new abductees, we couldn't move very fast, so my position was a very important one. The Ugandan army could easily catch up with us, so we expected an attack at any moment. An hour after we passed the deserted village, we came to a big rock from which we could see the entire area. Usually we used these places for navigation and scouting, but this time we were in a hurry to get as much distance between us and St Mary's College as humanly possible, so we didn't stop at the rock to survey the situation.

We came into a small valley and then up another hill. At the top of this hill I looked back to check whether we were being trailed. That was when I saw them for the first time. On the other side of the hill were three people following us. One of them was a white sister wearing a nun's habit, one was a well-dressed black man, and the last was a black woman who looked like a local villager. The white lady and the man were waving at me and they were even shouting things, but because of the distance I couldn't hear what it was. The moment I saw this I sent for a dedication officer, the lowest officer in rank, and I told him to run up to the commander of the blocking force to report this. In the meantime, I gathered some boys to check out our visitors. While the visitors walked down the hill there was a brief moment when they were out of our view. We used this moment to line up, and I sent out some boys to see if these three had been followed by the army. When they came into sight again, we had an ambush prepared. Suddenly they were staring into the barrels of our guns.

We stared at each other face to face. It was clear that they feared us, but there was also a very strange determination within these people, like they were ready to die. The nun immediately started to talk. She introduced herself as Sister Rachelle and she asked to talk to our commander. I wasn't sure what to do. I could kill her immediately or I could take her to the commander. Both these things might anger the hotheaded Agira, so I was very relieved when the senior commander of the blocking force appeared. He took over the discussions from me and ordered me to take the party to Commander Agira.

I walked in front and the three followed me until we came to the main body. The moment the Aboke girls saw the nun, they started crying, as if they had the feeling that their salvation had come. Somehow I admired the white lady and her two followers. I had got used to people who fled when they saw us, and rarely had I seen such brave but stupid determination. She was very much aware of the risk she was taking in following us, but she had shown us that she wasn't afraid to die. I saw the surprise on the faces of my colleagues. They were all wondering what these three people were thinking. The white lady especially attracted a lot of attention.

As soon as we were in front of the commander, the lady started to talk, but the commander made it very clear that he would be the one asking the questions. He asked if she spoke Acholi and she confirmed that she understood Langi, which was very much related to Acholi. The commander questioned where they had been when we attacked the school.

'I was in Lira with Sister Alba, who was sick,' she replied. 'When I came back, I saw what had happened and I decided to follow you, to ask you if I can have my girls back.'

From her bag she pulled hundreds of thousands of shillings and put them into the hands of the commander, but he wasn't interested in the money. She offered medicine or anything else that they could provide in exchange for the girls. I don't know what it was with this commander. He was one of the most brutal commanders within the LRA, responsible for the beating and murder of the Otieno family in Awach. This man was vicious, ruthless and very dangerous. He could have killed her with one blink of his eye and normally he would surely have done so. But instead he began to smile and then he said to the woman, 'Don't you worry – you will get your girls back.'

The moment I heard this, I was taken by surprise. I had expected that at any moment I would be given the order to shoot this nun. After the commander had made this strange promise, he gave the order to move on again and to line up the girls on the top of the hill. There they would talk further. I was ordered to stay in the main group and help to guard the girls. As we walked, the commander talked to the nun as if he had known her all his life, telling her about battles he had fought and the things the LRA had achieved. Agira also called Kony through the satellite phone.

We kept on climbing the hill and when we were at the top, we were told to line up the Aboke girls. Agira's second wife, a girl who was barely fifteen years old, unrolled a plastic sheet on which the nun and the other visitors were told to sit. The sister started negotiating again; she told the commander that she would give him anything and everything he wanted, from medicine to money. But the commander was very clear; he declined everything and told her that she shouldn't worry so much, and that she would get the girls.

Just then we heard the distant noise of a helicopter approaching. Immediately the commander started screaming orders. Everybody was to take cover so that the helicopter didn't spot us. The sister was forced to take off her white cap and the black man who was escorting her had to take off his white shirt. It was too late. The helicopter had already spotted us. As the helicopter disappeared over the horizon, we were told to pack our gear and to start moving. We knew that the Ugandan army was now aware of our position, so we had to clear out of there as soon as possible. We had to push the girls to walk faster. After ten minutes the helicopter came back looking for us. We tried to disappear under the bushes, but because there were so many of us, it was difficult to hide. So we continued marching. Several hours later, we crossed a railway line that had been out of use for more than a decade and was slowly disappearing under the tall grass. Once across the tracks, the advance party walked into the first ambush.

The main body was able to go around it and, along with several dozen experienced soldiers, I was selected to reinforce the advance party. When we came to the frontline it was chaos. The UPDF had been waiting for us and had set up good defensive positions. This wasn't going to be an easy battle. Furthermore, the helicopter was still circling above us, and it was equipped with a heavy machine gun. When we arrived, the sixty warriors of the advance party were under heavy fire. We came just in time to prevent the UPDF from destroying them. We immediately set up defensive positions and I took command of the left wing. A fierce battle unfolded in which neither side could advance.

Within minutes, the blocking force came to our aid and provided another fifty experienced soldiers. We finally managed to eliminate the enemy. We also tried to shoot down the helicopter with the B-10, but we didn't manage to hit it. The blast was enough, however, to make the helicopter retreat. It then didn't take long to catch up with the main group again.

When we found them, the sister was still negotiating with Commander Agira. A small group of the girls was selected to stay among the rebels, while a much larger group was set apart. Even from a distance we could see that the sister was upset. When we came closer, we heard that Agira had given her back 109 girls, while we kept thirty of the strongest and the most beautiful. Not for a single moment did I consider this offer to be unfair. From my perspective, we could have willingly and easily killed this nun and taken all the girls, so giving back so many of them seemed to me to be an extremely generous gift. It was clear that the sister didn't accept this offer. As she was talking to the girls, I could see tears were in her eyes.

She begged Agira to take her and let the girls go. She even went on her knees and held her rosary in her hand. At this point Agira was nearly at his breaking point. He became extremely wild and he started to scream at the old nun.

'Do you know me? ANSWER ME . . . DO YOU KNOW ME?! I will kill you if I hear just one other word from you. You don't know me. I can kill you any second from now if I want to. Either you stop begging now, or I take all the girls.'

Sister Rachelle was clearly startled by Agira's sudden outburst of anger. As he walked away, she offered him her apologies. She got the message: either she would back down, or the commander would carry out his threat. The sister had no choice but to accept. The commander told her to note the names of the girls left behind. One of the girls had to assist the sister in writing down the names, because her hands were shaking uncontrollably.

When this had been done, Agira ordered the nun to join him in prayer. We all knelt down as the commander praised the Lord and the Holy Spirit who had taken hold of our leader Joseph Kony. After the prayer Sister Rachelle showed Agira a list with thirty names and she was forced to call all the names so each girl came forward. One of the thirty girls hid in the larger group. The sister realised Agira's anger at this, so she asked some of the girls to bring the missing girl forward.

By this time, it was late in the day and getting dark. The commander gave the sister a flashlight and told her to go. The sister ordered all the girls to say thank you to the commander. Agira asked the girls if he had mistreated them, or if he had mistreated the sister, and both times the girls replied no. He told them not to run away the next time he visited their school. As the sister was departing, the commander gave her another abducted girl, who was barely ten years old. She had been abducted from the last village and may have been the child of the local village lady who had come with the nun. Sister Rachelle took the child and left with 110 children.

We proceeded for another few hours until we came to a deserted village. Here we set up camp for the night. The thirty Aboke girls were forced into one hut while all the other abductees were separated into the other huts. Each hut had a few guards stationed inside; the rest of us soldiers had to sleep under the open sky. At first light, we packed our gear to move out.

I was ordered to be in the blocking force again and I watched the advance party and the very large main body as they set out. Because there were so many abductees in the main body, Agira decided to reinforce it with troops from the blocking force. Because of this, the blocking force was left with only about ten people. Leading us was Captain Ojara. I was the second-in-command. After the main body was long gone, we followed their trail. We marched for maybe an hour and a half when we walked into a terrible ambush. Somehow neither the advance party nor the main body had noticed it, and for some reason the UPDF hadn't opened fire on these groups; instead they had reserved it all for the ten of us. It was Captain Ojara who saw them first, a lot of soldiers lined up about a hundred metres away from us, on the top of yet another hill. At first, we thought that it was people from the main body, so we walked up to them without even expecting an attack. Then it began.

Our enemies held the high ground and they were lined up in great numbers, so when they started firing, we really stood no chance. Although it was forbidden in the LRA, we all squatted down and hid behind some trees. Captain Ojara ordered one of his escorts to run with the walkie-talkie to get within talking distance of the main body and to request reinforcements. Luckily the main body had already heard the shooting and they immediately dispatched a battle group to support us. This group was under the command of Opiro Anaka. When they came to reinforce us, they were bare-chested and ready for battle. We removed our shirts as well and lined up to fight. Captain Ojara, who was also in the artillery department, loaded the mortar and began firing back at our enemies. A serious gun battle ensued. As we advanced up the hill Captain Ojara was shot in the belly. When I saw this, I brought him back to safety as my colleagues continued to fight. Ojara's injury was very severe. He must have been hit by some kind of bomb and part of his belly had been removed, and all his intestines were out. I tried to get him back to a safe distance, but he died on the way. Minutes later Opiro Anaka, now in command of this entire battalion, had his thirty reinforcements in position to help us. Opiro fired his mortar and I fired Captain Ojara's mortar.

In the meantime, two helicopters came to reinforce our enemies. One of the helicopters was a gunship – another name for an attack helicopter – and caused us serious trouble. The other didn't engage us; it was just there to scare us. In the first few minutes the gunship did a lot of damage. Finally, some of my friends from the Juba training fired the B-10 at the helicopter and it immediately left the battlefield. We were still greatly outnumbered by the UPDF soldiers and the battle continued fiercely for hours. By three in the afternoon, we had managed to scatter our enemies a bit. But they kept on fighting, shooting at us with mortars from all different directions.

That day our enemies suffered very high losses, but so did we, particularly in the blocking force. From the ten people who started in the force that morning, I was the only one who emerged unwounded. Three others in the group were severely wounded and the rest were shot dead. Throughout the fight we continually received reinforcements and many of them also got shot. Somehow I managed to survive.

I deeply regretted the loss of my colleagues, especially Captain Ojara. He was the nicest commander in the LRA. He truly cared for his soldiers and he always wanted us to survive in battle. When we first walked into the ambush, he allowed us to take cover and wait for reinforcements, instead of sending us into our deaths as so many other commanders would have done. This battle was the heaviest that I had fought in Uganda and one of the heaviest of all the fights while I was in the LRA. We lost more than fifty people that day, and once again I was angry. I always experienced such rage from these battles. This time I blamed the Aboke girls for all our trouble. On several occasions I openly cursed them, as did many of my colleagues. Why were they so fucking special? Hadn't we all been innocent children when we were abducted? Where was the Ugandan army then? Where was all the fucking media attention when we were stolen from our parents? Where were the white people coming to rescue us? It was as if nobody gave a shit about us, only about those damned girls from Aboke. I fumed that we had lost almost fifty of our best fighters and commanders, men such as Ojara, just to abduct some girls who would mean nothing but trouble to us.

After the battle we moved back into Lalogi parish, where we rested in the middle of the bush. At night one of the Aboke girls tried to escape. A guard had seen somebody slipping away in the distance and we were immediately awakened and told to pursue the girl. Not far from our position we found a hut inhabited by a large family and we ordered them to come out. The commander questioned them about the girl. The family claimed that they hadn't seen her, but some soldiers searched the house and found her. The reaction of the commander was frightening. He was extremely angry. He beat the girl and also the family until they were all unconscious and nearly dead. For the rest of the night we stayed near the hut. Around nine in the morning we began to move out again. Just before we left our commander beat the girl and the family some more, and we left them there to be killed by the blocking force.

We then returned to our sickbay near Gulu town, under Atwa Hill. The sickbay was located in the thick bush at the foot of the hill. Ironically, on the top of this hill were the barracks of the UPDF. The only thing separating our sickbay from the barracks was a thick line of trees. But they never knew about our sickbay and this was the last place they would ever look for it. It was only much later that they found out about it. The only problem was that we had to remain silent in this area, and this was difficult for the badly wounded.

We stayed in the sickbay for several hours while we waited for all the lightly wounded to be treated. Afterwards we went to a village called Ogul, where we stayed for almost a week. Ogul was a friendly place for us where we never mistreated any of the civilians. This is why we had their full support. They always made sure that we had enough to eat – we even paid them for our food – and in return they didn't disclose anything to the Ugandan army. In Ogul we continued training all the new abductees. Some of the new recruits, for example the boys from Samuel Baker, were given guns and all the initiating rituals were performed. Agira had the authority to bless the new soldiers and he did so readily, because we badly needed to replenish our forces. Some of the recruits who had received a bit more training were given power over the other recruits. In this way they could improve their own position within the LRA, and we had some new guards for the other abductees.

By the time we left Ogul, every abductee had been anointed and everybody's name was written. It was one of the LRA guidelines that all the newly abducted people had to be anointed within four days, but only after their name had been written. Hundreds of recruits were seriously beaten and afterwards Commander Agira anointed all of them with shea oil. All the new abductees were told that they belonged to us now and that they would all become fierce warriors.

From Ogul we set out for Kitgum, where we were supposed to have a gathering with all our other battalions operating in Uganda at that time. Just before we crossed the Achwa River, there was a big meeting of the commanders of several of the battalions. I think that three or four battalions were present, and they all had abductees. From here they started selecting people to go back to Sudan, while others were to stay in Uganda. Many of the new soldiers that we abducted at the beginning of the mission, who had already received their training and guns, were staying in Uganda, while the newest recruits were going to Sudan. In all around 500 abductees from the different battalions were sent to Sudan. To escort them, there was another full battalion, selected from all the experienced soldiers of the different battalions. I was among them.

On our way to Sudan we were constantly disturbed by helicopters, which were trying to scatter us and separate the girls from us. But they couldn't do this, because the abductees were surrounded by experienced soldiers at all times. The entire day we kept on moving and the helicopter continued firing at us. It was so terrible. Many of the new recruits were actually hit by the shooting. It was as if the government forces didn't care about the new recruits or the rest of us; they only held their fire where the Aboke girls were located. After a while, I was selected – with a second lieutenant and another sergeant – to take out the helicopter. We assembled the B-10 and when the helicopter came into view the second lieutenant stood in the open without moving. Although we all had our army uniforms on, the helicopter didn't see us until it was too late. We managed to shoot the helicopter down. We saw it burning and sinking slowly. When it passed behind a hill, that was the last we saw of the helicopter. Without this distraction we continued to move the whole night through and for two more days, until we were near the river that separates Uganda from Sudan.

That morning we came to the area of the last big settlements in Uganda. This was our only chance to gather enough food for all the new recruits to survive the journey, so we attacked some very large settlements. Once we had gathered as much food and as many jerrycans as we could find, we crossed into Sudan. It took us several hours to reach the river and here another disaster awaited us.

It was November, which is the time of the short rainy season in northern Uganda, and there had been some very heavy rainstorms the past few days. This meant that the river was extremely wild. We had tied the rope over the water and about a hundred of our experienced soldiers crossed successfully before they forced the abductees to do the same. At one point there were too many people on the rope; it sagged, and everybody went under the water. I saw five of these new recruits dragged away and I think that they all drowned. I was one of the last to cross the river.

All the jerrycans had been filled at the river, so we were ready to start the long march towards Aru. We were still wary of an attack by the SPLA, who had surely been warned by the UPDF, but what happened next was unexpected. A few kilometres from the river, the UPDF had also crossed into Sudan and prepared one last great attack. We walked straight into their ambush. Once more, a heavy fight followed. The UPDF were trying their very best to rescue the Aboke girls. Never before had I seen them so determined. With one full battalion they came after us with the sole purpose of rescuing the girls, but they had underestimated our resilience. We also had an entire battalion of determined soldiers. The battle lasted for several hours, but in the end, we again managed to win it. As in the last battle, we suffered very heavy losses but not as bad as the UPDF.

Throughout this battle I fought side by side with the second lieutenant who I had shot down the helicopter with. He and I were very similar, and we had become close, at least by LRA standards. Like me, he was a courageous warrior who fought as if he was willing to die. Both of us were fearless, which really scared our enemies. I do not remember how many enemies I shot during this battle, but again they were many, and again not even a splinter hit me. It almost seemed as if I was invincible.

After the battle had raged for several hours, the UPDF finally sounded their retreat and they were forced to leave the Aboke girls behind. Among the newly abducted, the Aboke girls were now the most hated recruits of them all, but also the most protected. All the action that was taken by the outside world to release the girls only made their life within the LRA worse.

The Kitgum Massacres

The march back to Aru Junction went painstakingly slowly, and it was one of the most difficult journeys that I had ever taken. First, the distance to Aru was much longer than the distance to Palutaka. Second, because Palutaka was now occupied by the SPLA, we had to avoid it, meaning that we were also avoiding the greener areas. Third, it was now sometime in early November, and while it was wet in Uganda, in Sudan the dry season had begun. By the third day after filling our jerrycans at the river, I had run out of water. This was just before we reached the 'bad place', an area near the mountains where the rocks were burning under the hot sun. This was by far the toughest part of the journey. The gumboots I was wearing turned into ovens as we walked over those rocks. Many people suffered during this part of our march. The heat didn't discriminate between senior soldiers or junior recruits, men or women, young or old. It affected us all.

While we were walking over the baking-hot rocks, I was on the verge of collapsing. I violently took the water of a few new recruits, reducing their only hope of surviving this march. This brought back memories of the time when I was a new recruit, making my way across the deserts of southern Sudan to Palutaka, not knowing how far I still had to go and terribly afraid of the madmen with their guns. On this march, I was one of the madmen and I had little sympathy for the new recruits.

In total it took us seven days of this hellish journey before we finally reached Aru. On the second day the commander called the headquarters and told them that none of us would survive if they didn't bring us water. Finally, on the fifth day, a large group came to our rescue with dozens of jerrycans filled with water. By then, out of the 800 people who had started the march to Sudan, about a hundred had died from thirst and sheer exhaustion. I don't know what happened to those boys from whom I took the water, but I wouldn't be surprised if they were among the dead.

When we reached Aru hundreds of my colleagues came to greet us by sprinkling water over us. We were so relieved to have survived. The moment we entered the camp we were told to line up and to parade. A short ceremony followed in which all the experienced soldiers were honoured, but I don't think that any of us cared about it. We just wanted to reach our huts and collapse in peace. Luckily that ceremony didn't take long, and we were excused to go and rest. The new recruits had to stay behind while the more elaborate welcoming ceremony for them began. This was an orientation ritual in which the rules and regulations of camp life were explained. Finally, the selection began in which all high-ranking commanders hoped to get one of the Aboke girls.

As I walked towards my hut, I met the commander of my unit, the Mzee, and the overall commander of the Stockree artillery. They were both heading towards the selection ceremony. I saluted them as they passed and the Mzee asked me about the mission, and whether I had brought an Aboke girl back for him, but I was almost too exhausted to answer him. For weeks I had been under constant military attack, risking my life almost around the clock. The last few days hadn't been any better, as I had been struggling with malnutrition, exhaustion and, most of all, thirst. I was in no state of mind to say anything positive about the mission. Instead I said something incredibly dangerous and stupid.

'The mission went well, sir. I have killed many Ugandan soldiers and I have brought you the girls, but if you ever send me to Uganda again, I will surely escape.'

I had uttered these words out loud without thinking about the implications of such a statement. Even thinking about escaping could cost me a serious beating and now I had said the words out loud, and in front of a captain and a major. The penalty for talking about escape was death and during my two years in the LRA I had seen many people being executed for much lesser offences. But I was lucky. Instead of giving me a punishment, both commanders started to laugh. I had rarely seen the Mzee laughing like this and it even put a smile on my face, although there was nothing to laugh about.

'And where would you go, Attiena? You are a holy soldier now. If people find you, you will be killed. Out there you only have enemies. Accept it, boy, we are your only family now.'

Both commanders continued laughing as they went to the selection ceremony, telling each other how funny I was. It did not occur to them that I could have been serious about escaping. Of course, I wasn't actually inclined to escape. I had been with them for almost two years and I had built a reputation as a fierce warrior. I wasn't a ruthless killer – I never took pleasure in killing innocent civilians, like many of the young boys who so quickly climbed the promotion ladder – they knew that. But I was well respected for my conduct in battle and had become a favourite of many commanders. No one would expect me to want to escape. I was used to life with the rebels, so I even surprised myself with my words.

The only time in the past year that I had seriously thought about leaving the LRA was when we passed my village, and even then, escape never truly crossed my mind. I just wanted a short leave to reconnect and have tea and cookies with my parents and to chat a little about my new life. I had had so many opportunities to escape in the past, but I was a soldier and had a duty to dethrone Museveni before I could even think about leaving the rebels.

A moment before I entered my hut, I saw Nyeko. I immediately felt the urge to shoot him, but I kept my cool even though I hated him so much. Luckily, he had his back turned and I didn't have to look him in the eye. I went into my hut and fell into a deep sleep.

The next day I saw that our unit had received twenty new recruits. This included one of the Aboke girls, who would be married to the top commander of the artillery department in the Stockree Brigade. The new boys and girls in our unit had to undergo military training, which became my primary responsibility. After a few days' rest, the training began. Every day I took them for long marches. When the sun was at its peak, I made them run over the dusty landscape until they collapsed from exhaustion. I really made them suffer during the training, but I believed that they would thank me later. Once they were confronted by a well-armed enemy with the intent to kill them, they would appreciate the extra stamina that the training built.

This first week of their training was mainly marching, marching and more marching. I seriously caned the ones who couldn't keep up with the others and I gave them hot exercises. It was the same training I had endured almost two years earlier. After the first week I also introduced some gun training, but the main activity was still marching. Because my recruits would become artillerymen one day, I introduced the mortar and RPG launcher to them, but for now they were still much too junior to touch these kinds of weapons. All in all, the training took four weeks, and by then it was well into December. The recruits were sent on their first military test to attack some Dinka villages and replenish our food stocks. Happily, I wasn't selected to join them.

Christmas time was very special within the LRA. The day before Christmas the festivities began with a big ceremony, in which hundreds of soldiers were promoted to a higher rank. Everyone except those who stood guard was invited to watch the celebrations. We didn't know ahead of time who would receive a promotion, so I was really anxious for myself. I had fought very well during the last mission and I expected to be promoted for my outstanding service. Being a sergeant was OK, but my life would be much better in the position of second lieutenant. Sergeants could be beaten for no clear reason by any of the ranks that exceeded theirs. But lieutenants were not beaten like this.

The ceremony began with the lowest promotions. First there were the ordinary soldiers who were promoted to corporal or dedication officer. Then existing corporals and the dedication officers were promoted to sergeant, and after there were ordinary soldiers who skipped the first two steps of the ladder and got promoted directly to sergeant. When they were done with this group, I became excited for my turn. They started naming the list of sergeants who were being promoted to second lieutenant, but my name wasn't among them. It completely ruined the rest of my day, even though it was a day of celebration. The next day our Christmas celebrations began.

Christmas was really nice and because of all the fun festivities, I forgot about my frustrations of the previous day. It started early in the morning with prayers. Kony stepped up to the stage to celebrate the birth of Jesus. He told the classic story of Mary's journey to Bethlehem, where Jesus was born, but the story was also mixed up with military propaganda. Kony announced that the Spirit Lakwena had revealed to him the date that the Ugandan government would fall. It was to be a few weeks later, on 12 January 1997. With this revelation everybody clapped and cheered, even me. Even though many previous deadlines had passed, we still believed in the Spirit: every revelation gave us renewed hope. Every time Kony said that Museveni would fall on a certain date, I believed him. Lakwena's revelation filled me with joy. In about three weeks we would conquer Kampala and then I could finally go home in peace and with honour.

After morning prayer, the dances began. Our choir sang traditional Acholi songs and all the soldiers joined in to perform the dances. It started with the Larakaraka dance, which was a kind of courtship dance, and afterwards we performed my favourite, the warrior dance. For several hours we danced and whenever I wasn't dancing, I spent time joking with my Juba friends and a new friend I had got to know during the retreat from Uganda. After the dancing all the senior soldiers got some beans and potatoes. Throughout the month I had been starving due to the ongoing famine in Aru, so this food was really welcome. I had become a valuable asset to the LRA because of my superior training, so they wouldn't allow me to starve to death. However, there was rarely enough to take away the hunger. So the Christmas dinner was a great surprise. This was truly a happy day for me.

The juniors got only a small portion of watery soup, while they watched us eating all the good stuff. Many of them were close to starvation, so observing us eating beans and potatoes must have been a real torture for them. Although I noticed that they were looking at us, I didn't feel any sympathy. We didn't care about the new recruits any more. Hundreds of them were now being brought in every month. At the same time dozens of them died from starvation, diseases or executions. It was a waste of time to grow attached to any of them, as we never knew who would survive and who would die.

Two days after the Christmas celebrations they started the selection for another big mission, and I was very pleased that I wasn't chosen. I had completely had it with the missions to Uganda. It was not only the difficult journey that I despised, but also the constant threat of being killed and the horrible suffering we inflicted on the civilians. During the last mission we had been in such heavy fights that I was not anxious to return. Again, the group that had been selected was given a few days of training in which they were well fed and well rested.

The goal of the new mission that was under preparation was punishment. Its one purpose was to teach the people of Kitgum a lesson. During the last few months the civilians had uncovered several of our arms depots and revealed them to the Ugandan army. This was totally unacceptable. The resistance of the Acholi people was getting worse over time, even though we were fighting for them. This had to stop.

In the meantime, the new recruits had returned from their food-gathering mission and I was supervising them on all kinds of tasks. Just after Christmas I had taken fifteen new recruits to fetch water. When we came back, we were told to gather with others at the gate of Control Altar. Senior staff had assembled several boys and girls, some of them experienced soldiers, who all came from Kitgum. Then they explained that Kitgum civilians always betrayed our movements to the Ugandan government and they were always searching to uncover our arms depots. The boys and girls were told to take off their shirts and they were made to suffer for what their people had done to us. All of them received a heavy punishment of a hundred strokes. By the time the beating was over, some of them weren't breathing any more, while the rest were severely wounded.

One of the boys almost beaten to death came from the artillery department of Stockree. I knew him quite well and he was made to suffer for the conduct of his people, even though he had been with us in the rebel movement for over a year. This boy was meant to go on the mission to Kitgum, but because of his injuries he couldn't. The Mzee came up to me and he told me that I had to take his place. It made me really angry. Immediately my escape threat of a month earlier came back to mind, but I kept my anger in check and didn't reveal it to the commander.

After the beating ceremony we were told to stay within the gated area of Control Altar, where we got a good meal. The next day we each received our supplies, including extra arms, plus water and food for the journey. The water wasn't enough to reach Uganda, but we were told that the Arabs would provide us with more on the way. We then got the briefing for what would be a very bizarre and contradictory mission.

Three small battalions would invade Kitgum, with each battalion having different objectives. The battalion from Sagnia Brigade was instructed to hand out medical supplies in the villages to win the hearts and minds of the people of Kitgum. The Gilba Battalion would then visit the same villages and order the people to move out of Kitgum or suffer the consequences. Afterwards Stockree

Brigade would come in and kill every civilian that hadn't obeyed Gilba Battalion's orders.

In effect, the mission had two goals that in retrospect seemed to be very contradictory, but at the time appeared to make perfect sense. Handing out medical supplies was intended to change opinions in Kitgum, so they wouldn't turn against us any more. Those who wouldn't go away when we asked them nicely were probably the same people who gave away valuable information to the enemy, so they would be executed.

The second goal was to effectively depopulate the entire Kitgum District. We wanted all the civilians to leave Kitgum so that we could have the terrain where we would destroy the armies of Uganda, before we set out to Kampala. Depopulating Kitgum was a measure to protect the civilians from being harmed in the battle – at least, that was what we were told. In the meantime, we also had to teach them a lesson so they would stop aiding the Ugandan army.

Soon after the briefing we set out on another horrible march. It was 1 January, exactly two years from the time that I had been abducted. January was the hottest period of the year and it meant that this trip would be harder than any I had experienced before. At around nine, we set out with little over 300 combatants. Whenever we went to Uganda, we had to carry a lot of ammunition, and therefore the trip went very slowly. As promised, the Arabs provided us with water along the way, but not with food. On the first day out, we passed several Arab camps where we refilled our jerrycans. At the last Arab camp, we were given some time to sleep. The rest of the journey was very difficult. In the sweltering January heat there was no grass and no water, and we ran out of food.

I had very heavy luggage and could not move well. At one point I just couldn't move any further, so I sat down. I threw all my gear on the ground and lay down against a tree. At first I thought that I would rest for a minute, but I came to the conclusion that it was nice to lie here, and I couldn't bring myself to stand up. My best friend Joe, from the Aboke mission, walked up to me and encouraged me to move on.

'Do you want to sit here for ever?'

He persuaded me to continue and finally he even started to beat me, after which I slowly got up and went on my way. He surely saved my life that day because, on my own initiative, I would not have continued. I had witnessed many people saying that they would stop to rest for a minute, never to stand up again, dying on the spot they chose to rest. Determination and persistence were key to survival in the LRA.

As we continued, I was struggling to keep up with the rest. I had been selected well after the others, so I hadn't received the benefit of extra food before the mission, and I was really feeling the lack of energy. Several hours after Joe had persuaded me to get up, I had to sit down again for a few minutes. Joe was now in front of me, so I didn't have his words of encouragement to count on, but I didn't really need them. I realised the danger of staying seated, so I was planning to sit for just a few minutes. But a captain called Langole found me. This man had recently transferred from Sagnia Brigade to Stockree and he had become good friends with Nyeko. This made him a natural enemy of mine. Nyeko had probably told him stories about me, but we had not had any more confrontations and most of the time I ignored him and his friends. Until now, that was. Langole asked, 'Attiena, why I are you sitting here like this?'

'Please, sir, I am just resting, but I will continue in a minute.'

At this point he became really angry with me. He said, 'OK, if the luggage is too heavy for you, we will take it away.'

The moment he said this he took away my ammunition.

'And the gun – you can't carry the gun any more. Here, I will take it.'

At that moment he kicked me and violently took my gun while I tried to hold on to it. From the first moment that I had received my gun I had never allowed anyone else to handle it. They had told us clearly that the gun was our mother who nurtured us and our father who protected us and we should never let go of it, and now I was being stripped of my gun. Then the captain told his body-guards to strip me of my clothes as well. I struggled against them, but there was nothing that I could do to prevent this. In the mean-time, some people asked him what he was doing, but he threatened to give them the same treatment if they interfered with his busi-ness. He told everybody to continue marching. He didn't want the battalion to witness what he was about to do, so all the soldiers, except for his bodyguards, were told to move on.

It took a few minutes for the battalion to pass and in the mean-time two bodyguards tied me up with my own shirt. After the group had passed, Langole put the barrel of his gun into my mouth. At that moment I really thought that it was the end. In my head I was already saying goodbye to the world. I anxiously tried to look for ways out of this, but all possible escape routes would end the same way: with me being killed. But I refused to be killed like a defenceless chicken. If I had to die this way, I would at least take a few people out with me. I had managed to loosen the T-shirt and my arms were almost free. One of the guards stood one metre away and held his gun loosely in his hand. My plan was to take his gun to try to shoot Langole before I was executed.

The captain took the gun out of my mouth and backed up a few steps to attach the bayonet. That is when I understood his plan: he didn't want to shoot me, he wanted to spear me so I died a slow death, and he hoped no one would notice.

By now I had already accepted that I would be executed; I just hadn't accepted the terms. I had seen many people killed by bayonet before and it was a horrible death. If I was to be killed, it would be by a bullet in a proper gunfight. When he stepped back, I saw my chance. Everything happened as if it were being played in slow motion. Just as I decided to reach for the bodyguard's gun, I heard a voice, shouting: 'LANGOLE, WHAT ON EARTH DO YOU THINK YOU ARE DOING?'

Once again, I was rescued at the last possible moment. The overall commander of the brigade, a colonel named Wall Okot, came running towards us, probably because he had heard that I was about to be executed. He could march very quickly – his ambitious marching speed was one of the reasons that I was almost executed – but at least he had some sympathy. He was not overly aggressive like the other commanders. He normally talked very slowly and whenever a soldier was lagging behind, he would give them encouragement instead of beatings. The two commanders began quarrelling with each other. Wall Okot asked: 'Why have you tied this sergeant up?'

The captain explained his story, claiming that he was only trying to scare me. At this Okot became really angry.

'I know you were planning to kill this sergeant. So you want to kill all our soldiers one by one? Then how are we going to win the war?'

Okot ordered him to give me back my clothes and gear and instructed Langole's bodyguards to cane him seriously. Afterwards he ordered Langole to take charge of the advance party, while I was to stay close to Okot. Okot gave me some water and *posho* (cooked maize meal) and told me to drink and eat. He explained that my failure to walk was caused by my lack of energy. Both the near-death experience and the extra food and water gave me renewed energy, and although I was still struggling a bit, I managed to keep up with the colonel.

In a day we reached the river near the Uganda–Sudan border. Here I spotted something that no one else had seen: the footprints of a leopard. I saw that the tracks were still fresh, so the leopard had to be close. I immediately told the commander. He asked me how I knew this and I showed him the footprints. At that point he ordered three of us to follow them and try to shoot the animal. We set off as silently as we could. Everyone was extremely careful, because we all knew how dangerous these animals could be, espe-cially for young people like us. Several minutes later we saw the leopard sitting high up in a tree. It started to make a lot of noise and even came down the tree to attack us. We opened fire and continued shooting until it was dead. I quickly ran back to the commander to report and he immediately called Kony, using his satellite telephone. Leopards were considered to be spiritual ani-mals and if we killed one it was a spiritual affair, which required the consultation of our highest spiritual leader.

From Kony we received instructions that we were allowed to eat the animal, but that the skin had to be brought back to Aru imme-diately. So we skinned the leopard and then boiled the meat. Because the leopard was very wild, the meat also tasted very wild. It was not all that nice to eat. After the meal, two boys were selected to take the skin back, while the rest of us continued on our mission.

After we crossed the river, we moved through the place with all the bees and later we reached the Padwat reserve. Here we hid some of our weapons and were allowed to rest for a few hours. Then the brigades separated and each of the three battalions left to carry out their missions. This was the starting point of the most horrible mission that I had had to participate in to date, and probably one of the worst prolonged massacres that the LRA had ever conducted. Just before we set out, we received some very clear instructions from the man I now hated even more than I hated Nyeko.

'We are God's vengeance to the people of Kitgum, who are trying to sabotage our holy war. Let's have no misunderstanding here: we are here not only to kill, but also to make the people from Kitgum suffer as they have never suffered before. They will be made to understand the consequences of resistance. In Aru they want to hear about the massacre on the radio. They even want to hear it in the international news. Do not make a mistake of disobeying rules and disobeying a command to kill, because if you do, you will be killed next.'

The horrendous slaughter started with a large village. We arrived in the wake of Gilba Battalion and many people in the village were still packing their stuff to move out, as they had been instructed to. But they were too late. As we surrounded the village, we were ordered to arrest all the civilians and place them in the centre, regardless of their age or gender. Dozens of them were lined up. We bound their hands with ropes and then the killing started. The people never knew what they had done wrong and didn't understand what was happening to them. Our commander began beating the crap out of those people and the rest of us were told to gather large stones. I will never forget the images from that day. We were ordered to take the rocks and bash in the heads of the civilians. Usually people didn't die with the first blow, so we had to hit them over and over again. The whole time their neighbours were watching it, knowing that they would be next. Even the small toddlers, who couldn't possibly have done us any harm, had their heads bashed in, one after the other. While we were doing this, some other colleagues killed all the animals. We left nothing alive in that village, nothing at all. The last living soul had been a small baby and this life was ended in a kind of brutal game of tennis. It was so cruel and so horrible.

Other villages followed. Several hours after the first massacre we came across a small group of hunters. Again we lined them up and tied them tightly together with ropes. Then Commander Langole shot them with their own bows and arrows. He didn't aim for any vital organs, so that the killing was drawn out into something like a game for him. The hunters were screaming out in pain and the harder they screamed, the more fun Langole appeared to have. At that point I really wanted to take up my gun and shoot the bastard, but I knew that his bodyguards would then kill me. Langole eventually grew bored and he just shot all the hunters in the heart, ending the game. We continued, with the three battalions criss-crossing the countryside and the civilians never realising what was happening around them until it was too late.

We visited village after village, brutally killing every living thing we found. I witnessed hundreds of different ways to kill someone. Sometimes we massacred civilians using a brick and branches, other times we would use bayonets and spear them to death. The next day we would wipe out a whole village by decapitating them with axes. When we were done with the killing, we would sometimes set the village on fire. Then, while the huts were still burning, we took any babies and young toddlers that were still alive and threw them into the burning huts. There were even occasions in which we forced the villagers to mutilate, torture and kill each other.

One day Langole instructed a mother to boil her own children and then to eat them. She killed both her boys, but when she couldn't bring herself to eat them, she was beaten to death with a padlock. In another village, two boys were armed with large sticks and they were told to kill each other. We promised the victor that we would let him live. We all watched it like it was a rooster fight, some of us cheering for one boy while the rest encouraged the other. Langole waited until one boy had beaten the other to death and afterwards the victor was also slain, using a machete. Langole's justification was: 'It is the time for killing, not the time for letting people live.'

For a week we continued with this killing spree in village after village. We killed hundreds upon hundreds of villagers and even this wasn't enough to please our commanders. The radios reported the killings and in Aru they heard about it. When the national news and finally even the BBC started reporting on it, it still wasn't enough.

As the massacres continued, I was slowly losing it. I felt I was going completely mad. Each time there was another cruel murder, I felt that something was dying inside me. We often talked with our victims, taunting them as they pleaded with us.

'Brother, please, why are you killing me?'

'What did I do to you?'

'Please God, what have I done to deserve this?'

'Please don't kill my baby, please don't kill my baby!'

'Boy, if you do this, you will for ever burn in hell.'

'In the name of the Son and the Holy Spirit, have mercy on us, boy, please have mercy.'

'Mamma, mamma! You killed my mother, please don't kill my father!'

All these sentences kept repeating over and over in my head. I couldn't sleep without hearing these voices, couldn't eat without hearing them, couldn't walk or go for a long or short call without hearing them. I couldn't even kill without the voices of a hundred people resonating through my head, amplifying the one voice of the person I was about to kill. At night I saw their spirits coming back for me, provoking me, laughing at me and hurting me. I woke up with terrible pains in my chest and in my head, as if the spirits in my dream had done some kind of horrible physical damage to my body. I wanted desperately to stop this madness, stop the killings, but there was nothing I could do. If I refused to kill, I would be the one to die.

While the killing continued, the Ugandan army started a massive military campaign against us, employing all their heavy fighting equipment. Helicopters constantly flew overhead, so that whenever we set a village ablaze, we had to move away from it very quickly. The moment the army learned of our position, not only would a gunship start hovering over us, but they would also send tanks, APCs, artillery pieces and other major equipment. Apart from the heavy machinery, several battalions were patrolling through Kitgum trying to catch us. We met these foot soldiers on many occasions, but usually the fights with them were very short. As the soldiers followed our trail, they passed village after village where everybody was already dead. No one was spared. The seasonal heat caused the bodies to decompose very quickly. These sights were very demoralising for them, and whenever the foot soldiers found us, it didn't take more than a couple of bullets to send them away screaming.

Sometime during the second week of the mission we came under our first heavy attack from the Ugandan army. We were in a village somewhere near the main road that had been almost deserted except for some elders who couldn't move too well. After we had killed the elders, we settled down and started to roast some chickens. It was while we were eating the chicken, at around 2 p.m., that we were taken by surprise by a UPDF mobile unit that included several tanks. When they started shooting at us, they were still far in the distance, but well within firing range. Their first shell killed several of our soldiers. The moment this shell exploded we all ran through the valley and up the other hill, where we could disappear into the treeline.

I had already covered a few hundred metres when I realised I'd made a huge mistake: I had left the mortar behind. The LRA regulations were very clear about leaving artillery pieces behind. Langole had been searching for an excuse to have me executed for a week and now I had presented him with the best of reasons. There was only one option out of this for me to survive: I had to go back and retrieve the artillery piece.

So while the bombs were falling around me, I ran back towards the village. The only thing that was in my mind was to get back at least a piece of the artillery. I had no fear or any other emotions. By the time I reached the village, I saw that they hadn't reached my position: I had one opportunity to grab the mortar and escape. I ran towards it and at that point all the foot soldiers started to open fire. I grabbed the mortar's barrel and started running like crazy, while the bullets were flying all around me. I was the only rebel now in clear range, so many guns were targeted on me. Luckily there was still some distance between them and me, and there were huts and other obstacles that prevented them from having a clear shot, so they started chasing me. There was also a tank on the road with the barrel facing me, but I didn't know this at the time. I was only focused on reaching the treeline on the other side of the valley when I heard a very big BOOM!

I found myself on the ground and for a moment everything darkened in front of my eyes. When the light came back seconds later, I saw a small crater next to me and I heard a high-pitched ringing in my ears. The moment I regained consciousness, I got up, took the 60 mm barrel and started running again. The UPDF soldiers opened fire again, but I was only slightly aware of this. I saw the bullets impacting everything beside me, but it was like it wasn't real. As I kept running, the ringing began to diminish a bit and slowly my senses returned. With that, I finally realised the danger I was in.

By now I was down the valley and, just as I started to go up the hill, the LRA opened fire on the soldiers who were chasing me. From the hill my colleagues had seen everything: the retrieval of the mortar, the chase and the tank blast that nearly blew me to pieces. When I reached the hill, people immediately came to my assistance and took the barrel from me. They told me that I had been shot.

'No, I haven't been shot – they missed me.'

But they insisted: 'No, you have been shot. Look at you, you are bleeding. Just look at all the blood.'

They helped me to remove my shirt and that was when I realised that I had indeed been shot. As they removed the clothes from me, I looked at my stomach and I saw a very big hole in my underbelly, and I started to panic. I thought that my stomach had been completely shot away. Apart from the wound I also had some burns on my stomach and back. While my colleagues were attending to me, I blacked out. Every few hours I woke up and noticed that they were dragging me on a makeshift stretcher, but I never stayed conscious for long.

They took me to a sickbay at a secret location in Kitgum. The doctors and nurses there took good care of me. The wound, which at first seemed very bad, was actually not so severe. A grenade splinter had scratched me, leaving a deep cut, but it never entered my body. The burns were also not that bad. After one day I was getting bored and I asked the doctor to release me and to let me go back to my unit. This was not allowed, but after two days in sickbay my unit came back to collect me.

Langole immediately started to give me a hard time. He hit me in the face and shouted at me about leaving the artillery behind. Luckily there was a lieutenant who defended me, arguing that by going back to collect the mortar I had shown extraordinary bravery. Yet it was clear that Langole wasn't satisfied. He clearly wanted to see me punished or even killed.

Our rivalry had actually started back on the day we first set out from Sudan. Langole had selected me to become his personal escort, but I had repeatedly refused. In my mind I was too high in rank to be the escort of a captain – a colonel perhaps, but not a captain. So throughout the mission, the captain kept asking me to cook him food, slaughter a chicken, bring his chair and other tasks, but I refused to do these things. This really pissed him off, and he grew more and more irritated. He knew very well that I had the support of the overall commander, so he couldn't just kill me; instead he was always looking for other reasons to have me executed. The fact that I had left the artillery was one such reason, but because of my extreme bravery I now had the support of all my colleagues. They had all seen me retrieve the weapon and, days later, they were still talking about it. Word quickly reached Wall Okot. This irritated Langole even more. By becoming a hero, I had made it even harder for him to execute me.

But Langole found other ways to make things difficult for me. He was the commander of my battalion and that meant that, although we didn't like each other, I still had to follow his commands. If I systematically refused military orders the colonel himself would find out, and I would lose all support from him and be executed.

A few days after I left sickbay, he started placing me in dangerous military situations. I was always selected to be the first man in any fight that we encountered. Whenever we were retreating, I would be the very last man to hold off the enemy forces. Weeks passed like this and I was always in mortal danger. Whenever we met one another he would cane me or quarrel with me for no reason. He even speared me once with his bayonet. It was not a deep wound and he didn't intend to kill me; he just wanted to scare and hurt me.

Because of this treatment, I was starting to evaluate my life in the LRA. I realised that this guy would someday become the cause of my death. That is when I started to develop a plan to escape. I even revealed this to certain people I trusted, but they laughed, as if it were a joke. I was now their hero, so there was no way that I would escape. They never believed me, but I was dead serious.

In the meantime, the killing in Kitgum continued, slowly depopulating the area, but still it wasn't enough for our leaders. Sometimes we walked for days in areas we had already passed through, where we would only encounter burning villages and dead bodies everywhere. The stench was unbearable. Whenever we saw groups of storks and vultures circling above a village, we knew that we had been there earlier. We could spot these villages from up to twenty miles away by watching the marabous and vultures.

I wasn't the only one who was haunted by the voices of the victims. After several weeks many of us started to hate the killing of
innocent civilians. We couldn't bear all the pain any more, even
though we were the ones causing it. We had become completely
traumatised. After so much killing over such an extended time, we
all went a little crazy. Any human being was viewed as someone we
might have to kill. Even though deep inside we didn't want to kill
that person, it might be a reflexive act. For this reason, fights
started occurring between our soldiers, and these fights could turn
very deadly in a few seconds. Sometimes our soldiers just shot
their guns at bushes, saying that there were people hiding in them,
even though there was nobody there.

By February, I remembered the prophecy that by now we should
have conquered Kampala, as the Spirit Lakwena had revealed in all
his wisdom. But we were still struggling in Kitgum, not even close
to destroying our enemy forces and only targeting civilians, the
majority of whom had never done us any harm. I felt betrayed. We
had been promised that the war would be over by now, but instead
things had only got worse.

To make matters even worse for me personally, the overall commander, Wall Okot, became gravely ill. He had a severe case of
diarrhoea, to the point that he was on the verge of death. He was
in such a bad condition that he could no longer even wear trousers. The diarrhoea was constant. I saw him on several occasions
when we had joint meetings with all the battalions, and each time
his illness seemed to be worse. He was my only guarantee that
Langole wouldn't execute me. The last time I saw him was after we
had been in Kitgum for nearly two months. We had gathered for
another joint battalion meeting, the 'RV meeting', which they
sometimes called 'rendezvous'. The people of Sagnia Brigade

carried him in on a stretcher. We stayed in the RV meeting for two days and the whole time we saw Okot's condition deteriorating, to the point where he was more dead than alive.

Soon after this, when all the battalions had split up, the Gilba Battalion suffered a huge attack. They had called in for reinforcements and, as always, Langole selected me as the very first soldier to go. I never got a moment of rest around him. During the RV meeting I had been constantly on guard without relief, so I hadn't slept for more than two days. I was very, very tired. Commander Langole treated me like a new recruit, assigning me the nastiest and the most dangerous of missions. No other soldier suffered the way I did. But there was no way of refusing his orders. If I refused a direct order I would be shot on the spot. Langole was just hoping and waiting for such an opportunity.

I had a very bad feeling about the mission, but there was nothing I could do to avoid it. As we passed the RV point we could already hear the battle unfolding. I was leading a group of twenty people, but I was struggling to keep my focus. When we arrived at the battleground, we saw that Gilba had walked into an ambush. They were being attacked by all types of artillery, tanks, APCs, foot soldiers and helicopters. The battle started somewhere at around four and continued for hours until nightfall, by which time we finally received heavy reinforcements from Sagnia and Stockree brigades. The helicopter flew away because of the darkness, and our enemies finally started to retreat. By then, dozens of our soldiers had died, including several boys and girls from the group I was leading. Luckily, I came out of the battle without a scratch.

We started to move north again, and I was afraid that we were on our way back to Sudan. I had the idea that if I followed them into Sudan, I would stay there for ever. If I was to escape, this was the time for me to do so. Once again, I told some other soldiers that I wanted to escape. I wanted to find out – because they had been complaining about the mission – if there was a chance they would join me. But they started laughing, thinking that I was joking. This time I was dead serious.

Because of Okot's deteriorating condition and the fact that it was almost impossible to find villages where we hadn't been before, Langole, who was now practically first-in-command, sounded our retreat to Sudan, almost two months after our mission had started. We set out, and after a day and a half we were getting close to the river and the border with Sudan. I knew that once we crossed the river, my chances of escaping would be very slim. I knew that if I wanted to escape, I had to do so while we were in Uganda. Never before had I felt such determination to leave the LRA. My opportunity came when we were nearly at the border.

Part V
The Life After

Escape

As we were nearing the river, the UPDF ambushed us, taking us by surprise. Langole was far away from me, which meant that he was in no position to give me the order to advance, as if I were some kind of one-man army capable of destroying an entire UPDF battalion. As the battle unfolded and my colleagues were falling all around me, I knew that my opportunity to escape had arrived. Everyone was preoccupied with the action, so nobody saw me as I slowly crawled backwards, away from the gun battle. When I was far enough, I stood up and ran. The area was covered in dense forest, and although I could still hear the gunfight, it didn't take me long to be out of sight. It was dangerous to follow the trail, but close to it was a dry riverbed so I went downhill to follow that instead. I knew that both Gilba and Sagnia battalions were near and that by now they would have been called in to come to our aid, so any minute that I was out in the open presented a real threat to me. I had to find a place where I could hide until they had passed.

After about twenty minutes I found the perfect hiding place. It was a little cave between the roots of the trees that grew on top of the riverbank. The cave was covered with long yellow grass and it was one of the few places that hadn't been destroyed by wildfire. It was somehow miraculous that I had seen the cave, as it was covered by grass and was about two metres above the riverbed. I climbed up the riverbank and over the roots and branches of the trees. I reached the cave, carefully pushed aside the grass and crawled in. The cave was too shallow for a grown man, but for me it was just perfect. I carried two landmines with me, a mortar, several grenades, my gun and my knife. I put the landmines and the mortars into the back of the cave and made some space for myself. I covered the cave opening with the yellow grass as carefully and precisely as I could. Then I waited.

From the distance I could hear the gun battle. It lasted for several hours before finally dying out. All this time I lay there, not minding all the insects and trying to stay awake. I wondered who had won the battle and for the first time in more than two years, I actually hoped it was the UPDF. Not that I suddenly favoured them – I still hated them as much as I had done a day earlier – but at least they wouldn't be looking for me. More hours passed. I considered leaving my hiding place to check whether everything was clear, but then I remembered that I had made this mistake once before, on the day I was first captured, and that had caused my life to turn into a living hell.

After a long while I started to hear voices. It was two boys from my unit, whom I had led into battle on several occasions. From my position I could hear what they were saying, and it was clear that they were searching for me. Suddenly I also heard voices from up ahead. There were more soldiers directly above me, maybe even standing on my cave. One of the boys said that he had found another footprint and they were slowly walking in the direction of the cave. As they came closer, I could even see them through the grass. Luckily the cave was very dark, so they couldn't see me, but my tracks led them right towards the cave.

As the two boys followed my tracks, they suddenly saw the cave and I was listening to what they were saying. One boy told the other that the cave would be a nice place to hide in and then they came even closer. I took a grenade and, as silently as I could, I set my gun on sharp. Luckily, they hadn't heard it. By now they were standing only a metre away from me, both of them looking at my footprints and afterwards looking at the cave. Suddenly I heard a familiar voice from up above. It was Langole!

'Have you found him yet?'

Inside the cave I was nearly dying of fear. I was positive that these were the last moments of my life. I held my gun and the grenade in front of me and I was ready to say goodbye to the world in one last spectacular move that would take out the two boys with me and maybe others. I only hoped for the opportunity to take out Langole first. It was inconceivable that I could make it out of this alive. Suddenly the boy who stood closest to me replied, 'No, we haven't found him. He must be further ahead of us.'

'Then go, dammit,' Langole replied.

The boys took one last look at the cave and continued on their way.

As the boys left, I could finally breathe again. I wondered what dissuaded them from entering the cave. Maybe they thought I wasn't there or maybe they feared for their own lives. Perhaps they had realised that I was there, but they felt sympathy because of the way that the commander treated me. I will never know the answer, but at least I was alive.

By the time the soldiers left it was around noon, and I stayed in the cave all day and night. While I was lying there my stomach was aching from hunger. It was near the end of February, a time the Spirit Lakwena had determined was a time for repenting, which meant that every soldier, even the highest commanders, must fast. So I hadn't eaten anything for days. My hunger was extraordinary.

Early in the morning of the following day I slowly crept out of my cave. I left the mortar and the landmines behind, but I took my gun and the hand grenades. I lay in the sun for a while, because I was quite cold, and I needed the vitamin D. After half an hour I started to move on. I was in the middle of the bush, but still way too close to the LRA trail, so I decided to move as far away as possible. I climbed to the top of the hill on the far side of the riverbed, where I could see the mountains of Sudan. Those bloody mountains had almost killed me several times, but seeing them now caused me to smile. I knew that I would never have to pass them again. I felt freedom for the first time and with it extreme joy and relief. I was free. No longer did I have to put my life in the balance because someone ordered me to do so. No longer did I have to kill anyone because someone else told me to do so. At that moment, I had never felt so free. But I knew that I was in more imminent danger than ever before. Even though Langole had sounded the retreat to Sudan, he would go out of his way to find me so that he could torture me to death himself.

I was in hostile territory infested with people who meant me a lot of harm. If the LRA found me I would be killed. If the Ugandan army found me I would be killed. Even civilians would do anything in their power to kill me. Despite my sense of freedom, I also felt extremely lonely. I was on my own now and there was nobody to cover my back. I had to proceed with great care.

As I stood there on top of the hill, I saw the vultures and the marabous circling in the distance, and I decided to go in that direction. If I was to survive all my enemies, I needed to get some food. The village I entered was completely ravaged and everyone was dead. There was no smell of decomposition, so I knew that this was a fresh massacre. It was important to move quickly. Massacres always attracted the attention of the UPDF, and the LRA might also return at any time. It was one of those rare occasions on which my colleagues had left some animals alive, so I caught a few chickens and I took them to an empty hut. Within the hut I made a small fire that didn't smoke. Making a smokeless fire was a unique guerrilla trick that I had learned in Juba. I slaughtered the chickens and plucked the feathers. I was getting very excited about the nice meal that I was preparing.

While I was roasting the first two chickens I suddenly heard the sound of a hundred gumboots coming in my direction. I panicked. By now the soldiers were in the village, so there was no time to run away. I immediately threw some sand over the chickens and the fire to take away the scent, but it was already too late. They had found me.

'Attiena! Attiena Mortar, I immediately want you to leave the hut. You are under arrest for attempted escape. Come out immediately with your hands up.'

There was a large crack in the mud wall of the hut through which I saw that several of my former colleagues were approaching the door. It was Stockree Battalion that had found me. When the soldiers approached the hut I put my gun through the crack and I was ready to blast everybody away. It was the last man in our row, an older man called Otim, who spotted the barrel. He screamed for everyone to take cover and at that moment all the soldiers ran away.

In my head I heard two voices contradicting each other. One told me to stay in the hut and fight, while the other told me to run and never stop running. As the group started to disperse, it appeared that those few seconds lasted for several minutes. I decided that there was only one way to survive: I had to go!

The fleeing soldiers had their backs turned to me, so I ran out of the hut. I was surrounded on all sides by my former colleagues who were standing just metres away from me. I was in the middle of a circle of people who started shooting at me, but their bullets missed, and instead endangered the lives of the other rebels. I heard somebody scream to stop firing and to catch me alive. In the commotion I ran straight through a group of three rebels and they tried to catch me, but I was too fast for them. I broke out of the circle and at that moment everybody started to fire at me. I ran as I had never run before, but still it seemed to be in slow motion. Bullets were all around me, ripping my sleeves and my shirt. I could feel the blast waves of the bullets whistling millimetres over my head, but somehow none of them appeared to hit me. I kept on running, ten times faster than was humanly possible, and I never looked behind me. I was sure they were following me. I knew how badly Langole wanted me dead, especially now that I had escaped his little kingdom, so he would not give up easily. Against all the odds in the world I had escaped from the ambush and I kept on running and running and running.

I kept this up for three to four hours. From the time the sun was at its peak until it had gone down to the horizon, I ran. I finally came to appreciate the benefit of all the training sessions in which we had to run in the heat of the day. It had prepared me for exactly this moment. After I had run at full speed for half an hour, I adjusted my speed but still kept on moving, using the energy from the boost of adrenaline that was rushing through my body. Sometimes I thought I heard my former colleagues approaching again and then I got a new burst of energy, but after many hours, I finally collapsed. My body just gave in. My mind wanted to continue, but my body couldn't take another step. I hadn't taken a single bite of my chicken and by running all day I had depleted all my energy. With my last bit of strength I hauled myself into some dense bushes and I sank in. I instantly fell asleep.

I woke up in the middle of the night, not knowing where I was or if my colleagues were still following me. I felt terribly weak and even though I wanted to move, I had no strength to do so. I stayed where I was until morning. In the early light, I saw that I was lying close to some banana trees. The bananas were not ripe, but I ate them anyway to restore some energy. Nearby there was a little stream where I drank some water.

I had no clue where I was, only that I had been in the area before. The last two months we had been in almost every corner of Kitgum, and this district was very large. I was in the middle of the bush, so I chose to move in a random direction, away from where I had approached. Several hours later I came to a small village in which everybody was long dead. The stench of decomposing bodies made me sick. I quickly searched the village for food, but I couldn't find anything. Soon the voice in my head told me to get out of there, and so I moved on. The village was connected to a road, but I didn't dare to take it because the UPDF were always patrolling.

I returned to the bush. Two days and nights passed in which I never saw a single soul. It appeared that I was walking in very large circles. I was completely lost. My hunger had only grown worse. The bananas had helped a little, but their effect was short-lived. I needed something for a real energy boost. I have no idea where I was when I finally found my opportunity to fill my stomach, but I think it was close to Limu. As I was walking, I spotted a very large beehive. I knew that if I could get to the honey, it would provide me with all the energy I needed. I was only a child when I was abducted, and nobody had ever taught me how to harvest honey from a beehive, but I was determined to get it. I took off my jacket and T-shirt and I bound the T-shirt around my head, and then pulled on the jacket again. From my previous experiences in Limu I had learned that the bees only stung those areas not covered by clothes, so I tried to cover every inch of my body with clothing.

I took my AK-47 and pointed it at the beehive. I was still contemplating whether to shoot the hive from a distance or to open it by hand, using my gun as a precaution, when I realised that shooting might attract some unwanted attention to my position. I slowly approached the hive with my gun pointed at it. At a distance of twenty metres all was fine. There were some bees buzzing around me, but none of them stung me. At ten metres away from the hive I was still untouched. It was when I was almost there, within three metres, that they all came out to attack me.

Thousands upon thousands of those bees suddenly swarmed out, each of them intent on harming me. They started to sting all the uncovered areas, like around my eyes and on my hands, but soon they found all the cracks in my clothing. I ran away as quickly as I could, but it didn't do me any good. The bees were faster than I was. After I had run for several metres, I threw away my gun and I started to undress while they kept on stinging me. After I had moved for maybe half a kilometre, the bees finally gave up. By that time, I had been stung at least a hundred times, especially on the areas surrounding my eyes and my hands, but also all over my body. It was so painful. Everything began to swell. The world grew dark. I could only see when I lifted the swelling round my eyes with my swollen hands, but touching the swellings really hurt.

I stayed on the spot where the bees had left me, unable to stand, sit or lie down because of the extreme pain. I stayed there for hours. Night was falling and somehow I managed to fall asleep. When I woke up very early in the morning, the swelling was gone and instead of burning all over I was shivering from the cold. As I lay there, the first light started to appear on the eastern sky and I collected all my clothes again. My gun was lying very close to the hive, but there was no way on earth that I would continue without taking it. From previous experiences in Limu I knew that bees were less active at night, so when I was close to the hive, I ran towards my gun and continued on my way.

It was getting light all around me and by now I was almost starving to death. With every step I took I felt how the energy was draining from my body. I needed to eat something very soon, or I would collapse and never stand up again. Halfway through the morning, I came to another village. It was deserted and there were only the bodies of two elderly people lying around, which was a clear sign that the village had been abandoned before the rebels attacked. In this village I found some chickens. I didn't have the energy to catch them, so I shot them with my gun. I knew that the sound would attract the attention of anyone within a range of five kilometres, so I quickly took the first chicken and ate it raw. Of course, it wasn't tasty to eat raw chicken, but at that time the meal tasted as if it came straight from heaven. Within minutes I had devoured all the edible parts of the first chicken and I brought the second and third chickens with me to eat later. I then went back to hide in the bush, where I slept until it was dark again.

There was a small road, not even big enough for a car, heading out of the village. I knew it would eventually come out at a main road and although I was still terribly afraid of the UPDF patrolling the roads, I realised I had to take my chances. For nearly a week, my reluctance to follow roads had only caused me to walk in circles. The longer I kept on walking like this the greater the chances I would run into the LRA again, so I had to change my strategy. When it was completely dark, I started to follow the village road. After about an hour, the road led me to a bigger road that went in an east–west direction, if I'd read the stars properly. This was another skill they taught us in Juba.

Some memories were unfolding that I had long forgotten; memories of my early school years, long before my life had turned into hell. I remembered very well that my teacher had explained the geography of Uganda. He taught us that north of Uganda we could find Sudan, the biggest country in Africa. In the west there was Zaire, in the east Kenya, and in the south was Tanzania. I also remembered the history lessons in which we were told that out of all these countries, Kenya had always been the most stable and peaceful. So when I came to the road, in my head, I had two options. Either I would go to Kenya or to Zaire. I decided to go towards Kenya, and I hoped that once I got there, some Kenyan would be good enough to take me home to my parents.

I started moving in the eastern direction and all night I kept on walking. The moment it started to become light, I hid again. It was clear that on the main road, the UPDF was in charge. During the daylight hours, I saw many civilians moving over the road, but at night it was all quiet again. For two nights I moved like this. Every time I came close to a village, I would move around it through the bushes. All this time I felt so lonely.

I had eaten the chickens and I started to feel hungry again. This is when I completely lost hope. It seemed that I had escaped only to enter a world that was even more miserable. It was a world in which there was only me, and everybody else was my enemy. I feared every sound that I heard and every movement that I saw. I had to be sharp 24/7. There was nobody to cover for me or protect me. I had barely slept during the previous few weeks, and even in the moments that I did sleep, I was haunted by nightmares. Each time I closed my eyes, all the innocent faces and voices would come back to me, haunting me, torturing me. As the days passed, I became desperate. This life was even worse than what I had endured in the LRA. I just wanted to go home, but this seemed to be the one place I couldn't reach. I got to a point when I didn't care any more. I decided it was better to die, so I began to move on the road in clear daylight.

After half an hour of walking in the daylight I came across several civilians. The moment they saw me they wanted to run away, but I told them that if they ran, I would shoot them. I told them to turn around and so they did. I told them my story. I told them that I had escaped and that I wanted them to bring me to the UPDF barracks, where I would surrender. The men argued that they understood me very well, since they had children themselves who had been abducted, and they wanted to help me, but first I had to give up my gun. There was no way that I would agree to give my gun to the civilians. I was sure that they would shoot me as soon as I handed it over. I said that if they asked me again to give up my gun, I would shoot them.

'NOW, LEAD ME TO THE BARRACKS, DAMMIT!'

I pushed the men and reluctantly they went ahead. I told them not even to attempt to run, or I would kill every single last one of them. After we had walked for an hour or so I saw a large settlement appearing on the horizon. There was a hill with barracks on top and the settlement surrounding it. From a distance I could see that only the houses in the middle were proper huts; the rest were just shacks. It finally occurred to me that this was where many of the survivors of our massacres had fled to. I realised that every individual in the camp must have lost relatives because of actions that I was directly involved in. I knew I shouldn't expect a warm welcome.

As I entered the village, I still had my gun pointed at the two men who had led me there. All the villagers were looking at me, their eyes filled with pure hatred. As the Mzee had said earlier, they all wanted me dead. I ordered one of the men to go up the hill and warn the army, but the moment I excused him, he ran away in fear without going to the barracks. In the meantime, the soldiers up there were playing cards and had no clue what was unfolding below. The civilians were arming themselves with machetes, axes, shovels and all the other farming tools that they could get their hands on, and slowly they started to approach me. Since I had just entered the village, I hadn't been completely surrounded yet, so I knew that I stood a chance. As they came closer, I set an imaginary perimeter and I decided to shoot anyone who crossed it.

The whole situation was extremely volatile, and could get out of control at any moment. I knew that I didn't have enough bullets to kill all the civilians before the first person reached me, but at least I would take as many with me as possible. Suddenly the whole situation broke loose as the civilians ran towards me. I cocked my gun and the moment I aimed to shoot the first man, I heard a lot of gunfire from up on the hill. The civilians who had been running towards me immediately dived on the ground to take cover. For a short moment you could see the sheer panic on everyone's faces, as people thought that they were under attack. But it was the army who had fired the guns, not my former colleagues. Right away soldiers appeared among the crowd. Before they surrounded and disarmed me, they started to beat up the civilians, and they ordered them to return to their shacks. Reluctantly, the civilians obeyed the orders. It took several minutes and the whole time I just stood there, completely perplexed at the fact that the UPDF had saved my life instead of ending it.

A Prisoner Again

After the troops had driven away the civilians, a soldier who spoke Acholi came and asked me if I was going to cause him any trouble. I replied that I was there to surrender and that I had no intention of harming anybody, but I also told him that I would defend myself if anyone attacked me.

'No one will attack you, 'cause you're under our protection now. Now follow me.'

My answer seemed to satisfy him since he left me armed as he walked ahead of me. I knew that this was a defining moment. I had just given myself to my greatest enemy of the last two years and I anxiously held on to my gun. Considering what we had done throughout Kitgum for the last two and a half months, they had every reason to execute me on the spot without asking me a single question. This is what we would have done to any surrendering UPDF soldier. We would probably even torture him before doing so, not only to get information, but for the fun of it.

It was merely two weeks ago that I was still fighting for the LRA and shooting at the colleagues of the men that now escorted me. Maybe I had even been involved in fights with these individuals as well. All the stories I had been told about the UPDF were still fresh in my mind. If the stories were true, they would torture and poison me. Judging from the stories they told us in the LRA, I stood a better chance of survival with the villagers below than I would up here in the barracks, surrounded by soldiers who had all lost friends because of little boys like me. But so far, my enemy didn't seem to be interested in killing me.

I could no longer tell friend from foe and I had run out of options. I was very thirsty and hungry, lost and desperate. I still wanted to reach Kenya, but I simply had no idea where I was. The worst thing was the loneliness. For the last two weeks I had been alone, with no one making choices for me and no one giving me any encouragement. Although I still thought a lot in 'we' terms, I realised that there was no 'we' any more. There was just me.

The LRA had originally taken me against my will. I would never have committed any of the terrible crimes on my own. I was a child trying to survive in a bad situation. It was these thoughts that sparked my hope that the UPDF wouldn't execute me. If they hadn't failed to protect me from abduction in the first place, I would have never fought against them. If the UPDF hadn't been defeated in the defining battle that now seemed so long ago, I would have never been abducted. It was their fault that I had fought them, and surely they couldn't hold me responsible for their mistakes. These were the arguments that I planned to use in my defence.

I knew that I had already passed the point of no return when I entered the camp, and there was nothing I could do but wait and see what would happen. Still fully armed, I came to the top of the hill where we entered the barracks. When I looked back, I saw that the civilians were pointing at me. I knew that my fate was now in the hands of the UPDF, who were the only ones that could protect me from the wrath of the civilians and the refugees below.

The barracks consisted of dozens of huts surrounded by mortars and big machine guns pointed towards the green edges of the bush; they had a good defensive position, but I doubted if this barracks would withstand an all-out LRA attack, especially if that attack were to take place at night.

In the middle of the barracks an elder commander waited for me. The soldiers saluted this man and they introduced me as 'another escapee'; so there had been others before me. The commander took a few moments to observe me. He walked around me, staring at me. The seconds crept by like snails in a sandstorm. When he finally started talking to me, he had already walked several circles around me.

'Who are you?'

I replied, 'Norman Okello, sir.'

'When and from where did you escape?'

'Sir, I escaped maybe two weeks ago, but I don't know from where because I am completely lost.'

These were the only two questions he asked me. After the questions he welcomed me to Lokung barracks. He complimented me on my escape, telling me that it took a lot of courage for a young boy to take this step. He said I didn't need to worry about anything and he would make sure that, in time, I could return to my family. But first he had to take my gun.

I knew that this was going to happen, and I also knew that I didn't have any other choice, but I surrendered my gun with great reluctance. For the last two years this gun had been my lifeline. All this time I had never let it out of my sight, nor had I ever given it to anyone else, with the exception of the Arabs in Juba. This gun was my safety net and especially here, in the lair of the lion, I felt nervous giving it away. My gun was the only barrier that stood between me and my enemies. I would feel naked without it, and unable to protect myself against whatever they wanted to do to me. Yet I knew this was inevitable. I had chosen to put my fate in the hands of my enemy, and now I had no choice but to follow through.

Reluctantly but voluntarily, I gave the commander my gun, my knife, my hand grenades and all my magazines. As I did so, I felt a strange relief coming over me. From this point onwards, my fate really wasn't in my hands any more. For the first time in a long while, I didn't need to make any decisions; instead they would be made for me. I was at my enemy's mercy and that of Almighty God, who hadn't been very merciful to me for the last few years of my life.

Soon after they took my gun, they brought me some food and some clean water. My last meal had been more than two days before, and I wanted nothing more than to drink and eat, but somehow I couldn't do it just yet. Trust has many different levels and although I had given away my gun and put my fate into their hands, I was not willing to eat their food and risk poisoning. I told myself that I hadn't survived all this shit only to die of poisoning at the hands of the cowardly UPDF. I didn't want to offend my new captors though, so I told them that I wasn't hungry. At that point the commander burst out laughing.

'So, you think that we are trying to poison you. Is that what they tell you?'

He drank some of my water and he ate some *posho* from my plate. When he had taken some large bites, he asked me again: 'Do you want me to eat all of this, or shall I leave a little for you?'

At that point I started to indulge, licking the plate clean once I had finished. They brought me some more and again the commander took the first bites to show me that they had no intention of poisoning me. When I had finished the second plate, I was really full. For the first time in a very long time my stomach ached, not because of hunger, but simply because I had eaten too much. After this huge meal, they took me to a shower where they allowed me to wash myself. As the water ran over me, I felt that all the innocent blood that had been spilt over the last two months was cleansed from my body. I stood under the shower for several minutes before they cut off the water. As I came out of the shower, they sent me to the army doctor, who refreshed the bandage that covered my stomach wounds and treated my burns with a special cream. Then he cut off my long dreadlocks, which had been growing for over two years. It felt like I was undergoing a complete metamorphosis and it felt good. I wondered whether it was possible to invoke the spirit of the civilian inside me once more.

I began to relax. Because they treated me very well, I slowly convinced myself that I might actually survive. This is when they started the hearings. Again, I had expected this to happen. I didn't really feel like answering any questions just then. I was so tired. Why couldn't they let me sleep for at least one day?

Above all, it was still not clear who my true enemy was. The UPDF had been my enemy for the last two years, and although my life in the LRA was full of hardships, I still felt sympathetic to their cause. It was the government that marginalised us Acholis. The LRA's cause was to liberate us from them with whatever means possible. Yet it was the LRA who had treated me so badly, while the UPDF gave me food, medical attention and a shower.

I remembered that much earlier I had wanted the UPDF to wipe out the LRA once and for all. Back then, I had seen the rebels as my greatest threat, not the UPDF. Although this was on the day of my abduction a little over two years ago, it seemed as if several lifetimes had passed since then.

Because I didn't know who to trust, I told myself that I wouldn't tell the UPDF everything. The hearing was conducted by the older commander who had taken my gun away from me and tasted my food to show me that it wasn't poisoned. At first the commander asked me all the questions in a very friendly manner, but I didn't feel like answering them. When I told the commander that I wanted to sleep and be left alone, I sparked a terrible rage in him. He hit me in the face really hard and he started screaming.

'You know what I can do to you if you don't cooperate, don't you? Remember that you are in the den of the lion and that we can treat you LRA scum in whichever way we want to! Remember the villagers below? They are just craving your blood, and my work here would become much easier if I had their goodwill. Your head on a stake can give me that goodwill. Now I will ask the questions again and you'd better answer them. How many rebels were you with when you escaped?'

Again, I felt the constraints of my freedom. I had never chosen for any of this to happen. I had really hoped to be free once I had escaped the rebels, but it became clear that freedom was still far away. All I wanted was to see my parents again, but I realised that this could only happen if I cooperated. There was nothing I could do but answer their stupid questions. But I could still answer them in the way that suited me best.

'Sir, I think we entered Uganda with several battalions, maybe

300 or 400 men, but I don't know how many of them have survived your attacks.'

'Where are they now?'

'Sir, they could be anywhere now. The rebels can march more than a hundred kilometres a day and I am just a simple recruit. They never tell me anything about where we are going.'

'So, what routes do you follow?'

'Sir, again, I don't know these things. I am a simple recruit and they don't tell me about routes.'

'But you walked over them, didn't you? How do you always enter Uganda?'

'Sir, we cross a river and afterwards we are in Uganda, but I don't know anything about routes. It is green and it all looks the same to me.'

The commander was clearly unsatisfied with my answers and he kept on persisting and repeating his questions, threatening me when I told him that I didn't know. He suspected that I was playing the fool, that I knew much more than I was giving him, and he was clear that I would spend the rest of my life in prison if I wasn't more forthcoming. I told the commander that I didn't feel like answering his questions, and that I wanted to see my parents first. He didn't want to hear this. He became really irritated and told me he would kill me right then and there if he didn't get satisfactory answers to the next few questions. He cocked his gun.

'So, I ask you again: what can you tell me about the place where you cross the border?'

I knew I had to give him something, even though I honestly didn't know the answer.

'Sir, I really don't know, but what I do know is that it is a place with many bees who like the oil in our guns. We always have to run when we cross the border.'

At that point the commander started to smile a bit.

'So, you cross the border near Limu then. I thought that Kony could master all beasts so that they wouldn't touch his troops, but it appears that the bees are just as much a nuisance for you as they are for us. Now I am going to ask you again, and you'd better answer. Who was the mastermind behind the Kitgum massacres?'

I knew that I had to give him something tangible. Although the commander was tough on me, it was the only way in which he could get some information out of me. Compared with the usual treatment that I had grown used to in the LRA, there was nothing that the UPDF could do to persuade me to talk, short of executing me, and this was exactly the thing they were threatening me with. When the older commander told me that he would kill me, there was no doubt in my mind that he could carry out this threat. My biggest ongoing challenge over the last two years had been the struggle to survive, and I wasn't going to let it slip now. Especially considering that the main purpose of my death would be to amuse the civilians below when they saw my head on a stake. I had to give the commander something to please him.

'What? I will ask you this question only once more and if you do not answer me, you will not live to see the coming sunset. Who is the mastermind behind all this madness in Kitgum and who is leading you?'

This time he put his gun against my head. For a short moment longer I was silent, which really agitated the commander. I needed some time to think, but I knew he wouldn't give me much time. Wall Okot and other higher commanders had been the master-minds behind the Kitgum massacres, but Wall Okot had saved my life from Langole, and although he already might have died from the disease he had, I didn't want to make him a target. Langole, on the other hand, would have executed me if Wall Okot hadn't saved me. It was at this point that I knew how to answer the question. I suddenly remembered who my true arch-enemies were: Langole and Nyeko. I wanted them dead. In the last two months I had constantly thought of ways how to kill Langole and now I had the opportunity to sign his death sentence at a UPDF hearing.

Click . . . The commander pulled the lever.

'Delay me for one more second and I will kill you!'

'Sir, it was the commander called Langole who was responsible for all the massacres.'

I told him the story of the Kitgum massacres as best as I could remember it, the only difference being that I replaced Wall Okot's name with Langole's. I told them that the whole mission was Langole's idea and that he was the prime suspect behind all the massacres. This actually wasn't too far from the truth. Langole was the one in charge of Stockree, and Stockree was responsible for the massacres. He was the one who had enjoyed the massacres and without his direct orders, none of us would have killed anybody.

I even brought up Nyeko and explained that he had played a vital role in the Kitgum massacres. Of course, this was all bullshit. Nyeko was just a first lieutenant and he wasn't even part of the mission. Nonetheless, I started to cast all the blame on these two gentlemen, hoping that they would become the prime targets of any UPDF military campaign. As I told this story in so much detail, the commander finally seemed to be satisfied with my answer.

Dozens of questions followed.

'What are the routes that you take?'

'Where are the weapon depots hidden?'

'Who is supplying you with the weapons?'

'Are there any more who have attempted to escape?'

'Who was your commander?'

'How long have you been with the rebels?'

'Where do you treat your wounded?'

'Where is the new rebel camp?'

'Tell me everything about the rebel camp.'

'Where are the girls from Aboke? What happened with them? Who are they married to?'

The older commander asked me the questions while a soldier noted my answers on a piece of paper. One of the most important topics of my questioning concerned the Aboke girls. Again I started to curse those girls. They almost seemed sacred. Whenever they were brought up, I always wondered why they were so damned fucking special. I wished that I had also been on the UPDF's priority list, but no one ever pitied me. I was just a boy who could simply be killed because I didn't give the right answers. Why hadn't there been a white lady who had come to my rescue? What about the thousands of other kids who had been abducted over the past few years? The whole LRA was composed of people my age, so why didn't the commander ask about their fate? Instead he kept on asking about the Aboke girls. I told the commander what I knew, which wasn't very much, but he seemed to be satisfied. Throughout the questioning session, I never mentioned my own role in the abduction of the Aboke girls.

The commander continued asking about the arms depots, but on this point, I persistently said that I didn't know anything and after a while he started to believe me. Next he started to question me about our camp at Aru Junction. The commander wanted to know everything.

'How large is the camp?'

'Is it located on top of a hill?'

'How do you get the water from there?'

'Where is Kony staying?'

There were many other questions as well. Where it was obvious I had to know the answer, I gave it, but for all the other questions I said I was an innocent abductee, a low-ranking recruit who didn't know anything.

The questioning stopped sometime in the afternoon. Finally they allowed me to sleep in one of the huts. They never bothered to put a guard on me, because they knew that the vengeful civilians of the surrounding refugee camp offered better protection against my escape than any guard or prison wall.

I stayed in the hut until the next morning. Although I was dead tired, I could hardly sleep. This was the first night in two weeks that I didn't need to be on high alert. What kept me awake was the uncertainty of what would happen next and the fear that crept into me at the thought of seeing my parents again. Although there was nothing I wanted more, I had no idea what to tell them or even how to greet them.

When sleep finally caught up with me, my dreams were very troubling. The moment I fell asleep all the images of the last two months came back to me. In particular, the image of a big brown lady who was killed in an extraordinarily brutal way kept on haunting me. This recurring dream always started harmlessly. She was cooking food while I was observing her from the bushes, just the way it had actually occurred several weeks earlier. But then we came out of the bush and the whole village turned into chaos. In my dreams, the big lady came for me and she started choking me. I kept on shooting her, but the bullets went straight through, as if they never even touched her. I tried to stab her with my knife, but again it went through her like she was made of air. In the meantime, her grip on my throat got stronger and I almost choked to death. It was at this point that I woke up, sweating like crazy. I decided that I wouldn't fall asleep again and I was really grateful when the first light touched the horizon.

Even before the sun appeared in the sky, the camp woke up and all around me there was activity. I got out of the hut and no one even bothered to check up on me. I was free to do whatever I wanted to do. I saw a large group of soldiers making themselves ready to go on patrol. They all got some eggs and chapatti, and finally, when every one of them had eaten, they started to march off. From the top of the rock I watched them until they disappeared in the bush. I was happy that I wasn't in their shoes. This was my first day in a while with limited worries. I still didn't know what would happen to me, but at least there was no fear of running into the rebels or the patrols that had just departed. While I was still sitting on the edge of the rock, the commander suddenly called my name.

'Norman, please come here and have some breakfast.'

He served me the leftovers of the patrol's breakfast, which I ate with several of the soldiers who had stayed behind to guard the barracks. The commander, who only yesterday had threatened to kill me, was very friendly this morning. After breakfast he took me aside and told me that he still had a few questions he wanted to ask me, but he did so in a really friendly manner, as if he regretted his earlier approach. The first topic of questioning was my uniform.

'This is a very fine uniform that you are wearing. Surely an innocent recruit who has never done anything and who doesn't know anything would not be rewarded with such a nice uniform. Tell me how you got it.'

The commander wanted to know about my position in the LRA, and he played it through my uniform, so I started to tell him the story about the uniform, which had got nothing to do with my rank. I told the commander that I had traded it at one point for some marijuana that I was growing myself. This was when we were still in Palutaka. In the LRA it was strictly forbidden to smoke anything, but they didn't mind us growing marijuana. The Arabs, on the other hand, didn't have our restrictions and their desire for marijuana, which they called *qat*, was boundless. Since we didn't have a money economy, I had to trade the marijuana for something, and if there was one thing that the Arabs had in abundance, it was military gear of all kinds. Uniforms, guns, compasses, boots. They had everything. So I traded several small plastic bags of marijuana for a very nice Arab uniform.

It was the smallest uniform they had but still it was several sizes too big for me. Nonetheless I was extremely happy with it once I got it. I decided that no one would ever take it from me. It was back in the days before I was given a rank and when I enjoyed next to no respect from anybody. I was so proud to show everybody my new uniform that I had even marched into the other brigades, which wasn't allowed for new recruits, so I received a mild punishment. Since that time, I had been through so much with this uniform. The uniform wore the same marks of war as I did. It had burns from the tank attack and it was shredded by the bullets that whistled past my body on the day when I was almost gunned down by my own colleagues.

It appeared that the story of my uniform amused the commander. When I had finished, the commander told me that it was a good story, and also that he wanted this uniform for himself.

'Your uniform is really so nice and now that you are a civilian, you don't have any use for it. Why don't you give me your uniform, and I will give you another one?'

The moment he said this I thought of the pact that I had signed with myself that no one would ever take my uniform. Apart from my gun, the uniform had been my second lifeline and now I was being asked to give this up as well. But I knew I didn't have much of a choice. The commander could still do with me whatever he wanted and refusing to give up the uniform might be interpreted as not giving up my soldier's life. This whole morning the commander had been friendly, so I didn't want to raise his anger again. When I gave him my uniform, I told him the promise I had made with myself and asked him to take good care of the uniform. The commander laughed and told me I shouldn't be so attached to things that I got in the LRA. In return he gave me a uniform from a Local Defence Unit. After the exchange, the commander was so happy with his new uniform that he stopped the questioning altogether. The rest of the day I could do whatever I wanted, as long as it didn't involve leaving or killing people.

I decided to sit on the rock again to observe the civilian life below. The refugee camp was quite big and extremely densely populated. I could almost see the entire camp. It appeared that everyone wanted to be as close to the barracks as possible. From my own experience I knew that it was useless to be in the centre, because whenever we attacked a camp, this was where we would round everybody up. However, with a very quick hit-and-run attack in a camp this large, the civilians in the middle might actually stand a chance.

Around the camp there was still some farmland, which the people no longer farmed as much because of their fear, and with good reason. Attacking a camp like this took some advance planning, but killing and abducting people from farmlands was always an easy undertaking.

I found that I enjoyed watching all the activity. There was a little market in the camp and several shops. Even though there was nothing to do in the camp, it still bustled with life. Men were drinking and playing cards. Children were playing games. Women were busy grinding millet and cleaning their huts. In front of the borehole stood a long line of women and girls with large twenty-litre jerrycans. Although I heard occasional laughter from the playing kids or the drunken men, the general mood in the camp was of depression.

After I'd sat on the rock for a while, people started to notice me. Even from a distance I saw people pointing at me. They were having some kind of discussion about me. The finger-pointing of one individual attracted the attention of the next, and within several minutes dozens of people were looking at me. They started to scream hateful things at me. I decided to leave this place on the edge of the rock and return to my hut. I didn't need their hatred.

It was around the same time that an army helicopter landed on a bare strip in the middle of the barracks. When the doors opened, I saw a small boy step out, being guided by two older soldiers. From his uniform and his dreadlocks, I immediately realised that he also came from the LRA, although I didn't recognise him. The boy screamed in pain when a soldier grabbed his arm, and then I saw that it was badly wounded. The boy was brought to the doctor and the few soldiers who were still present turned their attention to him. I went back to the edge of the rock to see whether the civilians had gone back to their normal lives, but instead the camp had shifted their attention to the rock. I think the helicopter had attracted their attention. When I peered over the edge, the civilians started to scream and point again. I knew all too well that they wanted me dead, and this was an unsettling feeling. They were screaming terrible things at me.

'Rebel, why don't you jump? Look at him, staring at us, probably planning to have us all executed.'

I couldn't stand it any more. Didn't they understand that I had only done what I was forced to do, and I had never liked the killing, unlike some of the boys in my unit? But they knew nothing of this.

With nothing else to do and no opportunity to stay at the rock, I went to see who the other boy was. After some minutes the doctor was done with him and he was brought to the same hut where I had tried to sleep the previous night. As I went in, the boy looked at me with great suspicion. It was clear that he wanted me to leave, but I wasn't intimidated that easily.

I introduced myself as Attiena Mortar, but he didn't recognise my name. I told him that I had been in Stockree and that I left the LRA because they wanted to kill me. I continued talking to him because I didn't have anything else to do. After a while the boy opened up. His name was Victor and he had been in Control Altar. Although his arm had just been bandaged, it was still bleeding heavily. Victor hadn't been given any medicine, so he was still in a lot of pain. Nonetheless, we started to talk to each other, and we shared our stories. While Victor was talking, I started to get the feeling that I knew him, but I was unable to pinpoint exactly how, since I was always in Stockree and he in Control Altar.

I decided to ask him. He told me that he didn't know me either, but that he was well known in the LRA because he had been a singer in the LRA choir. Then I remembered. I saw his face every Friday and Sunday during the prayers. It felt good to have someone around who understood what I had been through.

Although he was in terrible pain, we chatted throughout the day. He told me about his escape story, which was even worse than mine. He had escaped from Aru with three others when they went to the so-called 'river' to collect water. From the start they had done what I hadn't dared to do. They left their weapons behind, so that they wouldn't be seen as soldiers. On the second day this caused them a lot of problems, as they were attacked by wild pigs. Pigs can be very dangerous animals if you don't have a weapon. Then they were nearly captured by two Arab soldiers. Luckily they were faster than the Arabs, who never bothered to shoot at three unarmed children.

After several days they had stumbled upon a village and decided to enter it at night to steal some food, not knowing that this village was actually SPLA barracks. Once the SPLA detected them, they came under serious fire, but luckily none of them were hit. It was only at the border of Uganda that they walked into a real ambush and were all shot by the UPDF, even though they were unarmed. Victor was simply lucky that he had blacked out when they shot him. When he regained consciousness, he was on the helicopter heading to this base.

It was slowly starting to get dark and eventually the commander came in to bring us some food and water. We still didn't trust our captors, and Victor was especially terrified of them, so we made sure that others took a few bites and sips before we ate or drank. When it was finally dark, we tried to sleep.

This second night was pure agony. Not only did the same terrible dream reoccur, which caused me to wake up sweating all over, but lying awake was also awful. I tried to rest without falling asleep, but Victor was crying all night long because of the horrific pain. It reached the point that a soldier came in and told us that he would kill us if Victor didn't stop crying. But even with this warning he couldn't help himself. He just kept on crying. As the night wore on, a previous wound in my armpit began to swell and ache. Initially it was nothing, but the wound was never treated and now infection was setting in. It was a rough night.

In the morning we ate the leftovers of the patrolling units again. As we watched them disappearing into the bush, Victor and I were discussing all kinds of things up on the lookout rock. Another large group of the villagers were once again looking at us and pointing.

'Look at them. They have killed a lot of people and now they are eating while we are starving here.'

The civilians were enraged. If it weren't for the few remaining UPDF soldiers, they would have ripped us to pieces. The civilians couldn't have known that rebels could have a heart. They looked at Victor and me as if we were the embodiment of evil. When we were halfway through our meal, we decided to eat the rest in our hut, because we couldn't stand those hateful eyes and insults and threats any more. Soon four soldiers came to us, among them the Acholi who had been so friendly towards me the day I had surrendered. They told us that we had to go to the camp hospital for proper treatment of our wounds. This was a terrifying thought, since it meant that we had to face the crowd below. The hospital, if you could call it that, was at the other side of the camp. We would have to walk through all the enraged refugees unarmed, with only four soldiers protecting us. Except for the Acholi, I was really doubtful about their dedication to protect us.

It was still early in the morning when we started to walk down the hill. Below us the civilians gathered, and their intentions were clear. I completely despised them. These were people from my tribe who were supposed to protect their young, but instead they wanted us dead. Many of them probably had children of their own who were now fighting in the LRA. Instead of blaming their own children for the Kitgum massacres, we were the central focus of their hatred.

When we reached the foot of the hill the people all started to shout at us. It was really intimidating. I became very frightened. As the people drew closer, the soldiers closed in around us. From the rumble of the crowd, I heard very distinct threats:

'Make them pay!'

'Let's kill them!'

'You have killed my baby! It was you – I recognise you!'

These were the things that I heard among the thousands of horrors that they screamed at us. They started to throw stuff at us. When a big rock hit Victor's shoulder the soldiers had had enough. The Acholi fired into the air and one screamed very loudly that anyone who touched us would suffer the consequences.

'What is wrong with you? These children could be yours. Whatever they did was against their will and they had the courage to escape. You should embrace them instead of hating them.'

It was surreal to hear this out of the mouth of a UPDF soldier. For so long we had been told that they were the soldiers of the devil and that they would do everything in their power to hurt us as much as they could. Instead he was telling the civilians to embrace us instead of stoning us to death. These were the civilians on whose behalf we had been fighting for the last two years and the only reward we got for putting our lives in the balance thousands of times was unconditional hatred.

After this outburst the civilians stopped screaming and throwing things at us, but the way they continued to look at us remained very threatening.

Even though the atmosphere was volatile, and the civilians could turn against us any minute, it was actually good to have a short walk and to be out of the barracks for a little while. I had been observing the camp from above, but now that we walked through it, I had the sense that I was among the civilians again, even though they hated me. We walked past the little market, past the men drinking and playing cards, and past the little children playing. I enjoyed the children the most, both because of their happiness and their laughter, and because they were the only ones who didn't care about Victor and me.

At the hospital I could see the brutal evidence of our campaign in Kitgum. This gave me perspective on why the civilians hated us so much. What I saw there was terrible. There were people with missing limbs, people whose lips had been cut off and their eyes cut out. One mother held babies who had already been dead for some days. She was completely traumatised and unable to accept the deaths of her children. There was a terrible stench surrounding the hospital, and the sound of screams and cries was deafening. The hospital was one of the few stone buildings, but otherwise it clearly wasn't equipped to deal with the level of death and mutilation that we saw. This was a place of complete misery, a perfect example of hell on earth.

My little infection was minimal compared to these other traumas, but the lead soldier demanded that we would be helped first.

The nurse who was supposed to help me looked me straight in the eye exactly the same way the villagers did, with sheer hatred and contempt. At first, she flat out refused to do anything, but the soldiers strongly insisted that we needed medical attention. She screamed at me, 'So, you are more important than all the innocent victims over there.'

She pointed at the man who had lost a leg and was slowly bleeding to death.

'Did you hack off that leg? You are probably the one who caused all of this, aren't you?'

She pointed to all the victims around me and made such a scene that everybody shifted their attention to me. One of my escorts told the nurse to treat me instead of lecturing, and then went away to check up on Victor.

I was alone with the nurse and the fresh war victims and this was terrifying.

'You want me to treat your wound, do you?'

At this point she started to use her scalpel to slash my arm, which was already swollen. The pain was unbearable. I was screaming at her to stop, but she wouldn't listen. I was on the point of taking her scalpel away from her to stick it into her throat, when the soldier ran back, alarmed by my screams. When he saw what was happening, he became incredibly angry.

'What the fuck do you think you are doing? These boys provide us with important intelligence, and you are butchering them like they are cattle. They have been captured recently but they managed to escape. They deserve pity, not torture.'

She defended herself by stating that she was cutting open my wound to let the pus out. The soldier accepted this, but he also said that he would remain present for the rest of the operation. The sister made one more cut and she squeezed out all of the pus. There was a stench coming out of my wound and the nurse squeezed it as hard as she could. The more she squeezed the more it hurt, but this was also the way to treat it. Afterwards she put a bandage around my arm. While she walked away, I knew that she was silently cursing me.

At the same time they were treating Victor in another room. I could hear his screams as they removed the bullet from his arm. I suspected that his treatment wouldn't be any better than mine, and it even appeared that his screams somehow offered satisfaction to the other patients in the hospital. With every scream, Victor assuaged some of their vengeance towards us. While my operation was a matter of minutes, Victor's took much longer, maybe half an hour. All this time I had to listen to his screams and watch the dying patients around me. I was very relieved when the soldiers finally escorted us back to the barracks.

We stayed in Lokung barracks for over a week. Two days after Victor was flown in, two other combatants joined us. I knew these boys, Lamson and Vincent, because they were both in Gilba and they were involved in the same mission in Kitgum as me. The four of us were free to move around in the barracks, but our leisure time was occasionally interrupted by questioning. They tried to verify my story with the others, which worried me, since many of the things I had said about the last mission had been a lie. They first tried it with Victor, but since he had escaped straight from Sudan, he didn't know anything about the Kitgum mission. The other two boys knew more of the details, and that worried me the moment I saw them getting out of the helicopter. Luckily, they didn't start to question the others immediately and I had some time to brief them on my story. As I outranked both of them, I still enjoyed their respect. When I told them to cast the blame on Langole, who wasn't popular with anybody, they happily agreed.

After about a week, a convoy came with several large white vehicles with the letters UN printed on the sides. It was not announced to us that the UN would be coming, so when we saw those white vehicles entering the camp, we became very excited, especially when those cars came up to the barracks. When the doors of the vehicles opened, the four of us were all looking to these new people with awe and great expectations. Several black people were there and also one Filipina woman, called Fe Guevara, and a white man who introduced himself as Hervé Cheuzeville from France, who worked as the head of the emergency and relief sector of the World Food Programme. Back then we had no idea what this title actually meant, but I still remember the excitement we felt when he told us. It sounded like it was very important. Although we knew little about the UN and what they were doing in this country, we had the feeling that these were the good guys who would set us free.

Before the UN shifted their attention towards us, Hervé talked with the commander for a while. Afterwards they came to check up on us and ask us a few questions. While the woman inspected Victor's arm, Hervé conversed with the three of us. As he didn't speak Luo, he used a translator. The translator told us that the UN had come especially for us and that it was their mission to help us return back to society and to be reunited with our families again. The translator continued to talk, but I lost focus, as my thoughts started to dwell on my family. When I heard about the possible reunion, I became excited and nervous at the same time. I hadn't seen my parents for so long that I doubted if we would still remember each other. So much had happened since I last saw them and I wondered whether they were still alive and, if so, whether they would still recognise me and accept me as their son.

After Hervé had addressed us, he separated us for questioning. He started with Lamson and then with Vincent. While I waited for my turn, I experienced my first intense and joyful daydream for a very, very long time. It was as if long-imprisoned thoughts were being released. For the first time in two years, I dreamed about my parents without any reservations. The thoughts came without the fear that the Spirit Lakwena would read my dreams and use them against me, and that I would be forced to kill my parents if I ever saw them again. I pictured my mum digging in the cassava field and making us dinner, while my dad was plucking a chicken for our reunion meal. I dreamed of a big feast to which all of our family was invited, with enough to eat for everyone. I dreamed of my uncles, my aunts and my grandfather. I dreamed of going to school and telling my schoolmates about all my adventures, after which they would respect me, and I would become the most popular guy in school. I even dreamed of my younger siblings, whose images were very blurry.

'Norman . . . NORMAN!'

Hervé abruptly woke me up from my dream and started to question me.

'Tell me about your family – where can we contact them? When were you abducted? How did you escape?'

Hervé asked me a lot of questions, but he asked them very differently from the commander. Not that the commander was a bad man, but Hervé was so much more patient. It felt like he didn't judge me for what I had been forced to do. It appeared that he was the only one who didn't care so much about all the bloody details and that he was genuinely interested to connect me to my family. He never pushed me for more information or threatened me if I didn't want to answer.

The only thing that unnerved me about Hervé was that I didn't understand his kindness. Although there had been quite a number of people who had been kind to me when I was still in the LRA, this was a different type of kindness. In the LRA, any display of kindness usually accompanied the fact that there was something to be gained by being kind. That was the kindness that I understood. I couldn't figure out what this Frenchman wanted. All the time I was wondering how he would benefit from all of this. But I had little to lose and this man represented my best opportunity to be reunited with my family, so I told him about my abduction, which now seemed so long ago, and about who my parents were and where they could be found. I never told him anything about atrocities that I'd committed or the rank that I had achieved. In fact, Hervé never asked about these issues. While our conversation went through the translator, Herve was writing everything down. After we had answered all they had asked us, Hervé started to explain what would happen next.

'We will take you to another barracks in Kitgum, where you will find hundreds more of your former colleagues and where there are many more soldiers to protect you from possible attacks by the LRA. The camp that you are going to is called Pajimu. In Pajimu we separate the escapees and start the process of reuniting you with your families. The ones who are from Kitgum will remain in Pajimu for a while, and the rest must wait for transport from the UPDF, which will take you to Lira and Gulu. Here another department of the UN will take over and, in cooperation with the UPDF, we will try to reunite you with your family. However, be aware that the war is still not over and that this process can take time. Furthermore, it is possible that we will not be able to find your direct family. In that case you will be brought to other places where we can take care of you.'

Hervé continued to explain the procedure and afterwards we were told to step into one of the big UN vehicles. It was now around three or four in the afternoon. While we entered the back of a car in the middle of the convoy, Hervé and Fe Guevara went to a vehicle in the front. There were three UN vehicles and no UPDF armed convoy.

Our drive down the hill set off a massive commotion as hundreds of civilians ran towards the UN cars. They were armed with pangas and various sorts of crude weaponry, and even though we were in the hands of the UN, they still wanted to kill us. They tried to force open the doors of our vehicle, but we had quickly locked the doors from the inside. Some soldiers were escorting us through the camp and it required them to use considerable violence to get the civilians away. They knew very well that this was their last chance to hurt us, and they desperately wanted revenge. It took us a long while to clear the camp, as the civilians tried to stop us at every opportunity. Finally a soldier fired a round into the air, scaring the civilians away, and we could continue. Eventually we came to the dirt road at the outer edge of the camp, and the soldiers, our escorts, returned to their barracks.

As we left the camp, a new kind of anxiety washed over me. We were still in LRA territory and these convoys were very dangerous. The LRA could be hidden anywhere. From experience I knew how well a landmine could be hidden. I sensed that Lamson, Vincent and Victor were feeling the same thing, and we scouted the surrounding bushes very carefully. When we saw a fallen tree in front of us halfway over the road, we all held our breath. This was a classic way that the LRA prepared their ambushes. The tree blocked only half of the road, so I quickly scanned the other half to see whether the earth was the same colour everywhere, and luckily it was. As the first vehicle passed the tree at a high speed, I expected to hear a big bang, but nothing happened. Maybe the ambush had been deserted some time ago or maybe it wasn't even an ambush, just a fallen tree. Anyway, we were safe.

The trip took several hours and although we had all expected the worst, nothing happened. At times we had to slow down because of the extremely bad roads and then we would nearly shit our pants, but the trip remained uneventful. At dusk we reached our new destination, which was a large military camp in the vicinity of a trading centre.

We were brought to a high commander in this new camp. This man was in charge of all the escapees and, just like the commander of the other camp, he welcomed us with open arms. Hervé and Fe Guevara addressed us one last time, saying that we had to be patient and that eventually they would come for us. Afterwards they re-entered their vehicles, and together with Victor, who was being taken to hospital, they headed back in the direction of Kitgum.

Very quickly, the commander ordered some soldiers to put us with the rest of the escapees. What I saw next was simply overwhelming. As we were marched through the barracks, I saw that there were hundreds of us. Now I realised why the LRA had to constantly renew their abduction efforts.

The camp wasn't very different from the one that we had come from, except that it was much bigger and there were hundreds of us rather than only a few. I was immediately greeted by two boys I knew very well. One of them had been part of my unit and he was present when my former colleagues had trapped me in the hut. I knew the other boy from several fighting missions, including the abduction of the Aboke girls. I was extremely glad to see them, and we exchanged stories about how we got there. They asked about my escape and I told them everything.

Although the conditions in this camp were much worse than the previous one, time passed much faster here. We received very little food, but at least I had the company of many of my former colleagues. We were free to move around the barracks and nobody imprisoned us. Every day we played cards, we talked, and we even laughed with each other. Initially, the kind of topics we discussed were battles that we had narrowly survived, but after some time we also started to tell each other about the lives that we had before we were abducted. With the boy from my unit, I often talked about the day that they had cornered me in the ghost village. He told me that when Langole gave the command to shoot me, he had deliberately aimed around me. He said that was also the case for many others in the unit. It was on that day that he also decided to escape.

We only received food once a day, and it was usually served late at night. This one meal was barely enough for us to regain strength. The water situation was even worse. Although there was a borehole in this camp, it was reserved for the soldiers and their wives, and others who were strong enough to compete for it. In our weakened condition we had no access to this borehole. Instead we had to get our water from a pond that we shared with several groups of domestic pigs. Whenever we wanted to drink, we first had to chase away the pigs, and then wait for the water to settle so that it was at least a little bit fresh. We drank this water where the pigs swam and shat, and we also used this dirty pool to wash ourselves.

I developed an eye infection. Several days after the itching began, I could hardly see anything. Every day I washed my eyes with the dirty water, and it seemed that they were only getting worse. Luckily my friends took good care of me while I was blind. I couldn't compete for the limited food, but my friend Lamson always shared his food with me. He also guided me to the pond and sometimes he collected water for me. Even when we were playing cards, he would help me when I could no longer distinguish the hearts from the diamonds. Lamson asked the commander several times to send me to the doctor, but he constantly refused, saying that the eye sickness would resolve itself, and so it did. Just as fast as it had come, within a week it disappeared and I regained my vision.

I waited patiently for Hervé to come back and reunite me with my parents. After two weeks he did come back, but only as a bearer of bad news. He explained that his organisation had not yet located my parents and they also hadn't found another place for me, so I had to stay here. To comfort me, he had brought me some clothes that he had bought at the market. The same day that Hervé left, I took my friend to the nearby trading centre. Although I was terribly afraid of the civilians in the centre, nobody ever bothered us, probably because they didn't know that we were former rebels. In the trading centre we sold the new clothes. With the money we each bought sodas and a good meal.

This was the first time in years that I had walked among civilians as their equal and it felt good. Here nobody pointed at us. They probably thought that we were the children of the soldiers. We decided to stay in the trading centre until it was late in the afternoon. After that we decided to go more often, to observe how the civilians acted and to mimic their behaviour.

In the meantime, the conditions in the barracks also improved a bit. One day I had collected some water at the pig pond in a small plastic bottle. As I walked back to our quarters, I met a soldier's wife, who urged me to come over. When I came close, she took the bottle from me and said, 'Please, boy, you shouldn't be drinking this dirty water – it will make you sick.' Then she emptied the bottle and she took me with her to the borehole. From that day forward the woman always helped me to get clean water from the borehole.

With the little money I got from selling the clothes, we some-times could afford to buy some cassava and g-nuts (peanuts) in the trading centre. This additional nutrition to the food we received in the camp was critical, since more escapees came in every day and the food was decreasing. Eventually there were at least 300 of us, and there was a serious challenge in feeding us.

Amongst the escapees there were high-ranking individuals, such as first lieutenants and even a captain, but most of us were simple recruits. After about a month, a large UPDF truck finally came to take us to Gulu. There were 169 of us going to Lira and Gulu Dis-trict. I was forced to leave Lamson behind because he came from Kitgum. Although it was a really big truck, everybody was doubt-ful that we would all fit in it. To make matters even worse, the truck was carrying the bodies of several dead soldiers, which also had to be transported to Gulu. We had to share our space with them. The truck also contained the weaponry and ammunition that had been taken from all of us, so we were forced to stand on top of our own guns. We were pushed into the truck and it quickly moved out.

The soldiers who were guarding us were extremely unfriendly and they forced us to remain standing. We had nothing to hold on to but each other. With the bumpy road and the terrible speed, and the fact that we had to remain standing, people were pushed against the soldiers and the soldiers pushed back with the points of their bayonets. This really hurt and caused some of those in the truck to start bleeding. We once hit a really deep bump at a crazy high speed and some people fell onto the dead bodies. This angered our guards. A guard came to pull the boys off the dead bodies, hitting them with the butt of his gun. The attitudes of the soldiers towards us caused tempers to flare. Didn't they realise that they were pushing the wrong people around? We weren't on the road for even half an hour before the atmosphere deteriorated to the point where people could get killed.

I started the commotion. Among the escapees, all the commanders had been forced to remain in Kitgum. I saw that I was the highest-ranking individual on the truck. When we hit another bump, I fell against a soldier, who immediately started to threaten me and sting me with his bayonet. At this point I had taken enough abuse, and I addressed my former colleagues.

'Friends, the way that we are treated on this truck is unacceptable and I will not take this. Let us take our guns and show these soldiers a lesson.'

Most of the children on the truck knew very well who I was, and my words had a huge impact. All around me my colleagues started to scream, and the situation became rebellious.

'Let's go back – we don't need to be treated like animals.'

Some people actually bent over to reach for their guns. The commander, who was sitting in the co-driver's seat, noticed all the commotion. He ordered the driver to stop the truck and got out.

To make us quiet, he shot several rounds into the air with his pistol and demanded to know what was going on. I told him what had happened and what was going to happen if the soldiers wouldn't let us sit like normal human beings. The commander realised the volatility of the situation and knew that he was vastly outgunned. He gave us what we wanted and even more. Now we were allowed to sit down while the soldiers had to stand the rest of the way. Within a matter of minutes, the situation calmed down and we started to move again. We saw the shivering knees of the soldiers who were now standing, aware that we wouldn't take their mistreatment. They were scared shitless.

The rest of the journey was uneventful and soon we reached Lira. As it was getting late, the commander offloaded the Lira people as quickly as possible. More than forty people got off in Lira, which made the rest of the ride much more comfortable. We left Lira at dusk and when we reached Gulu it was pitch dark.

In Gulu we were taken to the barracks of the UPDF's Fourth Division, one of the largest barracks in Uganda, where we were ordered to line up once more.

'Name, place of birth, your unit in the LRA.'

Again more questions. It took a long while before they had noted all our details. Although we were really tired from the long journey, we had to remain standing. By the time we were allowed to sleep in some prison cells, it was already well into the night.

After a few hours of sleep we were woken up again. The condition of this place was even worse than the previous barracks. The prison cells were drastically overcrowded and filled with cockroaches and other vermin. The cells had tin roofs, which meant that they would get blazingly hot during the day. In the morning several of my colleagues were taken out of their cells for further questioning. Then it was my turn. I was taken to a stone building where I was seated opposite an older commander.

'So they call you Attiena Mortar. Sergeant Attiena Mortar, if I am not mistaken.'

It was at that point that I knew this would be a long day and that it would still be a while before I would see my parents again.

'Just an innocent recruit who knows nothing, are you? Give it up. We know you have been lying.'

Someone had told on me, probably to improve his or her own situation. A whole new round of questioning started, and I knew that this time I wouldn't get away with my lies so easily. The rest of the day was hell. They kept on asking me questions to which I didn't know the answers, or questions that I simply didn't want to answer. Whenever they weren't satisfied, which was with almost every answer, they slapped and threatened me. At the end of the day I was taken to another cell, where they kept the more senior soldiers and the commanders. The conditions in this cell were even worse than the previous one. It was overcrowded, dirty, blazingly hot and had a lack of food and water. If that wasn't enough, some of the people around me were indeed among the worst people within the LRA.

For two weeks the questioning continued and my reluctance to answer their questions grew with each day. The harder they hit me, the more the fire came back into my eyes. They told me that I would spend the rest of my days in jail if I didn't cooperate, and I responded that there was nothing they could do to touch me. The more unfriendly they became, the more my defiance was sparked. Whenever they told me that I was responsible for the death and destruction in Kitgum, I told them that it was their failure to protect me that got me into this situation in the first place.

Eventually my only goal was to defy them. They slapped me and reduced my food and water rations to an absolute minimum, but I didn't care. There was nothing they could throw at me that I hadn't already encountered in the LRA. They told me that they were going to enlist me in the army so that I could repay all the suffering I had caused. I told them that if they did so, I would escape and return to the LRA. This line of thought was real. After two weeks of unending questioning, I actually hoped that they would enlist me and give me a gun. I was extremely angry and aggressive at that time and truly willing to join the LRA again to take my vengeance. Luckily things didn't get that far.

After two weeks, a couple of people from World Vision came to visit the army barracks. They inspected all the cells and the moment they saw me they demanded to be allowed to talk to me. They asked me how I was treated, and I told them the blunt truth. They asked me about my age, when I was abducted, when I escaped, and other questions. Like Hervé, they asked the questions in a friendly way and they were very patient. When they took me aside, I was still extremely defiant, but they quickly managed to calm me down. After they questioned me for half an hour, they asked a soldier to escort me back to my cell, and to give me some food. They assured me that they would talk with the commanders to get me out.

When they left, no soldier came to question me again. It was pointless anyway. They knew very well that they couldn't extract any more information from me. Another few days passed in which my food rations improved. Then the two people from World Vision returned, accompanied by Hervé Cheuzeville.

The moment I saw Hervé I felt a calm coming over me. His reassuring smile gave me a strong feeling that things would be OK again. For two weeks Hervé had been the one person I was hoping to see more than anyone else. So far, he was the only stranger who appeared to be genuinely interested in my welfare, and what was more, he was a leader for an organisation called World Food. Considering my constant state of hunger, it was a title that had a magical sound to it.

Hervé asked me how I was doing, and I told him what had transpired since I last saw him. One of the others from World Vision acted as a translator. When I finished my story Hervé told me that he had good news this time. He handed me a piece of paper, but I was clueless as to what it said. My puzzled look gave me away.

'It is your release form, boy. You're finally free. You're no longer a prisoner. These two people from World Vision will take care of you now. In their hands you will be well off and you can rebuild your life once more. In the meantime, we are still looking for your parents, but I am sure we will find them soon.'

Freedom! I could hardly imagine what this meant. The first thing I wanted to do was to run all the way to my former home, but my legs went numb. I remained speechless for more than a minute, after which the lady from World Vision broke the silence.

'Come on, boy. Let's get you to a shower and a good bed.'

Still Trapped in the War

By the age of fourteen, I had killed more people than many of the most notorious serial killers the world has ever known. But that doesn't mean that I am an evil man, or that I am mentally ill. I never killed anyone out of pure cruelty or because of sheer hatred. I killed them because I had to. I had no other choice. It was either me or them. Or at least so I was told.

In World Vision's rehabilitation centre we had group sessions and individual counselling sessions almost every day. These sessions all revolved around one message: *It was not your fault; you are innocent.* Whatever I had done wasn't my fault, because the LRA had forced me to do it. Whatever had happened in the bush had happened against my will, and therefore I couldn't be held accountable. The LRA had abused me. They had brainwashed me and turned me into an errand boy for the Grim Reaper, the ultimate killing machine, free of remorse and sorrow. Whatever I had done, I held no responsibility. It was my commanders who were to blame; they had forced me to do all those horrible things.

The first day the counsellor told me that I was innocent and that it was the commanders who were to blame, I couldn't help but think back about those days when I was a commander myself. Even though my rank was very low, it was still a rank. I had ordered others to do unspeakable things and I had also threatened to kill them if they refused. So if I wasn't responsible as a juvenile commander, then who was? The ones who had commanded me? Most of them were also abducted at young ages and turned into killing machines. And what had age got to do with it anyway? My unit commander, the Mzee, had been quite old when they abducted him, but still he was as ruthless as I had been, even though he had been a schoolteacher before that time.

Every day the counsellors told me that I had had no other choice. But I clearly remembered several people who had been given orders to kill and who had refused to do so. Even though none of these people are alive today to tell about their bravery or foolishness – depending from which perspective you choose to look at it – they had made a clear choice. It was a choice that I could have made as well, if it was not for my lack of courage, my will to live, and the fact that I had valued my own life above that of dozens of others.

I do not regret my choices. If I had refused to kill, this story would not have been written. It might have been another man's story, a story of someone who might still be alive today, only because I had refused to kill him. That storyteller might have recalled a brave young boy who had refused to shoot him. But that would have been the end of it. Afterwards I would have been shot dead and no one but my parents would remember me, always hoping for the day I might come back. I am happy that my story has been written. I have no regrets over the choices that I have made; I am only sorry that my options were so limited. The counsellors at World Vision were definitely right about one thing: it was either them or me. The LRA was a kill-or-be-killed society, and I chose to live.

The time in the World Vision centre passed very slowly. I hated that they always treated me like a child, preaching about God, his forgiveness and my innocence. A few months earlier people had preached to me how it was right to kill in the name of God, and now all of a sudden it was a crime. For sure, I had always hated to kill innocent civilians, but killing on a battlefield was a whole other story. The vast majority of those who I had killed had died during battle, and I wasn't convinced about the immorality of this. Our enemies had shot at me, and I had shot back. Yes, I had killed women and children during combat missions, but letting those people live was a military liability.

The counsellors insisted that killing was a bad thing, no matter what the circumstances. They told me that I had no free will, no choice whatsoever. Everything had been done against my will and I was just a poor little boy who needed attention. Every day they kept on patronising me, treating me like some kind of victim, and I was getting sick of it. I was a soldier, a very good soldier, and yet they couldn't stop treating me like a child.

They tried to keep us constantly occupied so that we wouldn't have any time to reflect, but it wasn't working. At night the dreams would always come back. During the daytime we had all kinds of activities, starting with prayer, breakfast and then stupid games, followed by those counselling sessions. We had to do plays in which we simulated what had happened in the LRA and how we should behave in civilian society. It was supposed to make us ready for being a civilian again, but I wasn't impressed. I wanted to go back to school and to get on with my life. Mostly I wanted to be reunited with my parents. So far, there was still no sign of them; at least, no one ever told me about them. Several times I asked people if I could leave the compound, but the guards always refused. I was told I had to stay for my own good. I felt like a prisoner once again.

After a while, I couldn't take it any more and decided to escape. The escape itself couldn't have been easier: I walked through the gate while the guard had fallen asleep in the afternoon sun. The rehabilitation centre was in the middle of town, to protect the escapees from the wrath of the LRA. It was now the rainy season, but this day was very beautiful and for miles around I saw only blue skies.

As I was walking through the centre of Gulu I felt completely free. So far, I hadn't made a plan. I could walk to my village, but I knew it was a very long walk through LRA territory, so I decided to do something else. I only had two dreams, and since one of them was not yet in reach, I decided to satisfy the other.

After I had walked around for several kilometres, I came across a school. From outside I heard the children repeating phrases after the teacher in English. This was the class that I wanted to follow. I wanted to be able to speak English so that I could talk with all the white folks in their big Land Cruisers. I entered the school and when I came to the classroom where they taught English, I knocked on the door. For a moment the class went quiet, and the teacher, a lady, told me to enter. At that moment a strange fear came over me. What if the class wouldn't accept me? What if the teacher didn't want to teach me? I knocked on the door again. Again, the class fell silent and now I heard the footsteps of the teacher coming closer. When she opened the door, I could clearly see that she was in shock. I was still wearing the uniform that the old commander had given me and I still had a wild look in my eyes. She immediately looked around, expecting to see hundreds of others, but there was only me. With a shivering voice she asked me: 'Please, sir, how can I help you?'

I liked how she called me sir.

'I want to sit in on your class, madam.'

She refused and told me that the class was already full, but I saw that some school benches weren't occupied. That is when I got angry and I told her that I wanted to follow her class, or otherwise I would stab her to death. This woman was clearly terrified, but she let me in. Then she continued her class.

'Hi, friend, how are you doing today?'

The class repeated: 'Hi, friend, how are you doing today?'

She read the next sentence, which was written on the blackboard, and the class repeated again. This went on for several minutes, but it was clear that the class didn't have the same flow any more. The teacher was sweating; she was falling over her own words and the students' replies were only in whispers. It was clear that everybody was afraid of me and that I was an unwanted guest. Behind me I started to hear the conversation.

'He is a rebel. He can cut us into pieces if he wants to.'

'Yeah, but he is unarmed and alone; what can he possibly do against all of us?'

At that point I turned around and looked the boy in the eye. I felt an urge to hurt him. He was trying to set the class against me. In the LRA I would have killed him without even thinking about it. But I wasn't in the LRA any more. As I was looking this boy in the eye, he fell quiet, whispering a very soft 'sorry'.

The teacher immediately tried to avert this situation and she called out to me, 'This is for the new boy: please repeat after me and then translate the following sentence: "I am going to the church today – where are you going to?"'

At that point I had had it. First of all, I hated to be singled out. I was sure that the teacher was trying to make me look like a fool if I couldn't pronounce or translate her sentence right. Furthermore, the teacher and the students were all sweating out of fear. I had entered the classroom to be educated, not to be feared. At that moment I stood up and I left the classroom. I never repeated the sentences for the teacher.

By the time I reached the edge of the school compound, the police and World Vision had already been alerted. Several minutes later, a white vehicle came to pick me up. It was the people from World Vision, returning me back to my prison.

Once I was back at the centre I immediately had to talk to a counsellor. She asked me why I had entered the school and I told her about my wish to start learning again. She explained to me that I wasn't ready for that, but that soon they would send me to school and reunite me with my parents. I had to wait.

Several weeks later, I got a sudden visitor. From the first moment they told me about my visitor I was extremely excited. I fully expected that it would be either my mum or my dad, so when I saw Hervé Cheuzeville, I was slightly disappointed, although I was really happy that I finally had someone to talk to outside of World Vision, someone who might help me find my parents. Hervé gave me a firm handshake and he said that he wanted to know all about my last few weeks. I told him everything. I told him about the incident at the school, which actually made him laugh. I told him about World Vision and how I hated the way they treated me as a small child, but Hervé told me that I should be patient. He explained that these people really had the best intentions for me, but that they could only help me if I opened up to them.

I really liked Hervé. He was always so kind to me, but never in a patronising way. He was patient, and when he visited me, he always brought me a little something. When he saw that I was still wearing the military uniform, he took me to the market and bought me some new clothes. He never asked what had happened to the other set. We spent most of the day at World Vision and in Gulu market talking. We were still using a translator, as my English wasn't good enough for us to talk alone, so this made me even more eager to go back to school.

I asked Hervé about my parents, whether there was any news, but again he told me to be patient and to rely on World Vision, because they would surely do everything in their power to find my parents. When he brought me back to World Vision at the end of the day, I felt good. It had been a truly wonderful day. Hervé always made me feel understood and valued. He neither feared nor pitied me. I had the feeling that he was becoming a good friend, even though he was several times my age.

Weeks passed. My life at World Vision was becoming routine. The counselling sessions still continued, but they became less frequent. I noticed that I was slowly starting to change. I didn't despise the civilian counsellors as much as I did in the beginning, and slowly I began to see that they were only trying to help me. The more I accepted what they did, the less patronising it felt. Above all, during my little adventure at the school I had indeed come to realise that I wasn't ready for the world outside the gates.

Inside World Vision, I could say whatever I wanted to. I told the counsellors several times that I would cut them to pieces, but they always reacted very patiently. In the first few days, they let me talk and threaten them, but afterwards they started to ask me stupid questions. At first I really hated those questions.

'Norman, can you tell me why you want to cut me into pieces? What do you hope to achieve by killing me?'

Whenever they asked me this, I walked away. But later it made me realise that my threats were empty. I actually didn't want to cut those people into pieces. What did I want to achieve? I wanted them to leave me alone. But I was coming to understand that the world didn't work that way. They taught me that in the case of a conflict, I had to resolve the dispute with words, not violence. They told me that threats would not improve my life outside these gates. Instead, people would be scared of me and I would be alone. They asked me repeatedly what I wanted to achieve, and after a while I realised that the only thing I wanted was to be accepted by people and to live a normal life again.

Even the plays started to make sense. We simulated what would happen if we told someone that we would slit his or her throat. Afterwards we did the same scene over, but instead of making threats, we made conversations. I started to see how conversations were better than violence and threats. Gradually I was calming down. The rebel inside me was dozing, falling asleep, while the civilian slowly woke up. I learned the advantages of small talk once more. As I was lightening up, I gained new friends and sometimes World Vision allowed me outside the gates. At first there was always someone guiding me, but after several weeks of excellent behaviour, I could even walk outside all by myself.

World Vision could not, however, cure the dreams. Every night I was haunted by the most terrible nightmares. Often I was awakened in the middle of the night by my new friends, who had heard my screams. When they woke me up, I immediately started to thrash around, and it always took several people to calm me down. On several occasions I woke up and found myself at the other side of the compound, as I had a tendency to sleepwalk during my dreams. Every night I was afraid to fall asleep, but eventually I always did, and the dreams came to haunt me. As a result, I developed a chronic sleeping disorder, which meant that I slept very little at night, but I could fall asleep very quickly during the daytime hours.

I had been in World Vision for nearly three months when I finally received the long-awaited news. My parents had been found and that afternoon they would come to visit me. As I heard this news, my world began to shake. This was the one thing that I had been looking forward to ever since I had left the rebels, which was now almost six months ago. How many times had I asked about my parents? Always I was told that they were still looking for them, and now suddenly they were found, and I would see them soon.

Instead of joy, a terrible fear grew inside of me. I had been in World Vision long enough to know what could happen. In the past few months I had seen so many of my friends go to see their parents but return hours, sometimes even minutes later, rejected and utterly bitter. It was my worst fear that my parents wouldn't recognise me any more, or worse, that they wouldn't want me back because of the things I had done.

Before the visit I received some instructions. They told me that my parents would only visit for one hour and that I could not go with them afterwards. They were very clear about this. They told me that it was better for all of us to take things slowly. After I had been given some time to wash myself and put on my best clothes, I was told to follow one of the counsellors, who took me to another building five minutes from the rehabilitation centre. These were maybe the longest minutes of my life. When we entered the other room, I was told to sit in a white chamber with one of the head counsellors of World Vision. Minutes later my parents walked in. Almost two and a half years had passed since I had last seen them.

They looked sad and much older, but apart from that they were exactly how I remembered them. The moment they entered the room, tears started flowing across my face. I wanted to run over, but something held me back. When I saw the look on my parents' faces, it was like they were completely indifferent. As they looked at me, the sadness on their faces increased. Francis, the head counsellor, walked over to my parents and pointed to me, asking me if I was their son.

'Sorry, sir, but we have never seen this boy; this is not our son.'

Of all the shocks and disappointments in my life, this might have been the biggest that I ever faced. After years of imprisonment I stood just three metres from my parents. All this time I had missed them intensely, and now they rejected me. They didn't even recognise me as their son any more. My mum and dad looked at me again, but there was no sign of recognition. I fell on my knees and started crying.

'But it is me! How can you not recognise me while you are standing here? For the last two and a half years I have wanted nothing more than to see you again and now you reject me?'

For a moment it was silent, but then my dad mumbled: 'Norman . . . is that you?'

'Yes, Papa, it is me.'

At that point my mum and dad ran towards me and the three of us embraced. For a long time we couldn't say anything. My parents also started to cry, and at that moment, none of us were able to even speak. My mum was the first to break the silence.

'Norman, we heard you had been killed. We thought you were dead. Sorry that we didn't recognise you immediately. You look so different now.'

I wasn't able to speak. I just held on to my mum and dad. I was crying so hard. After about fifteen minutes my father asked me some questions about what had happened to me. I wasn't sure how to answer, but Francis intervened by saying that they should allow me time to find a way to talk about it. Instead, my dad told me about their lives after I was abducted. Whenever he forgot the smallest detail, my mum would jump in to tell the rest of the story.

A few days after my abduction, they decided to move to Gulu and leave everything behind. They now lived somewhere near the edge of Gulu town with my siblings, who were all doing well. Even though it was dangerous to do so, my parents still walked to our land every day to cultivate it, because it remained their only source of food. They left before the sun was up and returned only after it had sunk beneath the horizon, always walking through the thick vegetation to avoid encounters with the LRA. The long day was hard, and the trip was dangerous, but it was the only way to keep the family fed, and to pay the rent for the land they lived on.

My dad told me that he used to spy on the rebels who walked through his land in the hope of seeing me. He would also watch the rebels from the bush, putting himself in great personal danger for the chance to find me. He continued this spying until the day that he heard I had died.

When I asked how they had heard this, my mum started to speak of a friend, Moses, who had been taken on the same day as I was, and who escaped several months later. He informed people that I had been beaten to death and that they had dumped my body some place that he did not know. As we had been abducted on the same day by the same unit, everybody believed him. Initially my parents didn't want to believe it, but after a long while they accepted the sad news. So they were very surprised and almost angry when a World Vision representative came to them with the news that their son had been found.

I asked my mum about Francis, the boy from the neighbouring village who had been abducted on the same day as me, and whose name had been written the day before mine, and she told me that he had been released directly after they had written his name. All this time I was under the impression that they had killed him, so I was relieved to hear this. He had been so fearful and he had screamed so hard during the beating that the rebels didn't see any use for him. My mum also told me that he suffered from epilepsy, so it was a good thing, because he wouldn't have lasted very long. However, apart from that, he was still doing fine.

I had many more questions, but before we even realised it, the hour was over. There was still so much left to be said, but Francis, the head counsellor, was very strict. He told my parents that they were allowed to visit me again in three days, and this time for slightly longer than an hour. We gave each other a really long hug, and afterwards they had to go.

After this, my life in World Vision became easier. My family visited me regularly. Sometimes it would be only my mum or dad, and other times they came together or with a younger sibling. We always talked about lots of things: about the schooling of my younger siblings, about the family, our new home. I slowly started to unveil my life in the LRA, although I kept my deepest secrets hidden. There are certain things that happened that remained private, but as much as possible I was very open. My parents were often in shock when they learned about the hardships, but they never rejected me for it, nor did they ever cast any blame on me. Because of my parents' visits, I always had something to look forward to and time seemed to be passing much quicker. Also, Victor had been released from hospital, and he had come to World Vision. We quickly became best friends.

As the months passed, I was getting better at the conversation games; I stopped threatening people and using violence to solve my problems. After six months I was told that the time had come for me to leave World Vision. I could finally move home with my parents and go back to school.

This is when things started to get difficult again. The real world wasn't very friendly to former rebels. The neighbourhood was very hostile to me, and because of that, I resorted back to my old patterns of aggression, which only made things worse for me. It was like a vicious circle that was accelerated by my own actions.

My parents lived on the edge of Gulu town. Once I moved in with them, it didn't take long for the whole neighbourhood to know that I had been a rebel. Whenever I left my parents' hut to fetch water or to do other tasks, people would point at me and I could hear them whispering about me.

'There is that rebel again. Did you hear that he is responsible for the slaughter in Kitgum?'

I have no idea how people knew these things, but somehow Radio Kabi, the Acholi rumour system, worked in mysterious ways. My nightmares grew worse again, and every night I woke up screaming so loud that the whole neighbourhood heard me. Because of my screams and other behaviours, everyone became aware of me and my past. They started pointing at me and discriminating against me. I reacted to this in the way I had learned in the LRA, by becoming aggressive and by threatening people. Within a matter of days, I forgot everything that I had learned in the six months I spent at World Vision.

Because of my violent interactions with people, it didn't take long before I developed a bad reputation and people started fearing me. For example, when I played with my neighbours' children, I often lined them all up and started parading them and caning anybody who was parading out of line. Soon none of the children wanted to play with me any more – they were petrified. I threatened people in the most horrible ways when they discriminated against me. Somehow the threats worked in the short term and people had a tendency to shut up if I told them that I would eat their children if they wouldn't stop stigmatising me, but in the long run things only got worse.

Even my parents and siblings started to fear me. In the beginning, when they went to the land, they left me in control of my younger siblings. When they came back at night, we would have a conversation about my difficulties of the day. But soon my parents started taking my siblings with them, because they were too afraid to leave them with me. They would rather risk running into the rebels with my siblings than leave them with a rebel like me. Initially I slept with my siblings in one hut while my parents occupied another. But after only several days at home, all my siblings moved in with my parents, and I was left alone in the hut. They told me it was because it would be more comfortable for me, but I knew the real reason all too well.

When my parents came home after a long day of work, they had to listen to my neighbours' complaints regarding my behaviour, leaving little time to have a meaningful conversation with me. Our conversations were reduced to verbal fights. One night my father came up and hit me in the face, telling me to never cane my neighbours' children again. I reacted by kicking my dad and threatening to slit his throat in his sleep if he ever talked like that to me again. Minutes later I offered my apologies, but by then the damage was done. I became alienated from my parents and the whole neighbourhood hated me.

Sometimes I had these mood swings when, all of a sudden, I wanted to kill or destroy things, and I always did so. I would kick things to pieces, especially things that people had been working on for a long time. I would kill our neighbours' pets, including chickens and ducks that the people kept for special celebration days, like Christmas and Independence Day. The consequence of my actions was that I became completely isolated. I couldn't get anything at the shops any more because those folks were afraid of me. I didn't have intense conversations with my parents any more because they were afraid of me. I didn't play with the children in my neighbourhood because I scared them. The more I was alone and discriminated against, the worse my aggression got and the more isolated I became.

At school, things didn't go much better. Most of the time I was behaving quite decently and I tried to remember the behaviour lessons from World Vision. They had taught me that I would make mistakes, but they never told me that for every bad thing I did, I had to do more than a hundred good deeds to make up for it. For me this didn't work. Already in the first week, my fellow students started to gossip about me and after several days I lost my cool. I got into a fight with a fellow schoolmate whom I hit very hard. Seconds after the fight erupted, a teacher came and pulled me away from the other boy. The teacher told me that I was grounded and that I was not allowed to enter school for a week.

When I returned after that week, nobody had forgotten about the fight. The other students stopped bullying me, but no one talked to me either. I tried to behave at my very best, but all my good actions couldn't make up for the mistake I had made a week earlier. After that, I didn't get into a fight with anybody any more and I also stopped threatening the other students. But their behaviour towards me didn't change with my changed attitude.

I developed ringworm, and because of the infectious nature of the disease, I wasn't allowed to go to school any more. I think that everybody was relieved about this. I felt depressed, lonely and miserable. Once more my life had turned into a living hell. I knew that it was my own behaviour that was to blame for my isolation, but I was simply incapable of taking all the World Vision lessons to heart in the face of severe stigmatisation.

Yet again it was Hervé Cheuzeville who came to my rescue. He had come to visit me at World Vision but found that I had been sent home several weeks earlier. He came on a Sunday, just as I returned from church with my parents and my siblings. He arrived with a translator from World Vision, named Kaunda Kenneth. When Hervé showed up, I was very excited and eager to talk to him. I knew that he wasn't afraid of me and he would hear my stories without judging me or calling me a rebel. Hervé took me aside and I told him everything, from my experiences upon coming back home to my ringworm infection. Afterwards, Hervé went to my parents and he had a long conversation with them.

This was at a time when the rebel activity around Gulu was really bad. A few days before, the rebels had even penetrated Gulu town, near Lacor Hospital. Living on the outer edge of Gulu, I was extremely afraid of re-abduction. When Hervé heard all the stories and saw where I lived, he took me to the clinic and he bought antifungal medication. Then he took me to the Acholi Inn Hotel, where he applied the medication. He booked us a room for the night, because by then the rebel activities within town were serious and he didn't want me to live so close to the edge of town. We talked for a long time and he stressed that he could do very little for me at that point, and that I definitely had to stop threatening and bullying people.

The next morning, he bought me a nice school uniform and some sandals. He had to go back to Kampala, so he took me home. In the days that followed I remained in my hut as much as possible. I didn't feel like facing the people outside. Within my little space I had a lot of time to think about the things Hervé had said and I promised myself that I wouldn't threaten people any more, especially not my parents and siblings. Several days later my ringworm was almost gone and, armed with my new sandals, uniform and books, I went back to school.

From this time onwards, I tried as much as possible to behave. To avoid fights and other conflicts, I simply isolated myself from everyone. During the breaks I just sat down somewhere and tried to study far away from the other pupils. During the lessons, I tried to actively participate, but I had a very hard time concentrating. Images from the war kept coming back to me. Because of my chronic sleeping disorder, I often fell asleep in the middle of a class. Then the teacher would wake me up and tell me to focus, but with my sleepiness and the images of the war coming back, I simply couldn't. Normally, when a student fell asleep in class, everybody would laugh at him, but none of the other students dared to do that with me. When I returned home from school, I would go directly to my hut, where I would shut myself in for the rest of the day.

Although I wasn't causing any trouble now, things were not going well for me. I felt so alone. The terrible images of the war were increasingly tormenting me. I still had many anger attacks, but instead of destroying things, I tried to walk or run it out. Whenever I felt an attack, I started walking or running long distances. I would walk to the centre of Gulu, past World Vision, towards Lacor Hospital and back. Sometimes I still destroyed things, but I always tried to do this as far away from home as possible.

The only ones who still talked to me were my parents, and even though they were sympathetic and understanding, there was always this fear. Once I had a long conversation with my mother about my nightmares, the images of the war and my behaviour, and afterwards we started crying together and my mum repeated over and over that she wanted her son back. When I told her that I was here, she replied that I wasn't the same son that she had lost so long ago.

She was right. I wasn't the same boy any more. I had changed drastically and the son she remembered had indeed died a long time ago. The LRA had brainwashed me, and they had taught me the way of the gun and the laws of the bush. I wished so much that I could resurrect the son she remembered, but the LRA had forced me to become a different person. Had I not changed, I would not have survived. This was the sad truth. Her words, although they were meant to comfort me, deeply hurt me instead. It was the first time that someone else had told me that part of me had died, and this realisation hit me deep.

In many ways, I was still trapped in the war, which continued both in my head and in the physical world. I could not shake the images of all the horrible things I had seen. On top of that, we heard stories about the war every day from Radio Kabi. There were schools that were plundered, camps that came under attack, and new massacres in Kitgum. However, the most terrifying rumours were that the LRA was planning to capture Gulu town. Several times, the rebels had penetrated Gulu. One time, they even came all the way up to the police barracks, which were in the heart of town, in an area known as Pece, the same area where my parents had settled.

Because I lived close to the edge of town, I started night commuting with thousands of other kids from the surrounding area. Every night we would pack our stuff and head into the city centre of Gulu, as far away from the edge of town as possible, just to escape the threat of re-abduction. We slept on the streets and on the verandas, no matter what the weather conditions were. In the daytime, I went to school, but as the rumours of rebel activity outside Gulu grew, the lessons became increasingly tense. Whenever Radio Kabi was active, people looked at me. For some, I was the closest they had been to a real rebel. After I had been behaving well for several weeks, some classmates asked me about my time with the rebels, but I never answered them. I was not sure if they were reaching out to me or if they were trying to make a fool out of me.

Several months passed and it was time for our third-term holiday. I received my report card and the only thing it said was to pull up, try harder, and that I was a weak student. I was doing my best, but my traumas kept me from performing well. The first day of the holiday, I had another visit from Hervé Cheuzeville and he asked me if I wanted to spend the holiday with him in Kampala. By this time, I was completely depressed, and this offer really cheered me up. I ran to my parents to tell them the news and they were also happy. The rebel activity was really high at this time and they told me that I should go, as they wanted me to be safe. I suspected that their real joy was that for three weeks they would be free from the fear that I instilled in them and my siblings.

Hervé left that same day. I was to take the bus the next day with the World Vision translator Kaunda Kenneth, also a former child soldier. I had never been to Kampala before, so I was really excited to go. When we came to the bus park the next day, a guy named Richard was waiting for us. This man worked for the World Food Programme and he had been instructed by Hervé to make sure that we would be on the morning bus. He bought us two tickets and we got on the bus. By the time the bus left Gulu, our excitement had grown, even though we knew that we would pass through the heartland of LRA territory. The atmosphere on the bus was very tense. There was a chance that an RPG could hit us, so the bus drove at a staggering speed that was terrifying in itself.

It took us less than an hour before we came to the bridge across the Nile near Karuma. Once we'd crossed it, everybody relaxed – everybody but me, that is. We were out of LRA territory now and this meant that we were safe, but I couldn't help remembering the last time I was here. I recalled the charge over the bridge two years earlier as clearly as if it was the day before. This was a time that we felt invincible and all of us had the idea that we would march on straight to Kampala.

As we passed over the bridge with its stunning view across the Nile, all the images came back to me. There were images of soldiers running for their lives and the two civilians who were so-called informers who were shot through the head. Yet somehow I felt a strange kind of pride. Back then, we all thought that we would go to Kampala and we were all extremely disappointed when we were told to go back. Now, however, I was on my way to Kampala, and from this point onwards, nothing could stop us. It was Kaunda who took my focus away from the memories. Once we had crossed the bridge, everybody started talking in relief, including Kaunda and me. We bragged about what we had heard of Kampala and each of us tried to outdo the other, although neither of us had been in a city bigger than Gulu.

When we finally entered Kampala almost nine hours later, we entered a world that we had never imagined, and which was entirely new to us. We were amazed by the sheer size of the city, but even more so by all these people. Everywhere we looked we saw hundreds and hundreds of people. It all resembled a big ant-hill, where thousands of ants were running in every direction. It did not make any sense whatsoever. The traffic was chaotic. Never in my life had I seen so many vehicles. When we got to the bus park and finally left the bus, two boys came walking over and told us that Hervé had sent them to pick us up. We walked with them to the 'old taxi park', where we would take a minibus to his home. While we were walking there, we chatted a bit with the boys. Kaunda did most of the talking, because his English was so much better than mine.

In the meantime, we looked around in amazement. Until then, the highest building that I had ever seen in my life was two storeys high, but here there were buildings with even more than fifteen storeys. I didn't even know that men could build such things. Everywhere on the streets people were selling things. It didn't seem like I was still in the same country. It was also as if nobody cared about the war in the north. People were laughing and having fun. We passed several vendors selling newspapers, and the headlines were about the war in the north, but it didn't seem to matter to these people.

When we arrived at the old taxi park I was really perplexed. Just minutes before, when we had entered Kampala, I had told myself that never in my life had I seen so many cars, but what I saw now was really overwhelming. Below me it looked like there were at least a thousand cars all in one big taxi park. This was pure chaos. Taxis were constantly going in and out, but to me it didn't make any sense whatsoever. All the minivans looked exactly the same, white with blue stripes, but somehow our two guides knew exactly which van to take. As we got in, the two boys paid the fees and we moved on. It took us many minutes to clear the taxi park, but when we finally left it behind, the trip went really fast.

Kampala was built around many hills, and on almost every hill there was some kind of religious building. Large mosques and cathedrals dominated the view. After about a twenty-minute drive we came to a very posh neighbourhood, where we got out. With our two guides we walked past several villas until we stopped at a gate. The two boys knocked at the gate and a watchman opened it. Several seconds later Hervé greeted us with open arms.

When we entered Hervé's home, dinner was already being served. It was like they had made it especially for us; what we were served was a typical Acholi meal. Rice, beans and a sauce made of peanuts. Hervé asked us about our journey and both Kaunda and I recounted all the things we had seen, especially the large buildings and the unbelievable crowdedness of Kampala. Since we were so excited about Kampala, Hervé asked our two guides, who were the children of the housekeeper, to give us a tour through the city the next day.

We spent three weeks in Kampala. These were among the happiest days I had encountered. Very often we went into Kampala with the two boys and I was always amazed by everything. One day we went to the catacombs of the Bugandan kings. They were buried in their old palaces, which were the biggest huts that I had ever seen in my life, and according to our guide, the biggest in the world. Everything they showed us was impressive, but after the first week the overcrowding in Kampala was getting to be too much for me. I was happier staying at Hervé's place.

One day Hervé returned home with two visitors: Els De Temmerman, a journalist from Nairobi, and her husband, Johan Van Hecke, who worked in South Africa on democracy and other issues. Hervé told Els about me and my past as a child soldier. That day I had a conversation with Els and she wanted to know everything. Initially I was a little bit afraid and I didn't trust her, but because I was under Hervé's care and with her promises that she would pay my education till university, I started to tell her a brief version of my story. I told her about my abduction, Sudan and even some of the missions in Uganda, including the abduction of the Aboke girls. But I never told her any of the details or the fact that I was a commander. Els went on to write the book *Aboke Girls*, in which I played a large role, but this was all later.

Before I knew it, my weeks in Kampala were over and we had to get back to the north again. On our last evening, Hervé had a long conversation with Kaunda and me. He told us about a school in Masindi. It was for Sudanese students, many of whom had also been former child soldiers for the SPLA, our former enemy. Hervé told us that this was a very good school especially equipped to deal with former child soldiers. In this school, people would not whisper about us, nor would they be afraid. When we heard that the school was for Sudanese students, we were both a bit shocked and Kaunda told Hervé that he didn't want to go there. I had fewer reservations. My home situation was miserable. Although I was trying to be good, I was making my parents' lives difficult and I didn't want that. Above all, in Gulu, I would still be trapped in the middle of the war. Every night I would have to go night commuting and I would always run the risk of getting abducted again. Masindi, on the other hand, was just outside LRA territory, on the safe side of the Nile. After Hervé described the school, I decided to give it a shot. Hervé promised that he would come to visit once in a while and if I really didn't like it, he could always bring me back to Gulu. Once he said that, I made the decision not to return to Gulu yet.

The following day we set out for the north again. This time Hervé drove us himself. During the ride back, my feelings were very mixed. On one hand I was glad to leave Kampala. Even though I had had a wonderful time, the city was too big for me and in a place like this I would never completely at ease. I was a country boy and I felt most comfortable in the middle of nature. On the other hand, I realised that a whole new future lay ahead of me and this made me very anxious. Hervé had convinced me that going to Masindi was best for me and earlier on he had talked about it with my parents and they had also agreed. I realised that I had made the right choice by deciding to go to this school. But I would be all alone there, with no friends or family and mostly Sudanese people. While we were driving the atmosphere was relaxed and the three of us were actually making jokes and having a lot of fun, but all this time I had an anxious feeling of uncertainty.

We left Kampala at dusk and we reached my new home in the middle of the night. The school was called the Blessed Damian School and it was led by head teacher Sister Asiimwe Sophia. Sister Sophia was already waiting for me at the gate. Hervé walked with me and the nun to the main building and for a while he and Sister Sophia talked about all kinds of things, but mainly about me. Hervé told her about my past, my mood swings and my attacks of aggressiveness. At first, I didn't want Hervé to tell her all these things because I was ashamed of them, but from her reactions I saw that she understood my situation and that she had dealt with it before. After a while the sister came to me and she called me 'young mister'. She told me that I had made a good decision by coming here and that she would take very good care of me. Like Hervé, she talked to me without any sense of fear, even though she knew what I was capable of. She talked to me with respect; respect for my past and respect for what I had gone through, but not in a patronising way. She told me about the school and that I would soon have hundreds of new friends. Although I still felt very anxious about all this, she made me feel relaxed. We talked for a while and afterwards she showed me my new home and the bed I would be sleeping in for the next few years.

After the tour, I walked back to the car with Hervé and I thanked him for all the good things he had done for me. His compassion touched me deeply. Then he and Kaunda got back into the car and they drove off. Once they were out of sight, I turned back to the sister. She must have read my mind when she told me that I was very lucky to have a man like that taking care of me. We talked for a few more minutes and afterwards she guided me back to my bed. This was the beginning of a whole new chapter in my life.

The Return of Happiness

When I woke up the next day, I saw my new surroundings for the first time in daylight. I was sleeping in a large room that I shared with dozens of others. Each room had a leader and the moment I awoke, our room leader came to me and welcomed me in the name of all the people in the room. I knew perfectly well that this was a formality and that this would happen with any new kid, but still it made me feel welcome and less alone. To my surprise, the room leader introduced himself as Odong, which is an Acholi name. Although he was Sudanese, he was also an Acholi, and despite the different accents, we understood each other perfectly well. As soon as I was out of bed, the room leader showed me around the compound of the school and gave me an orientation lesson.

I learned that the school was founded by the Torit Diocese in southern Sudan. Initially, it was meant for only Sudanese children. Torit lay near the border of Uganda and this area in Sudan was tribally mixed between Acholis and Dinkas. So although there were quite a number of people who spoke Acholi, Odong explained that Acholi would not be the language we would learn here at school. Instead we were taught English and Arabic, and we were supposed to speak English among ourselves. This was still a problem for me. It was not that I couldn't speak any English, but it was generally very weak.

In the first few weeks I mainly hung out with Odong, and I really started to know him well. He told me about his past and his time spent serving in the SPLA to liberate their country from the Muslim invader. Like me, he was also a soldier who knew all the laws of the jungle. He had entered the SPLA voluntarily when he was thirteen years old, because Arabic militia had destroyed his village. Knowing that I had fled northern Uganda from the threat of the LRA, as Sophia had told the students in my block, he included some encounters with the LRA in his story. He told me that the LRA were always the worst and most fearless enemy. Deep inside, I felt some pride as he told me this, but I was trying very hard to conceal any kind of emotion. From that moment onwards, I decided that I would never reveal my past at this school. Only Sophia and the teachers knew, and I really wanted to keep it that way, as I found myself surrounded by my former enemies.

It was all very weird to me to be talking with my former enemies like we were best friends now. Just over a year ago, I would have shot them without any remorse, and now we were laughing with each other. Of course, Odong also asked me about my past, but I told him that I was a refugee from the war in Uganda. I never told him anything about my past as a soldier and although it didn't take very long for everybody to suspect that there was something more to my story than I had revealed, nobody ever asked me about it. In this school there were so many people with bad memories that we all left them for what they were, relics of the past. If someone didn't want to talk about it, people wouldn't ask.

As school began, I had great difficulty concentrating on the different topics. Somehow my mind was always mired in the war. The brutal images and the memories of the thousands of pleading voices completely took my mind away from the class at hand, whether it was economics, English or mathematics. Sometimes, during the middle of classes, I felt this strong urge to destroy. Whenever this happened, I would walk out of the classroom and start running until my legs couldn't carry me any further. Of course, this behaviour was noticed by my fellow schoolmates, but luckily no one ever asked about it. Fortunately, the teachers had all been informed about my past, and every time I seemed unfocused or ran out of the classroom, they understood, and they never punished me for it.

Somehow, it felt a little bit like World Vision again. Even though the outside world was hostile to me, in school people seemed to understand. Every week I had an appointment with Sophia to talk about my past, my progress and my future. She really was wonderful to me. She never got angry and she was always very patient. I started to fully trust her and then I became very open with her. We only talked about the war when I wanted to and when I was ready to talk about it. Otherwise she never asked. Sometimes she would help me with my homework and other times we would talk about nothing special. These were the conversations that I liked most. It wasn't long until I had told her almost everything about my past, even including the things that I hadn't dared to tell others, and somehow it comforted me. Every time we talked, no matter what topic, I felt better. Although the stories about the war always triggered nightmares, it felt good to share all this bad stuff with someone. The conversations actually helped me to focus and to concentrate more on the schoolwork. Slowly things were starting to get better.

My social life was also improving. Although people noticed my strange behaviour at times and they suspected that there was more to my story, I was not unusual here. There were so many former combatants in this school that neither my behaviour nor my treatment stood out. Even for the people who had never fought in the war, the vast majority of students had experienced it one way or the other. Everybody had some kind of war trauma. This shared trauma sometimes resulted in fierce fights between some students, but it also gave us a common identity and some strange feeling of belonging. Despite our unique individual experiences, we all had one shared goal: to forget about the past and to start concentrating on the future.

In the first few weeks, Odong introduced me to many of his friends. It wasn't long before I became a member of Odong's group, who were all Acholis. As some of them were former soldiers, they sometimes talked about the war. I would remain quiet or pretend to ask ignorant questions. Most of the time, however, we focused on the present and the future. We were always talking about girls, joking about things in the news, and the wonderful people we would become in the future. Most of our ultimate dreams were modest, ranging from being a farmer, a first-grade teacher, a policeman and an accountant, but there were two whose ambitions were a bit higher. One of the boys was certain that one day he would become the president of a liberated and independent South Sudan and we would always joke about it. Another guy wanted to be something called an astronaut. He had heard about this profession from an American aid worker, and ever since then he wanted to become the first Acholi to walk on the moon. When he first told me, I had never heard of the profession before and I didn't even know that there ever had been a man on the moon. The first thing

I did was to check this with Sister Sophia and to my great surprise she confirmed that it had happened sometime in the sixties. Every day I learned new things in this school, yet my own goal remained modest. I wanted to become an accountant for one of the white-man organisations that worked in Gulu, until the day that I would inherit my father's farm and become a farmer again.

As the months went by my English improved significantly. Thanks to the patience of Sister Sophia and the friendship with Odong and his friends, I was really starting to feel at ease in this school. This in turn affected my performance. While my first report was riddled with 'weaks', 'pull ups' and 'try harders', all the ones that followed showed significant improvement. My second report had a lot of 'fairs' and the last report of the year actually had quite a lot of 'goods'. While my performance in most topics was above average, I really excelled in English and economics. It was only in Arabic that I kept failing.

As my grades went up, so did my spirit. The location of the school was on the safe side of the River Nile and although the war in the north was raging more intensely than ever before, I rarely worried about it any more. We sometimes read the newspaper and when I saw reports of increased rebel activity in and around Gulu, I really worried about my family, but at least I didn't have to fear for my personal safety. Strangely, the Nile crossing was less than fifty kilometres away, but here we were, completely safe.

The longer I stayed in the school, the less often my memories went back to the bush. The nightmares continued, but they were becoming less frequent and I began to also experience happy dreams. Sometimes I was daydreaming during class and I imagined myself flirting with a girl or receiving my diploma at university. At those times I always had a smile on my face. I often joked with my friends, and we always had a lot of fun. Slowly, after many years of misery, I started to feel happy again.

It seemed like my years at the Blessed Damian School flew by much quicker than I had anticipated, and quicker than I liked. After several years I finished my primary level and afterwards Hervé Cheuzeville and Els De Temmerman paid for my Senior 1 and my Senior 2. During the holidays I mostly went back to my parents and sometimes to Hervé in Kampala. I especially liked the times that I hung out with my parents. The school affected my behaviour positively and my parents no longer feared me. After several holidays, they even let me be in charge of my siblings again. There were times that I wanted to join my dad at the farm, but he always strictly forbade me to go with him. He told me that he never wanted me to come close to the war again.

In the weeks that I spent in Gulu, and sometimes also in Kampala, I did interviews with Els De Temmerman. As she was paying my school fees, I started to trust her. I never told her my entire story, just the bits that I wanted to reveal.

It was also during my years in the Blessed Damian School that Hervé's contract with the World Food Programme ended and he was transferred to the AVSI Foundation as a programme manager for a landmine victim project. This meant that he moved from Kampala to Gulu town, although he maintained his house in Kampala. So whenever I went to Gulu in the holidays, I spent time with Hervé, and he even gave me a job as his gardener. During holiday breaks, while my parents were working in the fields, I made sure that Hervé's house was tidy. At the end of the working period, when my holiday came to an end, he always paid me some money and I always brought my salary to my parents immediately, who gladly accepted it.

The fact that I brought home some money really helped me in many ways, much more than Hervé could have ever guessed. Bringing home some money, although it wasn't much, meant that I mattered. Slowly people came to see me as a productive member of the society, rather than a mere child or worse, a rebel. Of course, the stigmatisation didn't stop overnight, but as I refrained from the use of violence, my status in the neighbourhood grew. The talking behind my back slowly dissipated and people started to appreciate me for who I was, not for what I had done. As I kept silent about my past, people slowly began to forget about it altogether. Not only did my status within society improve, but also within the family. When I was not working for Hervé, I was in full charge of my siblings again and my small contribution also helped my family to provide us with a bit more food. I really started to like the benefits of helping people and the appreciation I got.

I graduated in 2001 and afterwards I continued gardening at Hervé's house. Graduation day itself was among the best days in my life. Because of the war and the poverty, many of our parents, including mine, couldn't make it to our graduation. In a way I felt really bad that they couldn't be present, because I knew how extremely proud they would have been. But this didn't stop me from having fun.

After we received our diplomas, several friends and I sneaked out of the ceremony and we bought some small bottles of Ugandan Waragi, a very strong gin. I knew that the next day I would go back to Gulu, so this was my last day to spend with my Sudanese friends. Since the school was very religious, we did our drinking in the bush far from the school, where nobody could bother us. That evening was especially funny. At first everybody started talking about what they would do next and where they would go, but soon even the astronaut and the president couldn't manage to remain standing. This was the first time that I was really drunk, and man, I enjoyed it. By the time we got back to school I had real difficulty walking in a straight line and everything seemed ridiculously funny to me, even the disapproving eyes of the sisters and the teachers who saw us arriving late in the evening.

The next day, early in the morning, Sister Sophia awakened me and we had one last conversation. We mainly talked about my future and even though I had a headache, the conversation lifted me up even further. After our talk she wished me the best of luck in the rest of my life and she told me she would miss our conversations. As a last great act of compassion, she gave me the fare for the bus to Gulu and this was the last time I saw her.

As I entered Gulu, it was clear that a new phase of my life was unfolding in front of me. It was the end of 2001 and somehow the war wasn't as intense as it had been in the mid-nineties or the period during my captivity and after my escape. In the first months after my return, life was easy, and everything went the way it was supposed to. I shared my hut with my siblings and because the threat of the LRA had lessened, I didn't have to commute to the centre any more. Every day my parents woke up before dawn and in the morning, I would be in charge of feeding my siblings and taking them to school. Afterwards I would go to Hervé's house, where I made sure that the garden looked top notch. Hervé really helped me to settle down. He taught me how to cook and he always instructed me in a very friendly way how I should act and how to be a true gentleman. At the end of every month, Hervé gave me my salary, which really helped to improve the quality of our lives. After work I always hung out with my friends, including

Victor, who had moved from his village in Kitgum to Gulu Municipality. Sometimes we managed to get some money together and then we would get drunk on Waragi, but most of the time we just played football and joked about all sorts of things.

Most of my friends were from World Vision and shared similar pasts, but in a matter of weeks my group of friends extended to include people who had never been child soldiers, as we were now being called by all the NGOs. We weren't combatants or soldiers any more, but 'child soldiers', as if we were somewhat less than a soldier. When I came home after dark, I would have dinner with my family and afterwards I often enjoyed long conversations with my parents. Occasionally they asked me about the time I had spent in the bush, but we mostly avoided this topic. The months following my graduation were really nice. I did everything that I wanted, and nobody told me to do this or to do that.

One great surprise was that there were actually quite a number of former LRA high commanders living in Gulu who had taken advantage of the Amnesty Act and escaped from the LRA. The Amnesty Act was implemented by the Ugandan government in 2000, and it was meant to weaken the LRA from within. The act meant that any soldier or commander who returned from the LRA would receive a blanket amnesty. They broadcast the message for weeks on the radio until they were sure that it had reached the LRA camps in Sudan as well. It wasn't long after the broadcasts that the first commanders started to return. We would hear them on the radio, urging others to escape as well, and reporting that they were not being harmed and really had been forgiven.

Sometimes when I was walking in Gulu, I would meet former captains I had known very well when I was in the LRA, including people who had commanded me through the various missions in

Uganda, and I was reminded about these days. These men had been terrible killers, much worse than I ever was. They had done monstrous things against civilians. But now they walked freely among them. The Amnesty Act meant that they were forgiven, no matter what grave crimes they had ordered people like me to do. Although I remembered how these people used to treat us when I was still in the LRA, I was always friendly towards them. I always stopped to have a conversation with them, and they clearly remembered me as well. Had I met them two years earlier, they would have killed me and any relative of mine they could find for the act of escaping, but now we talked about the things that were in the news, the latest gossip, the places where one could find a good pork chop or a good barber, and sometimes we even talked about the war. At first it was strange to come across these men that I used to fear, but I got used to it very quickly. I didn't fear them any more. Here in civilian society we were equals. None of us had a rank, and no longer could they tell me what to do and what not to do.

In the first few months after I graduated my life was very enjoyable. I really felt like a rising star within my community, I was one of the few in my neighbourhood with an income, and I was gaining new friends by the day. Yet as my life entered a new era, so did the war. I still lived in a conflict zone and in the years following 2002, this would become painfully evident once more.

In March 2002 the UPDF started an offensive called Operation Iron Fist. The intent was to wipe out the LRA once and for all in a grand military campaign that would last for only three months. When I first heard about this, I couldn't help but laugh. Three months to end a war that had lasted for almost seventeen years was a ridiculous notion. For my entire life, the war had loomed over me like a dark shadow, and I refused to believe that it would end so easily. I really thought that somebody in the higher echelons of the Ugandan government had gone mad.

Earlier that year Museveni had managed to make the government of Sudan agree to stop supporting the LRA. As an act of faith and goodwill, Sudan allowed the Ugandan army to operate deep within Sudan to finally defeat the LRA. The governments managed to agree on a so-called 'Red Line of Operations', which allowed the UPDF to go all the way to Torit and Juba. This was in itself remarkable, as the war in northern Uganda and southern Sudan had partly been a proxy war between the governments of Sudan and Uganda, with both countries supporting their adversary's rebel movements, in a similar way as the Soviet Union and the United States had done during the Cold War. Yet it appeared that this era had now come to an end. Officially, the Sudanese government stopped supporting the LRA and as a result the LRA saw no other option but to call for a ceasefire, which was completely ignored by the Ugandan government. Instead, the UPDF decided that Kony would never agree to peace and they saw an opportunity to finish the job, deep in enemy territory.

Although I really wanted this war to end, I held a very ambiguous position towards this great offensive. As the newspapers started to herald the bravery of the Ugandan soldiers and their great successes in defeating Kony's strongholds, I couldn't help but recall the days when I had been a soldier myself. The LRA is made up of children who are forced to be soldiers against their will. Whenever the newspapers heralded another success, I thought about all those dead, putrefying bodies of girls and boys who had barely reached the age of ten. I had to think about the mothers who were fleeing with their babies in one arm and their gun in the other, while the bombs were falling all around them.

Despite all the stories about Kony's defeat in Kit Valley and in the Imatong Mountains, I knew one thing: Kony cannot be defeated. He can be weakened, yes. He can be pursued and hunted. But he will not be defeated. The Spirit Lakwena is strong and he always knows when the next attack will come. The Spirit knows all too well how to repel an attack or where to hide. While the articles reported that the UPDF had the winning hand, I knew that civilians were the ones who would suffer the consequences of this UPDF stupidity.

Whenever the UPDF or the SPLA attacked the LRA, we would retaliate against the civilians that they were supposed to protect in order to send our adversaries a clear message: *We can harm you more than you can ever harm us.* Even before our retaliation began, I already pitied the victims, just as I pitied the LRA soldiers whose hardships I knew. Although I had spent the worst years of my life in the LRA, I did feel sympathy for all those souls who would find their deaths during the offensive and the retaliations that would undoubtedly follow it.

The LRA was hit hard, that was clear. They fled from one base to another, until they had no bases left to fall back to. But I knew that the LRA didn't need a base. If necessity dictated, they could live in the bush and prey on the local population, which the UPDF systematically forgot. In any military campaign, the UPDF would concentrate fully on destroying the LRA, forgetting to protect all the civilians who lived in harm's way. The newspapers soon began to doubt whether the mission could be successful.

For sure, the LRA lost its bases in Sudan, but they were far from defeated. As the LRA withdrew deeper into Sudan, the UPDF pursued, causing tensions between the governments of Sudan and Uganda. It was not long before the LRA was so far into Sudan that they crossed the Juba–Torit red line. As a result, the UPDF supply line became stretched to its limit, making their military campaign difficult to sustain. They also had to be careful not to violate the agreement with Sudan.

For several months, we heard one success story after another, but we never saw the words that so many people were hoping for: 'Kony is captured, the war is at an end.' Instead, events unfolded exactly according to my predictions. The three months that were promised to end the war turned into six, and six months turned into a year. In the meantime, LRA forces started to trickle into Uganda again, carrying out brutalities on an unprecedented scale and reaching further than they had ever done before.

From 2002 till 2006 the war entered its worst phase of escalation. As I had anticipated, the LRA retaliated against the civilian population. To make up for the losses that they had sustained during Operation Iron Fist, they abducted young people at an incredible rate. One of the aims of the UPDF had always been to save the abducted children, but far more children were abducted in those years than they could ever rescue. Of all the tens of thousands of children who were abducted during the war, more than half of the abductions occurred during this phase. In the majority of cases, these children were never seen again. They were either killed or still serve the LRA today.

For the first time, the war reached other parts of Uganda, such as the southeastern parts of Lango and the Teso region, which had previously remained largely untouched. This led to an enormous surge in the numbers of internally displaced persons (IDPs). Once more, Radio Kabi was broadcasting overtime and there was not a day that went by that we didn't hear new stories of brutal massacres.

On 15 June 2003 the LRA entered the Teso regions and in its wake, Local Defence Units (LDUs) sprang up everywhere. The first to have successes against the LRA were the Arrow Boys, but success came at a high cost. Although initially they were very poorly equipped and also largely made up of units of young boys, as their name suggested, the government started to arm them. As a result, they managed to make LRA operations in that part of the country very difficult. In Lira District a local defence unit called Amuka, the Luo word for rhinoceros, was also beginning to cause problems for the LRA.

Newspaper articles, once heralding the UPDF, started to criticise Operation Iron Fist. The damage reports did not live up to Museveni's promise to end the war – quite the contrary. Within a year of the start of Iron Fist, the number of IDPs had doubled, areas previously left untouched by the war were now embroiled in it, the rate of abductions had never been as high, and never had there been so many deaths to mourn as in the year 2003.

In the following year the situation grew even worse. In February 2004, Okot Odhiambo, one of the leading figures within the LRA, commanded a massacre in Barlonyo that was even worse than the one in 1995, when Vincent Otti, then deputy leader of the LRA, burned Atiak to the ground, killing more than 200 members of his own clan. Only half a day after the Barlonyo massacre, reports from Radio Kabi and the official media started to appear. Barlonyo was an IDP camp in Lira that was under the defence of the Amuka boys. They proved to be no match for a full LRA battalion. At around five in the evening, the LRA began bombing the camp. We heard stories that the camp was defended by about forty to sixty Amuka members, who had bravely stood up against Odhiambo. Being outnumbered and outgunned, they were quickly overrun. What followed was a terrible onslaught. Rebels executed people on a massive scale and afterwards they set the entire place ablaze. In the carnage over 300 IDPs were killed. Then, as suddenly as the attack had begun, Odhiambo gave the order to retreat, long before the first UPDF soldiers managed to reach the camp.

Not long after, on 19 May 2004, another large massacre took place in Lukodi, less than twenty kilometres outside Gulu. The LRA had surrounded Lukodi camp with hundreds of soldiers, making sure that nobody was able to escape. They looted the huts and killed the people who tried to run away. A group of men and women were assembled who were abducted with the sole purpose to carry away all the looted goods. In less than an hour the LRA were on their way again. As they left, they set the camp ablaze, making sure the flames killed all those who were still alive. In this onslaught, fifty-three people were killed. When they were finally at their destination, all the male abductees were executed. Massacres like these continued throughout the year.

As the rebels infested Acholiland, my siblings and I were again forced to commute to the centre of town every evening to spend our nights on the verandas. We slept without mosquito nets and on mattresses that would become soaking wet during the rainy season. As the war intensified, I left the happy years of the Blessed Damian and the months following my graduation behind me. The atmosphere in Gulu became extremely tense. People began to discriminate against the former rebels again, especially the ones who had returned recently. Luckily for me, it had been years since my escape, and I knew perfectly well how to behave among the civilians. The stigma other rebels carried was not applied to me. Every day new rebels returned, causing a lot of suspicion among the people of Gulu. The friendliness that I had experienced during the months after my graduation slowly disappeared.

As the war intensified, my parents went less often to our fields, which meant that we were slowly growing hungry again. By now, I was twenty years old and in any normal circumstances, I would be earning a living or going to university, but the war once more paralysed life in the northern part of Uganda. The food supply to the markets dropped, prices went up drastically and some NGOs even closed their offices, as they could no longer go into the field. Although I continued to work for Hervé, my movement became restricted.

It was also during this time that the Ugandan army started to harass people. People were being arrested on a massive scale and detained for months without trial or justification. A curfew was established that prohibited movement after a certain time. Those who moved around after the curfew were seen as rebels and were arrested, or sometimes even shot. My suspicion of the UPDF had never ceased, so I tried to limit my movement as much as possible, meaning that I wasn't able to continue to go to Hervé every day. During these years the UPDF started to encounter heavy losses. As a large section of the UPDF remained in Sudan, they were unable to defend the entire north and this gave Kony the opportunity to spread havoc.

I still met my friends now and then, but our meetings were always short, as there were new regulations in Gulu prohibiting assembly. The one person I still met pretty often was Victor. Every time we met, we talked about the dire situation of those people who had only recently managed to escape the LRA. They were really treated badly. Because the rehabilitation centres were overcrowded with new escapees, their guidance was generally very poor. As soon as they left a rehabilitation centre, they entered a very hostile world where they were left to fend for themselves. There was nobody telling them how to behave and how to deal with their problems in a non-violent way. The more Victor and I talked about it, the more we realised that something needed to be done to help these poor people.

We noticed that there were many NGOs in northern Uganda, yet none of them employed former child soldiers or managed to do something for them in a constructive and lasting way. The more often Victor and I met, the more we came to realise that we needed to start an organisation that would help other child soldiers. We believed that as former combatants ourselves, we were the best ones to fully understand and help.

It was also during this period that we met some Dutch people who recorded a documentary about some of us and our stories, after having been inspired by the book *Aboke Girls* by Els De Temmerman. One of them was Maaike Engels, who recorded a documentary about us called *Strictly Eighteen*. We presented our desire to establish an organisation to help former child soldiers, and it was she who helped us in setting it up.

It was in the early months of 2004, at the same time that Kony was wreaking his worst havoc, that we founded an NGO called the War Affected Children Association (WACA). Initially we had very little funding, but nevertheless we did manage to make a real difference for many escapees. One of the first things we did was to start registering people. Before long we had registered 1,898 members, all former combatants in the LRA. Initially we had nine members on the executive board and all of us had a past in the LRA. We had all managed to escape in the mid- to late nineties and therefore we had all experienced how difficult life can be when you first return to civilisation.

With the help of Maaike we managed to rent an office and set up a computer centre. Using old computers donated from the Netherlands, we taught the escapees how to use them, so that they would at least gain some skills that could come in handy later in their lives. Apart from the computer centre, we also supported little microfinancing initiatives based on an idea that actually came from another group of former child soldiers we were working with.

It was during the registrations at WACA that we came into contact with this group. It was made up of twenty former child soldiers who each had a very small business from which they managed to earn about half a dollar a day, if not less. Nevertheless, the group came up with the idea that they would try to save a few shillings a day that would be put into the group's savings. This group met every week, and during the meetings, all the group members would put 100 or 200 shillings into a pot. Every week one member of this group would borrow this amount, so that he or she could extend his or her business. In this way everybody in the group got the opportunity to invest in their business and expand it without acquiring a loan from the bank or seeking the help of outside organisations. Once we saw the brilliant way this practice worked with one group, we started to teach other groups how to do this. At first we focused mainly on groups operating in Gulu town, as it was too dangerous to go further, but later we started to take the risk of visiting groups in camps nearby too.

On several occasions we also managed to get sufficient funds to buy food to distribute among our members in the camps surrounding Gulu, as it was the former child soldiers in these kinds of camps that suffered most from the food shortages. Although the distribution of food was really the work of the World Food Programme, their aid did not always reach the people in most need of it. This is not to criticise what the WFP has done for the people of northern Uganda, but in the camps the former child soldiers stood on the lowest step of the social ladder, and by the time the food provided by the WFP was distributed, there was very little left for them.

This situation also clearly resonated during the needs assessment, which we conducted at the same time as registering people. It was the young women who had returned from the LRA with children who suffered the most. As they returned, raped, and either pregnant or accompanied by a baby or toddler, society collectively turned its back. The general perception was that they had indulged in sinful behaviour, either willingly or not. The girls who returned from the LRA pregnant or with children were believed to be unfit for marriage. They were social outcasts who had lost their value, since their parents could no longer claim a dowry. These girls often found themselves rejected by the community and even their own families.

On some occasions, parents were willing to accept back their daughter, but not the grandchild she had brought back with her. In these cases, the girls had the difficult choice of either abandoning their child and letting it die, or trying to survive without the support of their families. For sure, some girls made the painful decision to desert their baby to secure their own existence, but most couldn't bear the thought of this. Even though their child was the direct result of months and sometimes years of sexual abuse, it was still theirs; and even though they had been trained to kill, they couldn't harm their own offspring. Because of this severe stigmatisation, these women lived in abysmal circumstances, often in extreme hunger and abject poverty. At times, they weren't even able to breastfeed their own children as their bodies did not have enough nutrients to produce milk, and quite a number of children died from malnutrition. With the funds we received from compassionate people in the Netherlands and Belgium, we were able to distribute some food to help these poor mothers, which might have meant the difference between life and death for their babies.

Even though these were some of the visible successes we logged in the first year of our operation, our main success was invisible. Apart from the computer centre, the microfinancing projects and the food distribution, our main task was to give peer counselling. Many of the new escapees had great difficulty adapting to civilian life and they caused a lot of problems. It was something of a downward spiral in which they found themselves, very similar to my own situation. The moment they returned, their behaviour became very violent, partly as a result of the discrimination they encountered from the local population. Whenever they acted violently, the bias of the local population was confirmed, which led to further discrimination and further violence. The other staff members at WACA had been through the same ordeal.

Although it had taken me several years, in the end I could talk from experience on how to reverse this negative spiral. I counselled people that the key was self-control. Whenever somebody is finger-pointing at you, you have to ignore it. When people are talking badly about you, treat them kindly. When you want to destroy, go for a walk and turn your aggression towards a tree or some other thing, but not at other people or their possessions or their animals. Our office was a place where people could tell their story, and they had several pairs of ears that would listen and could understand. When people needed to cry their lungs out, our office was the place where they could do so. When people wanted to laugh, we welcomed them. Even though the direct effects of this endeavour were largely invisible, we met many former child soldiers who were really grateful to us.

Every day, child soldiers came to our office to tell us their stories. Some even came from places far away, like Opit or Awach. By the time they left our office, they were always happy that they could tell their story without being judged and without being pitied in a patronising way. We listened, we understood, and we gave them good advice. Often we used our own stories as examples. Of course, we could not change their lives in a single visit, but every time we gave them counselling, their own behaviour became less aggressive, which resulted in more acceptance by the community.

Thus, while hell was reigning all around us in those dreadful years from 2002 till 2005, we managed to do some good. Once we founded WACA, I became so busy that I gave up my work for Hervé. I started to work full time for WACA. As I had envisioned during my years in the Blessed Damian, I had indeed become an accountant for one of the aid organisations, even though my dream had never included the possibility that the organisation would be my own. Despite all of the suffering and the hardships the work involved, I always felt proud when I walked to our office each morning. We had each climbed up out of our miserable situation following our escape, and now we were able to give the escapees the help that we ourselves had needed so much a few years earlier.

Although I was doing a lot of good, giving up my job with Hervé meant that I didn't have an income any more. The WACA funds were generally quite low, so we couldn't be paid wages for the hard work we did: all our work was voluntary. Despite my years of deprivation, the busy work with WACA caused time to fly by. My life took on a normal routine. In the morning I would return home with my siblings, hoping that my parents had managed to get enough food to allow us a breakfast. Often this wasn't the case, but there was always the hope. If my parents went to the field, I would leave my siblings with our neighbours and I would walk to the centre, where I worked throughout the day. The work consisted mostly of counselling in the early years, but I also had to do the accounting, reconciling our income with our expenses, and keeping the budgets. Whenever we received funding, usually from the Netherlands, and later also from supportive groups within Uganda, I would be really busy. On top of my other work, I also helped with buying the food and organising transportation, something that was very difficult during the war years. After work I always went back to my home, where we had some dinner with my parents. Later I would take a mattress and commute with my siblings to the city centre where we would spend the night.

With the stream of people entering our office, new stories came to us on a daily basis and soon our office became a central hub of Radio Kabi. We heard so many rumours of terrible things that sometimes at night I would just cry over all the misery in our country. If we were indeed the chosen people, as Kony always used to tell us, then why was God testing us so much? My busy schedule during the daytime meant that I had little time to think back about my own war experiences, but at night, when everything was quiet and the people around me were asleep, all the images came back to me, triggered by the terrible stories that had deeply entered my mind from the new escapees. I always hated the night, not because I was afraid of the dark, but I was afraid of the silence and the idleness. Most of all, I was afraid of the images of war and the spirits of the dead that came to haunt me.

When I was awake, I would often become sad by remembering what I had been through in my life. When I slept, my nightmares were getting worse because of the situation surrounding Gulu. I still suffered from my sleeping disorder, which meant that during the daytime I could doze off in a matter of seconds. Despite the heavy workload at WACA, my colleagues would often find me deeply asleep over the accounting books. At those times they made fun of me and when I finally woke up, I laughed with them. But deep inside I felt how my sleeping disorder was really disturbing my biological clock.

Little less than a year after we founded WACA, in January 2005, something happened that would have a profound impact on our war. Even before the insurgency in northern Uganda began, the people of southern Sudan had risen up against their Muslim government, which wanted to introduce Sharia law to its mainly Christian population in the south. After having suffered years of harassment by the Khartoum government and the Arabic militias they sponsored, the people of the south stood up and initiated the largest rebellion that has ever unfolded in Africa. The war that followed was as devastating as the war in Uganda, with the main difference being that the rebel movements of southern Sudan finally became a great success. In early 2005, the government of Sudan realised that it could no longer sustain the fighting. Their battle had come to a stalemate years earlier, and even though neither side had any big victories, the losses suffered on both sides were immense.

In January 2005 the warring parties signed a comprehensive peace agreement, which would give the SPLA some autonomy to govern the south of Sudan. This had a great effect on the LRA and, therefore, the war in northern Uganda. Even though the Sudanese government had officially stopped arming the LRA in 2002, it was clear that the LRA remained well armed during 2003 and 2004. But after the comprehensive peace agreement, it became almost impossible for Sudan to continue supplying the LRA without gravely violating the peace agreement. The peace deal also meant that southern Sudan was now governed by the SPLA and all the troops of north Sudan withdrew from the battlefield. This meant that the LRA could no longer maintain their bases in Sudan.

But the LRA kept on fighting and slaughtering. Throughout northern Uganda, Kony's soldiers had hidden large stockpiles of weapons and ammunition, which enabled them to keep up the war effort for a while longer. Throughout 2005 massacres continued to occur, even in the vicinity of Gulu town. Without the support of the Sudanese government and the loss of its safe havens, however, the LRA was unable to maintain the intensity of the preceding terrible years. Slowly Kony was losing ground. As the ammunition stock-piles ran down and the resistance of the Local Defence Units and UPDF intensified, especially in the Teso and Lango sub-regions, the LRA faced increased difficulties in sustaining their war effort.

Museveni had made an effort to fully arm the Arrow Boys and Amuka, and at a growing rate, the once disorganised militias started to win their battles. It was on 29 September 2005 that the last LRA commander died at the hands of the Arrow Boys at Iyal-akwe. Initially, Radio Kabi and the national media reported that it was Brigadier Dominic Ongwen who had been killed, one of the highest commanders, who I knew very well, but later it appeared that this was a lie to boost morale. But no matter who this commander was, his death marked the end of LRA activity in Teso.

After that, the retreat from Lango sub-region also became imminent. The Arrow Boys had shown that the LRA could be defeated in battle and this inspired the Amuka in Lango. Soon afterwards the LRA also started to sustain losses in Lira and Apac District, and they were forced to retreat from Lango as well. Even though there were still many pockets operating in Acholiland, they no longer had the strength to penetrate Gulu, which was now heavily fortified by the UPDF.

As the war lost its intensity in the last few months of 2005, the atmosphere in Gulu was slowly improving. I stopped commuting to the city centre with my siblings at night, and somehow I felt safe enough to stay on the edge of town. The schools opened again, and businesses slowly started to flourish. We began to realise that the years of real hardship might come to an end, and people began to pick up their lives again.

It was also during this year that another dream of mine came true. Thanks to the book *Aboke Girls*, Els De Temmerman was able to find some sponsors to pay for my university degree. When Els came to me to tell me this news, I was as excited as a small puppy. Four years earlier, it would have been utterly inconceivable for me to receive a university degree and now this opportunity was in reach.

I started my studies in accounting at Makerere University's regional centre in Gulu. It was a part-time study programme and most of my classes were at the weekends, making my life even more demanding than it already was. On the weekends and in the evenings, I studied, and during the weekdays I worked at the office. Escapees were returning every day, and with the improved security situation, we were also able to visit the camps more often.

While I was fully focused on my studies and my work for WACA, the LRA was in search of a new home. Sometime in September 2005 we saw in the newspapers that Vincent Otti, one of the most senior LRA commanders, had crossed into Congo, where he sought political asylum for the LRA. In the weeks following the LRA's decision to go into Congo, tensions between the governments of Uganda and Congo flared up, as the UPDF wanted to pursue the LRA deep into Congolese territory without the consent of its government. International pressure kept Uganda from following the LRA, and considering the horrific backfiring of Operation Iron Fist, we were all happy about this.

In 2006, the war completely lost its impetus. By then, the rebels operated in groups of a few fighters, and even though we still heard stories of terrible killings taking place in rural areas, the LRA at large no longer posed a serious threat. It was during this year that the remainder of the LRA crossed the Sudan-Congo border. With that move the war virtually came to an end. In August 2006 Vincent Otti declared a unilateral ceasefire, and to show that the LRA was serious about this, they withdrew from northern Uganda.

Kony saw no other option but to suspend operations and move to the Democratic Republic of the Congo (DRC). There the government was fighting numerous rebellion movements and couldn't be bothered with the LRA, as long as they stayed far away from the mineral mines. In the safety of Garamba National Park they started peace talks mediated by Riek Machar, the new vice president of South Sudan.

During the years that followed, happiness truly returned to my life. The curfews of the UPDF were lifted and once more we were allowed to assemble in public places. As the situation normalised, we started to mourn our missing and our dead. I started to meet up with my friends and the Ugandan Waragi occasionally started to flow in my veins. When I was not studying, sleeping or working, I hung out with my friends, and although all of us had lost relatives and endured the appalling years of 2003 to 2004, we managed to smile again. If this war had taught us Acholis one thing, it was that life continues, no matter what has happened in the past.

As the years went by, WACA was slowly growing into a professional organisation. Postwar rebuilding began, and our services continued to be required. In Acholiland, many people remained in the IDP camps, as they expected the war to return any moment. This meant that people remained hungry. As before, it was the former child soldiers who suffered the most. In WACA we started to educate the communities about what had been done to former members of the LRA, and make them aware of the effects of stigmatisation.

Everywhere in and around Gulu, our members started to organise themselves into community-based groups. They quickly learned that as former child soldiers, they stood much stronger together. In a group, they could help their weakest members to become strong and, above all, they would always have a group of friends who would understand where they were coming from. The groups started to write songs, and to perform dances and plays that, besides being fun and entertaining, also served to make the community aware of LRA members' histories and the way they were being treated by the civilian population. Slowly these efforts started to bear fruit.

After peace had prevailed for several months, people once more dared to go to the fields – some distance from the IDP camps – to start growing their own food. By early 2007, some people started to believe in the peace talks and returned to their villages. Soon others started to follow. Although northern Uganda was ravaged by the war and remained one of the poorest regions on earth, people were slowly picking up their lives again.

But of course, many hardships remained. The life in the IDP camps was hard and bleak. Drought, disease and floods continued to affect the population. Harvests failed and the seeds that people had somehow managed to collect got spoiled. As a result, children and elders continued to die because of malnutrition. Many people remained idle and there was a lot of alcohol abuse in the camps. These factors caused men to mistreat their women; rates of domestic and gender-based violence soared. In the IDP camps disease was rampant. The virus that people feared most was Ebola, which had broken out in 2005 near Gulu town. Even though this was the scariest of them all, other diseases killed too. Typhoid, cholera and malaria continued to claim many lives, especially within the camps because of the terrible hygiene situation and malnutrition. In addition, the number of people infected with HIV/AIDS was high in northern Uganda, among the highest in the country. Nevertheless life was slowly improving for most of us.

Throughout 2007 people continued to move back to their villages. Cows started to reappear on the Acholi landscape and extreme hunger slowly became a relic of the past. Cultural traditions that were lost in the war started to re-emerge – I saw people dancing the Larakaraka and elders telling stories around the campfire. The sounds of traditional songs that I hadn't heard in a very long time floated in the air.

At the end of the year, we collectively celebrated Christmas for the first time in ages. This was really wonderful. I spent Christmas Eve with my extended family and for the festivities we had slaughtered several ducks. The food was accompanied by beer and

Ugandan Waragi, which made the general atmosphere very cheery. This was so beautiful. The next day everyone in Gulu went to church. It was the first Christmas sermon that was full of hope. It had been peaceful now for one and a half years and slowly people started to believe that the peace would last.

From 2008 my life started to transform. I managed to let my old life go and embrace the future. The numerous interviews carried out for the writing of this book played an important role in my recovery process. Never before had I recounted my story in such detail, and usually the episodes I spoke about during the interviews came back to me in my sleep in all their horrible details. However, several weeks after I recorded the last interview, I noticed that the bad dreams slowly started to disappear, and also that my anger and trauma lessened. While I was telling my story, memories that I had suppressed but not forgotten came back to me and this must have helped me to come to terms with my past. It is a strange thing, but thinking back about my past and sharing it with others, I kept on forgetting. By visualising my past, I was able to give my suppressed memories a place. Of course, I will never forget what happened, but I managed to rid the memories of bad feelings and of trauma.

That year I went back to many of the locations where my story took place. I visited the place where I was abducted, the village where my colleagues almost shot me, St Mary's College in Aboke, and several of the massacre sites in Kitgum and other districts. In Kitgum I managed to find the cave where I hid during my escape and the LRA's long search. I had hoped to find all the things there that I had left behind so long ago, but someone had taken them. I even crossed the border of Uganda and Sudan to visit both Palu-taka and Pajok. Walking around these areas rekindled memories that had been deeply suppressed.

In Palutaka I could still see the ravages of the battle so long ago. The rusting ruins of the tanks and the mambas that had been blown up thirteen years earlier were still there. A close look revealed many empty shells on the ground. As I saw these things, flashes of memories came back to me. I once more saw the hordes of enemies coming towards me. I remembered the explosions in which the tanks and the mambas were blown up.

A few days later I visited Pajok and crossed the river in which I had seen several of my former colleagues drown. I remembered the white mercenaries that we fought there. It all came back to me in vivid detail. At the time I found it very difficult to let my mind dwell on my past. However, it was exactly this remembrance that cured me. As I visited these places, I was finally able to let the bad memories rest, to give them a special place, as some might say.

My friends helped me a lot. Out of all the former child soldiers working for WACA, I think I was the most traumatised. I was the only one who suffered from occasional depression, rage attacks and chronic insomnia. Of the three of my best friends there, I was the only one who still couldn't handle large crowds of people. This was also one of the reasons why I never went out clubbing. Too many people always made me aggressive.

Victor and another close friend called Richard, who was one of the members of WACA and who had served as Odhiambo's bodyguard, helped me to move through this. They always gave me advice, they were always ready to listen, and whenever I felt depressed, they were there to cheer me up. The three of us could always talk and we even managed to laugh out loud about some of the silly things we had encountered. My story about the bees is a constant source of amusement. Richard joined me when I went to visit the places of my story and, together with him, I managed to talk about what happened there. All of this helped me to get over my traumas.

Other things in my life also improved. On 23 May 2008 I managed to finish my diploma in strategic procurement and logistics management at Makerere University, Gulu Branch. Ten years earlier I had been a highly traumatised kid with behavioural problems and an uncertain future. Now I held my university diploma as one of the very few in northern Uganda, and I had founded and was managing an NGO. I found a wonderful girlfriend who deeply cared for me, and with whom I could also share my dreadful memories. My father gave me a considerable piece of land and I went back to the village, where I built a hut and cultivated the land. I was really starting to build up my own independent life and it felt good.

At WACA things also started to go really well. Our years of hard labour and voluntary work started to pay off. An organisation in the Netherlands managed to secure funds for a traditional agricultural project, which we implemented. With the Uganda Women's Finance Trust and funding from an Irish organisation called Trócaire we also trained over forty groups of former child soldiers and war victims in savings and loan concepts.

The humanitarian agency CARE International took an interest in our organisation and started a huge project with us called Hope: Harnessing Opportunity to Protect and End violence. It was mostly built around microfinancing and vocational skills training. Because of this project I became coordinator in Patiko sub-county, for which I received a small but decent salary. It was my job to train the community in village savings and loan associations and to train groups in selection, planning and management. Because of this job I spent most of my days in Patiko sub-county. Up to that point, I had almost forgotten the virtue of rural community life, the freedom and the helpfulness of the people around. It felt wonderful to help other war victims and to be embedded in a rural community once more. Every weekend I returned to my own land on my brand-new bicycle, which bears the name Prado Two-By-Two, to see how my harvest was doing and to visit my girlfriend. In November 2008 I brought in my first harvest of cassava, which I managed to sell at a good price.

The year 2009 was even better. My job at WACA continued, which meant that most of the time I was posted in Patiko and that I had a steady income. With the money from this job combined with my first harvest I bought one she-calf, several turkeys, twelve chickens and some ducks. I also bought two pigs, but this was mainly for my own joy, as pigs always make me happy because of the constant smile on their faces. I bought some more land and even though there was a bad drought, I managed to plant and cultivate some good crops. With my income, the profit from my harvest and the help of my family, I even managed to get a dowry together, and in October 2009 I married my girlfriend.

This was another defining moment. Marriage meant manhood, and now that I had a family of my own, it was my responsibility to feed and protect them. Even though my wife didn't really need my protection in her job as a policewoman, it was a nice responsibility to carry anyway. No longer was I a boy, and with this symbolic notion, I managed to let the boy soldier inside me disappear.

Two months after we married, on 1 December 2009, Emily gave birth to the most beautiful creature I had ever seen. We called our baby boy Lovis Arthur. Lovis Arthur had all my features and I fell in love with my baby from the moment I first laid eyes on him. As a proud father I showed off my child to all my family members and my friends, and I organised a big party to celebrate Lovis's birth.

During this party I made a promise to Lovis. I promised him that at all times he would get all the love and opportunity that I could possibly provide him and I promised him that he would never have to go through what I had been through. I am planning to keep this promise.

December 2009 was the happiest month in my life. Three weeks after the birth of Lovis, we celebrated a fourth peaceful Christmas in Acholiland. Besides celebrating the birth of Jesus, we celebrated the achievements of the Acholi people, who had rebuilt the country at an amazing pace since the end of the war. We were thankful that the prospects for the future of northern Uganda looked very bright. Where there used to be nothing but bush, gardens were flourishing, and severe, chronic malnutrition was a thing of the past. Even victims and perpetrators started to reconcile their differences. On New Year's Eve I went to celebrate in the clubs in town for the first time in my life. It was also the first time that I saw fireworks. All the clubs in town joined in the celebration with some really nice fireworks to announce the New Year. I realised then that gunpowder could also be used for good things. I spent that whole night in Havana Club, where I kept on dancing and drinking until very early in the morning. My fear of crowds had completely disappeared and this was one of the happiest nights in my life.

When I woke up the next day, I couldn't help but recall that it was exactly the same day, fifteen years earlier, that my true hell had begun and that my life was changed irreversibly. I wondered what would have happened in my life if I had decided to tag along with my mother on her trip to the market. For sure, if I had done so, I wouldn't have been abducted that day. But what was there to say that it wouldn't have happened at a later date, or that I wouldn't have been killed in those years as a powerless civilian? The only thing I know is that it did happen. I was abducted, I was a soldier and I have witnessed and done terrible things. I know that I will have to live with this for the rest of my life. No matter what, the memories will never disappear and also the nightmares will continue to haunt me for the rest of my life, even though they occur less often now than they did several years ago.

What has been done cannot be changed and even if it could, I don't know whether I want it to change. The story of the LRA is a part of my life. It made me into who I am today. I am a loving father now, a husband to a wonderful wife, and a satisfied employee of WACA. Every day of my life I can choose to improve the lives of others, first and foremost that of my son and wife, but also those of others who have suffered in the same way as I have. This is the thing that makes me happy now.

The most important reason why I have told this story is to make sure that my children will read it when they are old enough so that they can learn about the consequences of war and the value of peace. However, I will keep the promise that I gave Lovis Arthur and I will extend this promise to any future children. They will never learn it from first-hand experience as I did. I hope that this book will help people to understand the effects of war and make a contribution to a peaceful society. Let us all pray that the story you have just read will one day be a story of the past, no longer applicable to the modern world.

On the Fates of the People in this Book

More than two decades have passed since Norman Okello returned from LRA captivity. Despite significant instability in South Sudan that has brought a large influx of refugees, northern Uganda is relatively peaceful. Throughout this book, many individuals have been introduced. Like Norman, the people mentioned in this book are real and so are their stories.

In this epilogue I want to reflect on what happened to some of these individuals. In the years after Norman's return and even up to now, Norman still receives information regarding his former 'colleagues', as he calls them. For some people, including Norman's family, Hervé Cheuzeville, Victor Oloya and Kaunda Kenneth, the information we have is very reliable because Norman is still in contact with them, either in person or via email.

Norman's colleagues and commanders in the LRA

CAPTAIN OJARA was the man who abducted Norman and ordered his caning on the first day of his abduction. While Norman initially saw him as his personal nemesis, he grew attached to the man over time and he thinks that the military training he offered saved his life. Norman says that Ojara acted like a father figure, and while he was a brutal man, he was kind to his soldiers. Ojara's fate is described in the chapter 'The Girls of Aboke': he was shot in his belly after the girls were abducted. He died on the way to the sickbay from blood loss. Norman mourned his death.

MZEE was Norman's unit commander. He was the one who told Norman the stories about the history of the LRA and about Alice Lakwena. It is uncertain what happened to Mzee. Norman has heard two contradicting rumours about him. The first was that he got shot during Operation Iron Fist and died from his wounds. Norman heard this from a former colleague who was in the same brigade as he was. However, another of his former colleagues, who was in another unit in the same brigade, said that Mzee survived the bullet wound and that he was promoted to captain. Norman says that if this is the case and he is still alive today, then he has definitely been upgraded to the rank of major or higher.

NYEKO was the lieutenant who was on the verge of killing Norman when Brigade Major Oyet stopped him. Nyeko was shot with an RPG in Uganda. The blast broke his leg and several bomb splinters entered it. His leg was shattered, and lacking the medical equipment needed to treat him properly, the LRA doctors wanted to amputate it. Nyeko refused, saying he would kill anyone who touched his leg. Not long afterwards, his wounds got infected and he developed gangrene. He died an agonising death. Norman did not mourn him.

COMMANDER LANGOLE was Norman's other nemesis. He had also tried to kill Norman and was stopped by a superior commander, Wall Okot. When Wall Okot died from a severe illness, Langole was intent on killing Norman by sending him to the most dangerous spots in the frontline. Norman heard from a credible source that Commander Langole was killed in the Congo during combat. He doesn't know the specific date or location.

COMMANDER AGIRA was the leading commander of the mission to abduct the Aboke Girls, and the one who talked with Sister Rachelle after the Aboke mission. Norman said that Agira was a very dangerous man. He could kill people while smiling broadly, free of guilt and remorse. Agira died on the same day as Brigade Major Oyet, who saved Norman's life when Nyeko was trying to kill him. They died in Sudan during an attack on SPLA barracks that went horribly wrong. It was an attack in which the ambushers became the ambushed. As the two senior commanders of the attack, they were at the centre of the main body when an artillery barrage hit them and they died. Again, this story reached Norman through escapees who had been in that specific battle and who witnessed the deaths of both men.

COMMANDER OCAN led Stockree Brigade's artillery unit. He was the one who told Norman the LRA's rules after the opening speech by Raska Lukwiya on Norman's arrival in Palutaka. Ocan died in Kitgum District. He had gone to Kitgum to hide some weapons in

Padwat game reserve, when he walked into an ambush. Norman heard the story from other escapees who were in the same unit. He does not know the specific year or location.

ANYING, AYAA AND CHRISTINE, the three wives of Mzee, all escaped, Anying and Christine accompanied by their children. Norman has met Anying a number of times and she has been the source of much of the information on the fates of other LRA combatants mentioned above. Anying was in LRA captivity for a very long time and had a really difficult time readjusting to civilian life, where, as a woman, she is expected to be respectful and obedient to men. Nonetheless, she is doing fine. What exactly happened with Ayaa and Christine is unclear, but according to Anying, they are well.

ARTILLERY TRAINING RECRUITS: Norman was one out of twenty participants in the specialised military and artillery training in Juba. While Norman doesn't have the details of all twenty, he knows the fate of the five that were placed in Stockree Brigade. Of the five, three have died. As far as Norman knows, one is still in the LRA. He should have had the rank of captain by now. Norman is the only one who escaped.

VICTOR OLOYA is the boy with a severely wounded arm whom Norman met after his escape. Victor is doing well and today he continues to live in Gulu with his daughter. In 2004, Victor and Norman started the War Affected Children Association (WACA) and both worked tirelessly to help other ex-LRA combatants to readapt to civilian life. As the chairperson, Victor played an important role in the lives of many returnees. WACA ceased to exist in 2011, mostly because funding ran out, but also because it outlived its purpose, considering the few returnees as of 2011. After WACA closed down, Victor worked as a research assistant for dozens of university students and occasionally for journalists and PhD researchers, and continues to be available as a translator and research assistant.

LAMSON AND VINCENT were the two boys who came back from the bush after Victor Oloya. They were both from Stockree Brigade and Norman knew them well. The last Norman heard is that Lamson lives in Pajule, not far from Kitgum town, while Vincent is in Patiko, not far from Gulu town. However, Norman is not in contact with them any more.

The LRA top commanders

RASKA LUKWIYA was the brigadier general of Stockree Brigade when Norman was abducted, and at the time was one of the highest-ranking officers in the LRA. After Norman escaped, his star continued to rise. He was promoted to deputy army commander and later to army commander, the third-highest position after Joseph Kony and Vincent Otti. His ranking earned him a place on the International Criminal Court (ICC) 'most wanted' list, and in June 2005 the ICC issued an arrest warrant against him, charging him for war crimes and abduction of children. Lukwiya no longer needs to worry about this indictment. He died in clashes between the UPDF and the LRA in August 2006, after a ceasefire agreement had already taken effect.

VINCENT OTTI, deputy leader of the LRA, was rumoured to have been killed in October 2007 during a High Command meeting that Kony had convened at his base camp in Garamba. Allegedly, Otti was executed because there was a disagreement between him and Kony over the peace process. It is said that Otti initiated the peace process. Other rumours hold that Otti had plotted to kill Kony, and that he had been executed when this plan was unveiled. The LRA Crisis Tracker* claims that Kony hid in the house of his chief security officer while Okot Odhiambo oversaw the execution of Vincent Otti and other commanders loyal to him.

OKOT ODHIAMBO was rumoured to have died in late 2013 from wounds suffered during a clash between LRA forces and Ugandan troops. His body was exhumed in the Central African Republic on 20 March 2015. Odhiambo enforced the execution of Vincent Otti, and he took his place as second-in-command afterwards. He allegedly reorganised LRA's command structure and, after Otti's death, set up a new military base fifty kilometres east of Camp Swahili in Garamba National Park. Following operation Lightning Thunder in 2009, which was the UPDF's offensive against the LRA in the northeastern Democratic Republic of the Congo, Odhiambo was among the first to move into the Central African Republic, where he met his end.

DOMINIC ONGWEN was apprehended in 2014 by American forces after he had defected and surrendered. Handed over to the ICC, he made his first appearance before the court on 26 January 2015. On 23 March the ICC confirmed the seventy charges brought against him and committed him to trial, which began on 6 December

---

* The Crisis Tracker is a mapping tool that makes information on LRA attacks (and those of other armed groups operating in the same region) and other activities publicly available through a digital map, a news feed and other media.

2016, and is still ongoing at the time of writing in late 2019. The trial against Dominic Ongwen is unique, because, like Norman, Dominic was abducted when he was still a child and he worked his way up through the ranks, the main feature that his defence is based on. Of the five LRA commanders indicted by the ICC in 2005, Ongwen is the only one to appear before the ICC.

JOSEPH KONY'S fate remains shrouded in mystery. There was a time not long ago when Kony was the world's most wanted man. He made headlines on all major news broadcasts, and a short video produced by the American organisation Invisible Children had millions of people talking about the horrors he inflicted. Seven years after this video, *Kony 2012*, went viral, Kony has slid into obscurity. In 2017, Ugandan and US forces gave up the pursuit of Kony, having spent almost $800 million (according to a *New York Times* article dated 15 June 2017) on a manhunt that neither captured nor killed him. The last entry on Kony in the Crisis Tracker is dated 15 January 2016, when Kony reportedly ordered the execution of a sub-commander from Radom national part, in the border area of Sudan, South Sudan and Central African Republic. There are rumours that Kony has died from STDs or related illnesses, but there is no evidence of this. Without clarity on Kony's fate, his ghost will continue to haunt northern Uganda.

Civilians

FRANCIS is the boy whose name was written the night before Norman, and who was released afterwards because the LRA saw no use for him. While Francis escaped abduction that day, his story is tragic. He had epilepsy, which worsened significantly after the stress of his capture and caused friction in the family, leading to his mother and father splitting up. In 2001, when Francis was walking from his mother's home to his father's, he was allegedly arrested by the UPDF. This is the last that has ever been heard of him. His family think that either he was arrested and put in prison, or that he joined the army and might be fighting in Somalia or elsewhere, where the UPDF is currently deployed. However, this latter option is dubious, considering his epilepsy. While his parents still hope that he is alive, it is likely that he has been murdered. His parents have contacted the government several times, but the UPDF says that they know nothing. Ever since his disappearance, the parents have not found rest.

SISTER RACHELLE FASSERA served as a Superior General at the Comboni Missionary Sisters in Rome after the last Aboke girl was released by the LRA in 2009. In 2011, she was awarded the Servitor Pacis Award for her selfless bravery in the direct aftermath of the abduction.

HERVÉ CHEUZEVILLE played an important role in Norman's life after his return from the LRA and continues to do this in the lives of many others. In 1998, Hervé left the World Food Programme after having worked with them for almost ten years in Sudan, Malawi, Mozambique, Burundi, Rwanda and eventually Uganda. Afterwards he joined the Italian NGO AVSI, and he continued to work in Uganda throughout 1998 and 1999. Since then he has worked for a range of NGOs and for UNICEF in various African countries, including the DRC, Malawi, South Sudan and Chad, where his last assignment ended on 31 December 2013, with Aviation Sans Frontières.

Throughout his professional career, Hervé has gone the extra mile to help children affected by war. In 2004, he founded a Congolese NGO called Fondation Kadogo in Ituri, DRC, and with a group of dedicated Congolese volunteers sent many former child soldiers back to school, also following up on their social reinsertion into civilian society. In Bukavu, eastern DRC, while working for the NGO War Child Holland, Hervé set up a programme for street kids, children in conflict with the law and children accused of witchcraft, providing shelter and whatever aid they needed. In the same town he contributed to the promotion of the Congolese youth band Groupe Alliance, which has approximately forty young members who write songs about burning issues such as peace and reconciliation, HIV/AIDS, tribalism, corruption, child soldiers, street children and the ill-treatment of albinos.

Hervé has also written several books about his experiences, which can be found on his website, www.cheuzeville.net.

SISTER SOPHIA. Norman does not know what happened to Odong or his other friends at the Blessed Damian School. According to Hervé, who remained in contact with Sister Sophia, she is doing well.

KAUNDA KENNETH is the young man who accompanied Norman to Kampala when they visited Hervé Cheuzeville for the first time, and Norman is still good friends with him. At the time, Kenneth worked as a translator for World Vision. After this he learned about mechanics and became a vehicle technician at the Caltex fuel station in Gulu. Whenever Norman goes to Gulu, he makes sure that he meets Kaunda.

Norman's family

NORMAN'S COUSIN, who was present when he was abducted, has survived the war. While his cousin Francis was depicted as mentally disturbed, Norman says that this had to do with war traumas at the time. His mental disturbances have since disappeared, and he is doing well. His cousin is now a married man and he has one child, a baby girl. Francis never got much education. Due to the war and his war-trauma he stopped school at primary five and he never went for further education. He now lives a farmer's life in a peaceful village. Whenever Norman visits the village they often reminisce about what happened to them. Francis continues to voice his gratitude for Norman's efforts to save his life.

NORMAN'S UNCLE, also present when Norman was abducted, survived the war and is doing well. He left the IDP camp after the war ended and resumed village life, where he has become something of an entrepreneur. From the little money Norman's uncle got through his farming activities, he managed to buy a motorbike, which helped him transport his produce to town, where the profits were much higher. With these profits he bought a grinding machine, which is now being used by the whole village to grind their cassava. His relationship with Norman is very good. Whenever Norman is back in the village, he immediately stops what he is doing to come and visit Norman.

NORMAN'S FAMILY IN PARONGO survived the attack described in Chapter 7: 'The Person I Feared Becoming'. The village where they lived was approximately two kilometres away from Parongo trading centre, on the border of Murchison Falls National Park. The rebels did not reach there that day. Norman's uncles from his mother's side continue to do well. According to Norman, they live off farming, mostly rice farming, fishing in the River Nile and occasional poaching. Sometimes his uncles come to Gulu town to grind the rice into flour. Also, some of them have businesses and they buy their stock from Gulu, so every now and then they still come to see Norman.

NORMAN'S PARENTS are still alive, and they are doing very well. After the war, they moved back to the village and restarted the normal life that they used to know before the war, cultivating their large patch of land once more. While they initially had no start-up capital, the surplus crops they sold slowly increased their wealth. They have constructed six grass-thatched houses. With financial aid from Norman, they bought seven piglets that have now grown fat and are ready to be sold. They bought thirteen goats and they have over twenty chickens now. They even bought a cow, but they had to sell it because it failed to reproduce.

While this might seem a meagre wealth base by Western standards, in postwar northern Uganda it means that they are doing well. They can afford school fees and other things the children need. They don't spend much, as they live on a subsistence basis, which means that their wealth will continue to increase. While it will take a long time before they are back to prewar standards, Norman's father is confident that he will get there. His parents are very content with the family's happiness. They cherish every moment Norman spends with them when he is back in the village, and they are the proud grandparents of Norman's children.

*

NORMAN'S SIBLINGS are also doing well. His eldest sister got married and has given birth to a child. His brothers, who are much younger, have all graduated from various universities. Norman helped his father by providing their school fees.

Norman

Nine years have now passed since the last entry in the book on 1 January 2010. Much has happened in Norman's life since this date, psychologically, professionally and in his family. Let's start with the first. Norman was severely traumatised when I first met him in 2007. He would sometimes stand up in the middle of a conversation and run away. He suffered terribly from insomnia, because he didn't dare to sleep at night, being haunted by terrible nightmares of his wartime experiences. Norman claims that the research for this book helped him to get over the trauma. The research started in 2007, continued in 2008 for a period of five months, and ended in 2009. In 2009 he was already doing much better. By revisiting his memories in extreme detail, placing them in chronological order, sharing them extensively and revisiting many of the places in his story, he managed to put his memories to rest. He can now talk about his experiences freely, without fearing the repercussions of nightmares. While Norman still has some trust issues and prefers to share his story in person with very few people, he is no longer afraid to look back. He claims that the nightmares were the last remnant of his trauma, and he experienced his last nightmare in January 2013.

In 2012, three years after Norman got married, his second child was born, Lamara (meaning 'beautiful') Natasha, and a third child in 2014. Norman said that Lovis did so well at school that the school wanted to promote him fast through the primary stages, but Norman stopped them from doing that, commenting that they shouldn't rush Lovis's childhood too much. Norman is only too aware of the childhood that was stolen from him, so he wants his children to enjoy every minute of theirs. Norman is at his happiest when he is with his family.

In early 2012, around the same time as the birth of Lamara Natasha, Norman finished extensive training for a job in the security sector and found steady work in Kampala. Although his job takes him more than 300 kilometres away from his family, he talks with them every day. Every opportunity that he gets, he travels north to see them. Although he is far away from his family for most of the year, Norman is now the head of a household, which also means that it is his fatherly duty to provide and to protect. At the end of every month, he sends his earnings home so that his children can go to school and his wife can buy whatever is needed in the household. He even managed to save enough money to start building his own compound.

While he enjoys his job in the security business, Norman never stops looking ahead. Every month, he puts away a little bit of money, which will enable him to go back to school. His two passions are psychology and information technology. The first grew out of his own experiences in getting over his traumas. The second is inspired by the modern world and the opportunities that it brings. Norman sees IT as the future, while psychology is needed to heal the wounds of the past.

Norman is a self-made man who creates his own happiness and knows that his future is bright. His experience in the LRA has taught him one very important lesson: to reach your dreams, you need to be proactive and you need to do it yourself.

Without a doubt, he is the most inspirational person I have ever met.

Uganda: A History of Cyclical Violence

The origins of the conflict between Uganda's government and the Lord's Resistance Army, the longest-running civil war in sub-Saharan Africa, are complex and can be traced back to pre-colonial history, when the present-day territory of Uganda was divided into kingdoms and chiefdoms. Some of these groups traded, raided and intermarried, some fought wars and some cohabited peacefully. However, the idea that these various groups would one day ever be united under the same constitution, flag and leader was non-existent and for many reasons absurd.

In the early nineteenth century, current-day Acholiland was divided into sixty-five to seventy chiefdoms, all of which had autonomous political systems under the rule of a *rwot*, or chief, whose power was limited both because of the small size of the chiefdoms and because decision-making power was shared with the heads of all the village chiefs within the greater chiefdom.* By contrast, the vast majority of the Baganda, an ethnic group that inhabited the centre of current-day Uganda, were united under the

---

* Ronald R. Atkinson (2010), *The Roots of Ethnicity: The Origins of the Acholi of Uganda Before 1800*, Fountain Publishers, Kampala.

rule of the Kabaka, the absolute monarch, who by the nineteenth century was the source of power and wealth of every functionary of the state of Buganda.*

From the 1850s onwards, Arabic slave and ivory traders, referred to as the Kutoria, established three bases in modern-day Acholiland from which they organised their trade. This had devastating consequences for the Luo-speaking population of northern Uganda, many of whom ended up as slaves.

In the 1870s, the Egyptian government asked British explorer Samuel W. Baker to put an end to the slave trade in what is now modern-day Acholiland, which he did in 1872. The Egyptian government then named him the governor of the province of Equatoria, which included territories of current-day South Sudan and northern Uganda. The Luo-speaking populations of northern Uganda called this administration the Jadiya. Baker staked an exclusive claim for the ivory in the territory he controlled, employing violent military force to intimidate and brutally exploit the population. The Jadiya administration levied taxes, and razed whole villages if inhabitants failed to fulfil the quota or deliver porters for the ivory.

In 1883, the first rebellions against the Jadiya were initiated by the Madi and in 1888, the Acholi managed to defeat the Jadiya once and for all. However, having learned that foreign occupation had many violent consequences, they couldn't stop the tide of history.

In 1894 Uganda became a British protectorate. The British had no interest in establishing a fully fledged colony in Uganda as they had in Kenya; they came to Uganda first and foremost to extract raw materials for their own booming industrialised economy. The British had control over the central administration, the courts, and

---

* Samwiri Rubaraza Karugire (2010), *A Political History of Uganda*, Kampala, Fountain Publishers, Kampala.

maybe most importantly, the newly established King's African Rifles, the colonial army, which had British officers and African rank and file. Due to limited human resources, however, the British could only rule with the help of the local population. The political system of the Buganda kingdom proved perfect for their needs. The British crowned the Kabaka king of all Uganda in exchange for his loyalty to Her Majesty's government and good returns in raw materials.

When the British expanded colonial rule to include the area east and north of the Nile, the diffused political system they encountered offered a serious challenge to their rule. So they unseated the existing chiefs in Acholiland and installed replacements who were given unlimited judicial, legislative and executive powers on the condition that they were loyal to British rule and helped to collect taxes.* This, of course, provoked dispute and again violence was needed to subdue the local population.

Throughout the colonial era, a division of labour was created based on ethnicity that would have great consequences in post-independence Uganda. The British recruited in Acholiland for the King's African Rifles and for labour for the large farms in the south of Uganda, while discouraging farming in the north. Many of the Acholi who moved south found employment in the government as teachers, police officers, soldiers and civil servants. Especially in the security forces, the northerners became dominant, mostly because of the classic divide-and-rule strategy the British applied, in which they hired northerners to quell rebellions in the south. In the words of John Postlethwaite, the colonial administrator in

---

* Adam Branch (2011), *Displacing Human Rights: War and Intervention in Northern Uganda*, Oxford University Press, Oxford.

Buganda, the Acholi 'took to soldiering like ducks to water'.[*]

In the 1930s, the British rulers disbanded their appointed chiefs, as they had become too powerful, and reinstalled lineage-based chiefs. Later they created district and local councils that ruled alongside the chiefs. This system set the stage for party politics. In 1952, the Uganda National Congress was born, followed in 1954 by the Democratic Party. Both soon became national parties with nationalist ideologies, and when the winds of history changed and Britain prepared Uganda for independence, they became important in the negotiations. One of the main issues was what would happen with Buganda.[†] Due to its close relations with the British, Buganda had always enjoyed special privileges, and now wanted to ensure that it would keep them, which caused resentment elsewhere. To nullify the Bagandas' claim to such privilege, other political elites also started to play the ethnic card. For the first time in history, the Acholi wanted a paramount chief who would preside over all other chiefs, in order to give the Acholi a stronger voice within the political arena.[‡]

With support from the United Kingdom, Uganda gained independence relatively peacefully on 9 October 1962 and held its first democratic parliamentary election. The largest two contenders were the Democratic Party (DP) and the Ugandan People's Congress (UPC), which was a movement that had split from the Uganda National Congress. The kingdom of Buganda had been given a special status and didn't participate in the election. Instead, the king's party, Kabaka Yekka, automatically received twenty-one

---

[*] Sverker Finnström (2008), *Living with Bad Surroundings: War, History and Everyday Moments in Northern Uganda*, Duke University Press, Durham.

[†] Karugire, *A Political History of Uganda*.

[‡] Branch, *Displacing Human Rights*.

of the eighty-two seats in parliament. The UPC, under the leadership of Dr Milton Obote, a teacher from Lango, northern Uganda,
won the election, but with not enough votes for a parliamentary
majority, so the UPC formed an alliance with Kabaka Yekka.*

The early years of independence were a time of optimism and
relative prosperity. Exports were booming, and Uganda had the
highest per capita growth in eastern Africa. For the time being, a
spirit of cooperation and interdependence dominated. The Ugandan People's Congress drew supporters and members from across
Uganda, and Obote appointed ministerial positions from amongst
a range of tribal groups.† In 1963, Obote made the Buganda king,
Sir Edward Mutesa II, the first president of the country. The alliance would not last.

The 1962 independence constitution incorporated ten federal
districts, concentrated in the north and east, and five kingdoms, all
located in the south and west. The Buganda kingdom had a relatively high level of autonomy, with its own parliament, and Mutesa
had wide-ranging executive powers. The remaining four kingdoms
were given more limited forms of autonomy, while the federal districts came under the rule of district councils that did not enjoy
the autonomy granted to the kingdoms.‡ It was a system based on
ethnic inequality, and Obote, who came under the spell of social-
ism, sought to undo this. Inevitably, he found himself at logger-
heads with the political elites of the kingdoms, most notably the
Baganda. Obote needed the support of the military, which was
heavily dominated by northerners, most predominantly Acholi

---

* Dieter Nohlen, Michael Krennerich and Bernhard Thibaut (1999), *Elections in Africa:
  A Data Handbook*, p. 934.

† Ugandans at Heart, available at ugandansatheart.org

‡ Branch, *Displacing Human Rights*.

and Langi. So, while Obote tried to de-tribalise Uganda by dis-
banding the power of the kingdoms, he engaged in the very act of
tribalism to do so, further strengthening the north–south divide
created during British rule.*

In 1966, Obote dismissed Mutesa as president, and had members of his cabinet arrested and imprisoned.† The Buganda kingdom reacted violently and in turn, Obote ordered his army to
attack the Buganda palace and parliament. While the guards of the
Kabaka put up fierce resistance, they were no match for Obote's
forces, under the command of Commander Idi Amin.

Mutesa escaped to London, where he died in exile in 1969.
Obote disbanded the Buganda kingdom, dividing it into four distinct administrative units, and ordered the Ministry of Defence
to set up office in the former Bugandan parliament. A state of
emergency was declared and many Baganda were arrested, tortured and killed.

Obote became increasingly authoritarian and secretive, quickly
losing his legitimacy as a democratically elected leader. He alienated much of the Bantu-speaking south and west, and relied on the
largely northern army to enforce his rule and protect him from his
political enemies, while placing those he considered loyal to him
in key positions.‡ One such person was Idi Amin, who was
installed as the head of the army in 1966.

Amin was from mixed Kakwa and Lugbara origin, two ethnic
Sudanic groups from West Nile, a region in the northwest of
Uganda. Amin had served the King's African Rifles, and he had

---

* Branch, *Displacing Human Rights*.

† Martin Meredith (1997), *The State of Africa: A History of Fifty Years of Independence*,
Free Press.

‡ Finnström, *Living with Bad Surroundings*.

grown in rank because of his marksmanship, his athleticism and his perceived loyalty.* In the army, he engaged in boxing and for nine years, he was the heavyweight boxing champion in Uganda. During the Mau Mau Rebellion against colonial rule in Kenya, Amin was an interrogator for the King's African Rifles, a job he did extremely well because of his apparent lack of empathy and sheer brutality. As a reward for exceptional services, Amin was promoted to sergeant major, as one of only two Ugandans who were ever given that honour.†

On the eve of the Ugandan independence, Amin was accused of killing three Kenyans. British officers said that he should face criminal charges, but the Ugandan governor decided against it, saying that the prosecution of such a decorated native army commander would cause unrest.‡ Instead, he demanded that Amin should be redeployed to Uganda, where the new prime minister would deal with him. Milton Obote decided against a court martial and only reprimanded Amin. Thankful for the mere admonishment, Amin showed great loyalty to Obote, who regarded him as a simple soldier who would do his bidding. This proved a critical miscalculation.

While many regarded Amin as politically unintelligent, he turned out to be very shrewd when his own persona was involved. During his successful military career in post-independence Uganda, he installed Kakwa, Madi and Lugbara soldiers from his

---

* Meredith, *The State of Africa.*

† Ibid.

‡ Ibid.

own native West Nile region into key military positions, acquiring loyalty through ethnic allegiance.[*]

So when the relationship between Milton Obote and Idi Amin soured after an attempt on Obote's life in 1969, he was a force to be reckoned with.[†] In response, Obote declared a state of emergency and disbanded all political parties, becoming an absolute ruler, relying on the secret police, led by his cousin, for his personal security. Obote realised that Idi Amin had significantly increased his power base in the army and tried to place more Acholi and Langi officers in key positions. At the same time, he declared a move to the left, the government demanding a 60 per cent share – and hence control – of the banks and other large corporations operating in Uganda. Within the Cold War dynamics of the time, and as a member of the British Commonwealth, this raised suspicion in the West, especially in the UK. In effect, Obote did a remarkable job of creating enemies both nationally and internationally.

A clash was inevitable. Obote accused Amin of the murder of the army's deputy commander, who was of Acholi origin, and indicted him for the embezzlement of army funds. Having learned that Obote was going to arrest him for this latter allegation, it was Idi Amin who threw in the first decisive punch. In January 1971, while Obote was out of the country for a Commonwealth conference, Idi Amin launched a coup d'état.

The military takeover was met with surprisingly little resistance. As Amin went around the country to announce his victory, he was greeted as a hero and liberator of the people. Especially in the former Buganda kingdom, the public rejoiced and people dreamed

---

[*] Branch, *Displacing Human Rights*.

[†] Meredith, *The State of Africa*.

of the reinstatement of the Kabaka.[*] Internationally, Amin's take-over was also greeted with enthusiasm. Britain was keen to recognise his regime and did so precisely one week after the coup. He was lauded as a conquering hero in the British press. The jubilation wouldn't last long.

Idi Amin soon became known as the 'Butcher of Uganda'.[†] His regime was tyrannical, presiding over economic decline, social breakdown and very severe human rights violations. Almost immediately after the coup, Amin initiated mass executions of his opponents. In particular, he took revenge on Acholi and Langi ethnic groups because of their allegiance to Obote and their prevalence in the armed forces.[‡] This act of persecution was to have far-reaching consequences in encouraging the formation of the Lord's Resistance Army a decade and a half later.

In 1976, Amin declared himself 'President for Life'. A year later, Amnesty International estimated that between 50,000 and 300,000 may have died under his rule, including church leaders, cabinet ministers and the intellectual classes.[§] Amin claimed to eat the flesh of his slain enemies and was said to perform blood rituals with his victims. Under Amin's rule no one was safe. In 1972, he banished all people of Indian origin from Uganda, giving them a ninety-day ultimatum to leave the country. The Indians were brought to Uganda by the British to build a railway, but many stayed and became so prosperous that they were resented by the

---

* Branch, *Displacing Human Rights.*

† Biography.com editors, Idi Amin Biography, The Biography.com website, 7 August 2019, available at www.biography.com/people/idi-amin-9183487

‡ Finnström, *Living with Bad Surroundings.*

§ Amnesty International, available at www.amnesty.org/en/library/assetNWS21/003/ 1977/en/83de3d09-6d21-4f9a-8fdb-c42bcf58f127/nws210031977en.pdf

indigenous population. Inflation hit 1,000 per cent and, towards the end of his rule, the treasury ran out of funds and was unable to pay the soldiers, who consequently mutinied.* Hoping to calm the impending storm and to divert attention from his country's turmoil by uniting Uganda against a foreign adversary, Amin invaded Tanzanian territory in 1978.

Tanzania counterattacked, alongside Ugandans who had fled the country during Amin's years of terror. In the vanguard of the Tanzanian invasion was the Ugandan National Liberation Army (UNLA), a conglomeration of twenty-eight different rebel groups of Ugandans living in exile. Its leaders included Milton Obote and the then still relatively unknown Yoweri Museveni, who would become Uganda's longest-sitting president. Tanzania conquered Kampala and in 1979 Amin fled to Libya and later to permanent exile in Jeddah, Saudi Arabia, where he died in August 2003.†

Milton Obote returned triumphantly from exile and took power for a second term in what many claimed to be a rigged election. Even though a team of neutral election monitors, the Commonwealth Observer Group, declared itself satisfied with the legitimacy of the process, Ugandans criticised the observers for fearing civil war if the results were questioned.‡ Ironically, the anger and dismay created by the popular perception of a corrupt election fanned the flames of the very civil war that the Commonwealth Observer Group was trying to avoid.

Obote again surrounded himself with Langi and Acholi. Many key civil servants and army and police commanders from southern

---

* Meredith, *The State of Africa.*

† Ibid.

‡ Ibid.

tribes were forcibly removed while Obote supporters from the north took positions of power. The Acholi were again prominent in the military and, remembering well what had happened under Idi Amin, they retaliated against the Sudanic tribes in West Nile who had played a large role in the persecution of Acholi and Langi during Amin's reign.

The tribal politics of Obote did not win him any friends in the Bantu-speaking south, and shortly after Obote's government took office, Yoweri Museveni, a former Military Commission member from western Uganda, formed the National Resistance Army (NRA) and began a guerrilla campaign to overthrow Obote. The war that followed, popularly known as the Bush War, resulted in yet another cycle of violence that caused widespread destruction and an even greater loss of life than Amin's eight-year rule. A large area in central Uganda, north of Kampala, known as the Luwero Triangle, suffered the brunt of this conflict.

Reports of government atrocities, disappearances and torture increased. At the same time, the NRA also committed horrendous acts, often carried out by the *kadogos*, the child soldiers, who were numerous within the rank and file of the NRA.* Amnesty International documented the routine torture and killing of civilians by the military across southern and central Uganda. The death toll from 1981 to 1985 was estimated as high as 500,000. The mostly Acholi-led army realised that Obote was becoming a liability, and in 1985 a military council toppled him. Shortly after the coup, General Tito Okello took control of the de facto government. Obote fled to Zambia, taking with him, it was rumoured, as much plunder as he could carry.

---

* China Keitetsi (2002), *Child Soldier: Fighting for My Life*, Jacana.

Under the rule of the military council, Tito Okello's first objective was to end the war, which the UNLA was gradually losing. Okello invited all the armed groups in Uganda to the peace talks. While the NRA initially declined the invitation, they agreed when the location was changed to Nairobi, with Kenyan president Daniel Arap Moi as the chief mediator. The peace talks, which became cynically known as the Nairobi Peace Jokes, concluded successfully. The Nairobi Agreement was signed in December 1985 and included a ceasefire agreement, together with provisions for the demilitarisation of Kampala, the integration of the NRA into the national armed forces, political office for the NRA's leaders, and a commission of inquiry to investigate alleged war crimes and human rights violations.* This last provision caused uproar in the UNLA. Both parties violated the provisions of the peace agreement, and with the UNLA weakened by internal discontent, Yoweri Museveni took Kampala in January 1986 and installed himself as president. Fearing prosecution or worse, Okello's UNLA escaped north to their ethnic base in Acholi, where they reorganised. The NRA followed, embittered by what had been done in the Luwero Triangle and looking for vengeance.

This was the context that set the stage for what was to become the most protracted and infamous armed conflict in Uganda. This included hundreds of government atrocities, the wholesale theft of Acholi cattle by the government and Karamojong cattle rustlers, and the quick rise and slow fall of Joseph Kony, the most notorious warlord that Uganda has spawned, and, for a while, among the most wanted men on earth.

---

* Meredith, *The State of Africa*.

War in Northern Uganda and the Genesis of the Lord's Resistance Army

The LRA came into being two years into the war in northern Uganda. While Museveni's ascent marked the end of a period of political turmoil in central Uganda, it heralded a new one on its periphery. Smelling opportunity or fearing marginalisation and revenge killings, rebel movements mushroomed in all corners of Uganda. Some of these rebellions were short-lived, others continued for over a decade with horrible consequences for the civilian populations. The conflicts in the central north of Uganda gained international notoriety.

The National Resistance Army, Museveni's rebel-group-turned-government-army, entered northern Uganda in January 1986 and committed grave human rights abuses against the civilian population. In partial reaction to this, two distinct rebel groups emerged in northern Uganda. One was the Uganda People's Democratic Army (UPDA). It consisted mostly of soldiers from the UNLA, the former government army. Following their defeat, they had fled north across the border of Sudan and were relatively well armed, well trained in the art of war and battle-hardened. In the UPDA's shadow emerged another group, far less conventional, poorly armed, poorly trained and with very little military experience, but with the power to mobilise thousands and strike terror in the hearts of the enemy.

In the wake of the Bush War, many UNLA soldiers who fled north felt they needed spiritual redemption for the horrors they had inflicted upon others in the Luwero Triangle. Spiritual cleansing provided them solace. Acholi tradition demanded that the returning soldiers go through purifying rituals: 'Because they had killed, they brought *cen*, the spirits of the killed, to Acholi, thus threatening the lives of those who had stayed at home.'* They needed spiritual healers to free their spirits from those of the dead.

One such healer who could communicate with the spirit world was a young woman called Alice Auma. She was possessed by the spirit of an Italian World War I military engineer and fighter pilot who had died at the age of ninety-five, known as the Spirit Lakwena, the Messenger. Her cult soon became popular as she purified the souls of retreating UNLA soldiers and offered a mythology that could heal the devastation of their defeat by the NRA. Alice had the power to remove the stain of their *cen*, the corrupting effluence of the dead.

Alice Auma came from a poor family in Opit, a trading centre east of Gulu in northern Uganda. She was twenty-eight years old when she began her career as a resistance leader and founder of the Holy Spirit Movement (HSM). Alice believed that the pure soldier had no reason to fear the bullet, as their spirit would deflect

---

* Heike Behrend, 'Power to heal, power to kill: spirit possession and war in northern Uganda (1986–1994)', in H. Behrend et al. (eds, 1999), *Spirit Possession, Modernity and Power in Africa*, James Currey, Oxford.

enemy fire. She could also harness nature to her cause. During her semi-mythical 'journey to Paraa' in Murchison Falls National Park in May 1985, she claimed to have persuaded many animals and natural phenomena to become her allies. In battle her soldiers were joined by 140,000 spirits, bees, snakes, rivers, rocks and mountains. Her moral authority extended to embrace her environment, which she believed had also been polluted by the brutality of what had happened during the Bush War.

Her message was strengthened by harnessing aspects of Christianity that were beyond the reach of traditional Acholi healers. Her movement became known as the Holy Spirit Movement, or the Holy Spirit Mobile Forces (HSMF), and at the end of 1986 she had amassed an army of 10,000 'soldiers'. They began attacking NRA units based in Acholi and success attracted more followers. She was joined by soldiers from other movements, as well as peasants, school and college students, teachers, businessmen, a former government minister and numerous women and girls.[*]

Her followers were strictly disciplined, with rules including rejecting witchcraft, upholding chastity, no smoking, drinking or quarrelling, renouncing all sin, and concentrating solely on purifying the Acholi people and Uganda. The Spirit Lakwena guided her with his twenty Holy Spirit Safety Precautions, which included no walking sticks on the battlefield, no hiding behind anthills, and each man to have 'two testicles, neither more nor less'.[†] The Spirit Lakwena's orders forbade the soldiers to use weapons. Singing Catholic hymns, they entered battle with their bare torsos smothered in shea-nut oil – the bullets of the enemy would turn into

---

[*] Heike Behrend, *Alice Lakwena and the Holy Spirits: War in Northern Uganda, 1986–97*, Eastern African Studies series, James Currey, 1999.

[†] Ibid.

water and bounce off them. Nature became a key ally: if they 'bought' each river they crossed with coins and shells, water would block or drown the enemy. Stones would explode like grenades when thrown.

She became known as Alice Lakwena, and her attacks against the NRA were brave, selfless and remarkably effective. Faced with a mass of partly naked, oil-smeared men and women marching fearlessly towards them holding Bibles and singing hymns, the terrified NRA soldiers dropped their weapons and ran away.

Alice Lakwena's Holy Spirit Movement gained international attention. She was variously caricatured in the press as a voodoo priestess, a witch, the future queen of Uganda and a Jeanne d'Arc in the African wilderness.

In October 1987 Alice ordered her troops to leave northern Uganda and embark on a spectacular march through eastern Uganda, with Kampala as the ultimate target. By now, her threat as a popular movement and military unit was very real. Of course, they did not march all the way without shooting a single bullet. While the Holy Spirit Mobile Forces indeed used stones, they also threw hand grenades alongside the stones, which actually gave the visual effect that stones were exploding. Also, as they captured one military barracks after the other, their weapon arsenal steadily grew, and there were enough former UNLA soldiers among Alice's followers who knew how to use them. However, the fact remained that in terms of armament, the HSM was no match for the NRA.

During the battle in Iyolwa in Tororo, a battle the HSM won, Alice lost 202 men, which was the first indicator that her army wasn't invincible.* On 25 October, in the swamps of Magamaga,

---

* Klaas Castelein (2014), *Zo scherp als een pijl: het verhaal van de Arrow Boys uit Oost-Oeganda*, Afrika Studiecentrum, Leiden.

Alice Lakwena's glorious march finally came to an end. Less than a hundred kilometres from Kampala, the government soldiers set up an ambush. Faced with heavy artillery and a lot of firepower, the spiritual power of the poorly armed HSM finally gave way. Norman's commander claimed that Alice was defeated by the unfaithfulness of her followers, which caused the holy shea oil not to turn bullets into water. No matter what it was, the spell that Alice had over her enemies was broken. She escaped on a bicycle and lived in a refugee camp in northeast Kenya, where she died in 2007.

In the meantime, the armed struggle of the UPDA did not go as smoothly as its leaders had hoped. Realising that victory was no longer within reach and having heard what had happened to the HSM, some of the commanders opted for negotiations, which Museveni accepted, as he was still fighting numerous armed rebellions in other corners of the country. In exchange for political offices for the commanders, a large section of the UPDA, almost 10,000 in number, surrendered in Pece Stadium in Gulu town on 3 June 1988.

The remaining soldiers of the UPDA who refused to surrender either had the option to continue on their own under the leadership of Odong Latek, or to join one of the two remaining fighting forces left in the central north. One of these was led by Alice's father, Severino Lukoya, who tried to breathe new life into his daughter's failed rebellion. The other was led by a young man called Joseph Kony. Odong Latek decided to join Kony, which added to the strength of what was, until then, a very small fighting force.

Kony was born in the early 1960s in Odek, a village east of Gulu. He was the youngest of six children and not an outstanding student. He had a sense of humour, was pleasant, polite, loved soccer and was one of the best Larakaraka dancers (a traditional courtship dance in Acholi) at the school. It has been said that Kony is Alice's cousin, but the connection may not be as close as suggested. It is possible they shared a grandfather on their mother's side.

His father was a lay preacher in the Catholic Church and Kony was an altar boy for several years but stopped attending church and dropped out of school around the age of fifteen. It is reported that he joined his older brother Ginoni Okello, who was a witch doctor at a shrine outside Odek. Kony trained as an *ajwaka*, a healer or prophet (a medium for *jok*, which is translated as a spirit, force or power). He claimed to have been seized by the Spirit Lakwena and tried to form an alliance with Alice's HSM, but she turned him down. Kony was furious and his followers attacked and killed some of hers.[*]

Kony's partnership with Latek proved to be potent. Odong Latek was a ruthless and skillful guerrilla tactician. While Kony concentrated on the spiritual side, Latek organised the forces. Kony absorbed a huge amount from Latek's military experience and understanding of combat strategy. Latek was killed in 1989, but by then, Kony and his new military tactician, Vincent Otti, were well versed in the arts of guerrilla fighting.

In the meantime, Severino Lukoya's revival of the HSM had very little success, his spiritual powers being far less convincing than those of his daughter or of Joseph Kony.[†] On 26 July 1989, he surrendered to the local authorities in Gulu, leaving Joseph Kony as the only remaining rebel leader in the central north of Uganda.[‡]

In the early days, Kony's movement was known as the Lord's

---

[*] Tim Allen and Koen Vlassenroot, *The Lord's Resistance Army: Myth and Reality*, Zed Books, 2010.

[†] Ibid.

[‡] Behrend, *Alice Lakwena and the Holy Spirits*.

Salvation Army and later as the United Christian Democratic Army. In 1992, he renamed it the Lord's Resistance Army (LRA) to align it in opposition to Museveni's National Resistance Army. Kony's forces actively pursued the war, combining the guerrilla tactics of the UPDA with the spirituality of the HSM, which proved a powerful combination. While he enjoyed some popular support at the start of his military career, over time people grew tired of warfare, and Kony's tactic of plundering food did not gain him much popularity either.* Faced with a diminishing number of volunteers and dwindling support and supply, Kony had to rely on coercion and violence against civilians for his army's survival.

In March 1991, Major General David Tinyefuza of the NRA launched a huge government military offensive against Kony, codenamed Operation North. A state of emergency was declared, and the sub-regions of Acholi and Lira were closed to international press and humanitarian organisations. Believing that the LRA still enjoyed the support of the local population, Tinyefuza's forces only marginally distinguished between rebels and civilians. One of the most telling examples of this is the massacre that took place in Burcoro on 16 April 1991. The Ugandan NGO the Justice and Reconciliation Project described the massacre as follows:

> Between the 14th and the 18th of April 1991, Burcoro was the scene of a brutal operation carried out by the 22nd Battalion of the National Resistance Army (NRA) in which several hundred people were detained at Burcoro Primary School. They were released only after being interrogated, tortured and sexually abused throughout

---

* Government of the United States of America, The Anguish of Northern Uganda – Introduction, ReliefWeb, 2 October 1997, available at at reliefweb.int/report/uganda/anguish-northern-uganda-introduction

the four days of the operation. In this instance alone, government soldiers committed crimes including: murder, rape, sexual violence, torture, cruel treatment, deprivation of liberty, outrages upon personal dignity, attacking civilians, pillaging and other inhumane acts.*

Caught between murderous government forces and a rebel movement that was becoming increasingly predatory in nature, the Acholi population grew desperate. Three government officials of Acholi origin devised a strategy to protect the civilian population from the horrors of war. The Acholi colonel Fred Tolit, who was then the director of the Chieftaincy of Military Intelligence, had the idea to organise the civilian population into self-defence units. He shared this idea with the Minister of State for the Pacification of Northern Uganda, Betty Bigombe, one of the most famous peace activists from northern Uganda, who shared the idea with John Bosco Ochaya, the district head of Gulu. The groups became known as Arrow Groups and Wegi Atero (armed with bow and arrow). Ochaya appealed to the Acholi warrior identity to recruit fighters, although, as Bigombe stated, some young men simply joined up in order to receive a plate of *posho* and beans.†

Ochaya and other government officials managed to mobilise 6,000 civilians into arms against the LRA, even though they could not provide them with any weaponry, forcing them to use spears, bows and arrows. The religious leadership and political opposition

---

* Justice and Reconciliation Project (2013), 'The Beast of Burcoro: Recounting Atrocities by the NRA's 22nd Battalion in Burcoro Village in April 1991', JRP Field Note XVII, Gulu.

† Castelein, *Zo scherp als een pijl.*

criticised it, saying that violence would only spawn violence, and that innocent lives were at stake. Their assessment proved to be right.

Kony was outraged by what he saw as the betrayal of his just cause and promised to rid the genuine Acholi of the corrupt, false Acholi who were collaborating with the government, thereby advancing Alice Lakwena's ideals of spiritual purification into the realm of political cleansing. The LRA would decide who was 'clean' and who was 'tainted' by Museveni's government, giving Kony unlimited licence to slaughter those suspected of supporting the government. He controlled the rest of the Acholi population by asserting a series of rules, with violent consequences of maiming and death if broken. The rules appeared arbitrary and fluid and were constantly changing according to Kony's spiritual 'channelling', enforcing the LRA's authority by creating an environment of unpredictability and absolute fear.

The Ugandan government's response to the LRA swung back and forth between peace negotiations and military offensives to destroy the rebels. Operation North, which distinguished itself for its brutality and heavy-handedness,* succeeded mostly in antagonising the LRA into even more violent reprisals, while further alienating the civilian population at the same time. So in 1994 the government tried a different approach. Peace talks were started by Betty Bigombe, which initially seemed promising. She met Kony four times in the bush, without protection, and even though most of those who attended the first meeting with her were too terrified to go again, an uneasy ceasefire was arranged.

President Museveni's attitude was more belligerent, and the talks

---

* Government of the United States of America, The Anguish of Northern Uganda – Introduction.

collapsed when he issued an ultimatum for the LRA's surrender. He claimed to have received intelligence that the LRA were using the ceasefire to build up their military capacity and to negotiate assistance from the government of Sudan, which could well be true, but Museveni might have had ulterior motives for prolonging the war.

There has been much discussion that Museveni has used the war against the LRA to his government's political advantage. Andrew Mwenda, a prominent Ugandan journalist and critic of Museveni's government, suggests that the war has brought much benefit to Museveni's government from the USA in terms of diplomatic, financial, logistical, technological and moral support.[*] It has also allowed Museveni to establish a one-party system at a time when multi-party politics was being upheld; to denounce any opposition as collaborators with the north; to appeal to security issues to shut down dissent in the media; and to detain opposition candidates such as Kizza Besigye, former leader of the opposing Forum for Democratic Change party, on charges of treason and collusion with the LRA.[†]

The reason the LRA might have agreed to peace talks in 1994 was because it lost the support of the Acholi people, which made it difficult to sustain guerrilla warfare. Furthermore, while Operation North hadn't culminated in Kony's capture, it had weakened the LRA, and Kony had indeed used peace talks as a way to relieve military pressure and to provide time to reorganise the forces. Museveni might have been correct that Kony used the peace talks to negotiate assistance from the government of Sudan, because

---

[*] Andrew Mwenda, 'Uganda's politics of foreign aid and violent conflict: the political uses of the LRA rebellion', in Allen and Vlassenroot, *The Lord's Resistance Army*.

[†] For more information on the political use of the LRA, key authors who have written about this include Andrew Mwenda, Sverker Finnstrom, Adam Branch and Chris Dolan.

after the failed peace process, the government of Sudan did become the LRA's greatest ally.

In retaliation for the Ugandan government's support for the rebel Sudan People's Liberation Army (SPLA) led by John Garang, a long-time friend of Museveni's, the Sudanese government decided in 1994 to provide the LRA with arms, assistance and a military safe haven in Palutaka in Sudan. From there they could launch attacks into Uganda and retreat across the border to Sudan, where the NRA was unable to engage. In exchange, the LRA would help the government of Sudan to fight the SPLA. As Norman describes, Palutaka was divided into two military bases: the heavily armed military encampment of the Sudanese government army, and on the other side, the LRA camp of at least 5,000 soldiers. The two armies operated separately, but together they were at war with the SPLA, while Uganda and Sudan were in a proxy war, with both countries supporting rebel groups in the opposing country.

Sudan's bitter and bloody north–south divide provided the LRA with a significant opportunity for expansion. With the end of the Cold War in 1990, America began to see the threat of Islamic extremism as its enemy, rather than communism. In 1989, the Sudanese army under Omar al-Bashir seized power in Sudan and allied itself with the National Islamic Front (NIF) to form the government in Khartoum. America considered the regime a threat and began to finance the rebel SPLA. Uganda was the conduit of this assistance.[*]

In retaliation, Sudan provided the LRA with finance, military equipment and base camps like Palutaka. Support from Khartoum

---

[*] Mwenda, 'Uganda's politics of foreign aid and violent conflict'.

meant that the LRA no longer needed to win the hearts and minds of the Acholi people to continue its war. The LRA could operate without restraint.

Perhaps unintentionally, the government of Uganda gave the LRA another opportunity to advance their guerrilla warfare. From 1996 onwards, the government started to force people into IDP camps. Claimed to be for the civilians' protection, there was nothing civil about the establishment of the camps. People were given a forty-eight-hour ultimatum to get to the nearest IDP camp, after which the Ugandan army would start to shell surrounding villages with artillery fire, as they did, for example, in Awach IDP camp, according to several eyewitnesses.[*] Anyone who came after the deadline was considered a rebel, and could be shot or arrested.

As more civilians amassed, they started to surround the military units that were in the centre of some camps, which meant that the civilians acted as a protective shield for the military, instead of the other way around. In other camps, military bases were set up on the periphery of the camp, where the soldiers could only protect the camp if the LRA were to attack from that specific direction. Furthermore, the military units were often badly armed and understaffed, meaning that they were unable to repel a full-on attack.

By putting the population into IDP camps and leaving the farmlands fallow, the government was pursuing a scorched-earth strategy. If the civilians were in the camps, they were unable to cultivate the fields, which would mean that they couldn't feed the LRA or support them in any other way. What it also meant was that the IDP camps became death camps, where the malnourished

---

[*] Personal interview in Awach sub-county, September 2009.

and weak, living in insanitary conditions, succumbed to a range of diseases, from cholera to Ebola and many more.

With all the civilians removed from the rural areas, the bush belonged to the LRA. They could wander around undetected, hit the IDP camps, and clear out before the Ugandan military could ever respond.

The enslavement of the Acholi people into IDP camps was deplorable. For more than ten years, the people of Gulu District, where the forced migration started, lived in hunger, misery and fear. While humanitarian agencies such as the World Food Programme and others came in to provide people with vital necessities, the food provided was rarely enough. The civilian population knew that the government was unable to protect them in the camps, but they also knew that going back to the villages was no longer an option. First of all, in the camps there were food supplies, boreholes, schools and hospitals, while in the villages there was nothing. People would need to restart a whole cultivation cycle, which would mean that the first food would only be available in five months, at best. Secondly, the government would not allow them to move back to the villages, and they could be arrested as rebel collaborators. Third, before the IDP camps, civilians were scattered in so many places that the risks of encountering the LRA were dispersed, but now, unless all the IDPs were evacuated simultaneously, each camp provided a concentrated, easy target for the LRA. The Acholi proverb: '*Ka lyec ariyo tye ka lweny lum ayee deno can* – When two elephants fight, it is the grass that suffers', adequately describes the fates of the Acholi and some of the other affected ethnic groups, including the Langi and the Madi.

The LRA increased abductions to expand its army into the considerable force that Norman observed in Palutaka, where the LRA outnumbered the Sudanese government troops. It launched some of its most vicious attacks between 1995 and 1999, a number of which are graphically narrated by Norman in this account. The worst onslaught that happened during these years, one that was not witnessed by Norman, was the massacre in Atiak on 20 April 1995, in which the LRA killed between 200 and 300 civilians on a single day. Led by the LRA's second-in-command, Vincent Otti, who was from Atiak himself, this massacre was one of the most brutal in LRA history.

In a joint offensive with the SPLA, the Ugandan army, now renamed the Uganda People's Defence Force (UPDF), retaliated a year later when they attacked the LRA base in Palutaka. Norman described the attack as the worst onslaught that he witnessed in his young military career. The attack was considered a military success, but its effects didn't last. While Norman was sent on a mission to Uganda to stash some of the weapon arsenals that were saved from Palutaka, the skirmishes between the LRA and the UPDF/SPLA coalition continued. After Palutaka, as Norman narrates, the LRA set up a base in a place called Kit One. When the UPDF/SPLA coalition found the LRA there and defeated them, the LRA went to Kit Two, and history repeated itself. By the time Norman came back from his mission in Uganda, the LRA had established new barracks at Aru Junction, near Juba, deep into Sudan, where the UPDF couldn't follow without starting a full-out war with Sudan. Out of Uganda's reach once more, the LRA reorganised and strengthened its rank and file with new abductees and military training given by the Sudanese armed forces.

However, after 11 September 2001 and the al-Qaeda attacks on the US, the tide was turning and state sovereignty started to count for less in pursuit of the war against terror. A comprehensive attempt to wipe out the LRA was launched in March 2002, called Operation Iron Fist. Vicious attacks such as the Atiak massacre and the Aboke girls' abduction, in which Norman took part, had created international headlines and outrage. Further pressure was put on Sudan to cease supporting the LRA following the 9/11 terrorist attacks and by the addition of the LRA to the 'USA Patriot Act Terrorist Exclusion List'. Under international pressure, the Sudanese government conceded that the UPDF could hunt Kony on Sudanese territory, below an agreed 'red' line along the Torit–Juba highway. The UPDF, with US logistical support, attacked the LRA with an estimated 10,000 Ugandan troops and helicopter gunships. Hundreds were killed, many of whom were children no different from Norman, but Kony and his top commanders escaped. It appeared that, militarily, the LRA was too adept at skirmishing, evasion and dispersal. Norman's story, at the very least, is an astonishing account of the group's resilience and adaptability in the most extreme of environments.

The operation was a disaster. Forced from their bases in Sudan, the LRA fled Sudan and moved back to Uganda. Research from the Refugee Law Project in Kitgum District indicates that the year 2002 saw a very significant increase in armed violence, 2003 was the absolute peak year in terms of violence, and 2004 saw hundreds of massacres take place all over the central north. The conflict also spread to new regions, including the Teso sub-region and parts of the Lango sub-region. The government expanded its IDP policy to these new theatres of war, as well as the few areas within Acholiland and Lango sub-district that had thus far escaped forced displacement. By the end of 2003, over 95 per cent of the Acholi population, more than 1.7 million people, and large parts of the Iteso and Langi populations were displaced.

Again, the Ugandan army failed miserably to protect them from the LRA. Telling examples are the massacre in Abia on 4 February 2004, in which the LRA killed seventy-one people, and the massacre in Barlonyo on 21 February 2004, when between 200 and 300 civilians were killed* in an IDP camp, while the Ugandan army was nowhere to be seen. In response to such atrocities, the local population in Teso and Lango, who saw the LRA as foreign invaders, organised themselves into self-defence units and this time the government did provide them with weapons. Well armed and motivated to protect their own kin, the Arrow Boys in Teso and the Amuka (Rhino) in Lango proved much more adept in fighting the LRA than the Wegi Atero earlier in Acholi, who were only armed with bows and arrows and who were less motivated, as they were fighting their own kin. In Teso, the Arrow Boys were actually able to drive out the LRA almost by themselves.

However, it was mostly events on the international stage that began to undermine the LRA's ability to operate in Uganda. In January 2005 the Sudanese government and the Sudanese People's Liberation Army signed a comprehensive peace agreement that gave the SPLA autonomy to rule the south of Sudan. With the Sudanese army gone, the LRA lost its arms supplier and its military ally in the south of Sudan, and effectively lost its ability to continue the war. As a result, 2005 and 2006 saw a sharp decrease in the number of war crimes, although dozens of brutal massacres and hundreds of killings continued to take place.

In addition, in 2003, President Museveni referred the problem of the LRA to the International Criminal Court (ICC) and on

---

* There is a disagreement between the government and the community over the total number of deaths.

13 October 2005, ICC arrest warrants were issued for Joseph Kony and four other senior commanders of the LRA, charging them with crimes against humanity and war crimes, including murder, rape and sexual slavery. The ICC warrant stated that:

> The LRA has engaged in a cycle of violence and established a pat-
> tern of 'brutalisation of civilians' by acts including murder, abduc-
> tion, sexual enslavement, mutilation, as well as mass burnings of
> houses and looting of camp settlements; that abducted civilians,
> including children, are said to have been forcibly 'recruited' as
> fighters, porters and sex slaves to serve the LRA and to contribute
> to attacks against the Ugandan army and civilian communities.[*]

The ICC arrest warrants rattled the LRA. Incapable of sustaining the war effort because of arms shortages, and fearing arrest and prosecution, LRA deputy commander Vincent Otti contacted the BBC on 30 November 2005, suggesting that the LRA were willing to hold peace talks with the Ugandan government.

Peace talks began in Juba in Sudan between the LRA and the Ugandan government on 14 July 2006 and continued for nearly two years before falling apart. There has been considerable debate about whether the two sides were ever serious about an agreement. Rumours have circulated of manipulations to derail the talks, including secret cash payments to LRA members. Vincent Otti is said to have been caught up in the intrigue and was executed by Kony in October 2007.[†]

---

[*] International Criminal Court, Warrant of Arrest for Joseph Kony, issued on 8 July 2005, as amended on 27 September 2005.

[†] Ronald R. Atkinson, '"The realists in Juba"? An analysis of the Juba peace talks', in Allen and Vlassenroot, *The Lord's Resistance Army*.

David Matsanga, a former delegation leader at the peace talks, said: 'Instructions from General Joseph Kony were often at times confusing and he kept on shifting the goalposts. It's doubtful that any nations of the world will in future pay for any other [LRA] peace talks."*

Relative peace ensued in northern Uganda as the LRA redeployed to the Garamba Forest region in the Democratic Republic of the Congo. A final attempt to sign a peace agreement was made on 29–30 November 2008, but Kony failed to turn up. While some attempted to rescue the negotiations, Museveni's military strategists were preparing for war again. Less than a month after the last peace attempt, war continued in the DRC under the codename Operation Lightning Thunder. This operation once more promised to wipe out the LRA, and again, it was the civilians who suffered the brunt of the violence, while Kony and his cronies got away.

While the conflict rages on in the new theatres of war in the Democratic Republic of the Congo, South Sudan and the Central African Republic, northern Uganda has entered an era of improved security and economic recovery. While many post-conflict problems remain, children no longer need to be afraid of being abducted and people can farm their lands without having to worry about landmines or rebels. The former child soldiers who were fortunate to survive and escape the LRA have returned to rebuild their shattered lives and face the challenges of reintegration.

---

* Integrated Regional Information Networks report, 24 November 2009.

On Peace and Unending War

When Norman and his family celebrated Christmas in December 2009, a relative calm had returned to northern Uganda. Since the ceasefire in 2006, Uganda has had no more armed conflict within its national boundary. However, to say that Uganda is now at peace would not do justice to the thousands of war-affected people who continue to suffer the consequences of war and who do not experience peace, including those who fled ongoing wars in South Sudan and the Democratic Republic of the Congo.

Peace is more than the absence of armed violence. Peace is personal and public at the same time, located both in the realm of perception, within social networks and within real-time events. Peace needs recovery, healing, reconciliation and justice. This takes time and effort. While some individuals say that they experience peace, others continue to live in the war, even though the guns have fallen silent. Norman and many other survivors of this brutal conflict can attest to this.

In 2007, a year after the ceasefire agreement and ten years after his escape, Norman was most definitely not at peace. Every night he was haunted by nightmares of what he experienced in the bush, the toll of death weighing heavily upon him, causing severe insomnia and occasional rage attacks. In 2014, seventeen years after his escape from the LRA, Norman genuinely said that he had healed and that he lived in peace. Norman's story, no matter how horrific, is a success story. However, more than thirteen years after the conflict ended on Uganda's soil, there are others who continue to deal with the consequences of war on a daily basis.

Many parents weren't as lucky as Norman's. The families and friends of the thousands of abductees who didn't return and whose deaths Norman witnessed continue to live in a chronic state of suspended grief, ambiguity and powerlessness. While the exact number of missing persons remains unknown, there are indicators that they might well surpass the figure of 12,000.* While in some cases the relatives have received news that their child has died, most parents of the missing continue to live not knowing what happened to their children, never finding peace of mind. For research I conducted in 2013 about the coping strategies of families of missing persons, Esther, the mother of Akello, who was abducted in the mid-nineties, quite possibly by Norman's battalion, graphically explained the daily cycle of hope and despair: 'Every single morning [for the past seventeen years] I wake up hopeful that this might be the day that Akello will return, only to go to bed in the evening depressed and disappointed that it didn't happen.'†

Academic James Quesada said that wars produce a continuum of duress long after they end.‡ This is most certainly the case for

---

* The International Committee of the Red Cross (ICRC) came to this number by measuring the number of missing persons they documented in two sub-counties, and multiplying it by the number of sub-counties in the Acholi region: www.icrc.org/eng/resources/documents/photo-gallery/2013/08-30-uganda-disappeared-missing.htm

† Personal interview with Esther in Palabek, October 2013.

‡ James Quesada (1998), 'Suffering Child: An Embodiment of War and Its Aftermath in Post-Sandinista Nicaragua', *Medical Anthropology Quarterly*, vol. 12, no. 1, pp. 51–73.

the thousands of people who continue to be in the dark about the fates of their vanished family members. While most relatives of the deceased can eventually come to terms with their tragic loss and learn to pick up their lives, following the rituals of burial and culturally defined periods of mourning in which they receive sympathy and guidance, the stress of not knowing prevents such closure. Individuals whose direct relatives and close friends are missing are in a state of chronic grieving, with no rituals to guide them, no support groups and counsellors to help them.[*] For them, the war did not end with a ceasefire agreement in 2006.

Another group of victims who feel the continuum of duress are those people who were badly injured during the conflict. Disregarding political discourse on the purpose and outcomes of war, academic Elaine Scarry argues that 'the main purpose and outcome of war is injuring'.[†] As Norman clearly narrated, the tactics of the LRA were indeed intended to inflict bodily harm in order to communicate messages, and the government of Uganda did pretty much the same, for example through the act of raping men and women.[‡]

During the course of the war, tens, if not hundreds of thousands of people were badly injured, both mentally and physically. Many injured people have not been able to access medical care. For

---

[*] For more information about this topic, refer to Theo Hollander (2016), 'Ambiguous Loss and Complicated Grief: Understanding the Grief of Parents of the Disappeared in Northern Uganda', *Journal of Family Theory and Review*, vol. 8, issue 3.

[†] Elaine Scarry (1985), *The Body in Pain: The Making and Unmaking of the World*, Oxford University Press, Oxford, 1985.

[‡] Theo Hollander and Bani Gill (2014), 'Every Day the War Continues in My Body: Examining the Marked Body in Postconflict Northern Uganda', *International Journal of Transitional Justice*. For more information on the rape of men, the Refugee Law Project made a compelling video of one man's testimony called *They Slept with Me*, available at https://www.refugeelawproject.org/component/allvideoshare/video/they-slept-with-me-they-were-government-soldiers-in-the-late-1980s?Itemid=151

others, for example some of the mutilation victims, their wounds are so grave that they are beyond medical care, at least the type that is accessible in Uganda. These untreated wounds symbolise more than just a handicap. The wounds are the embodiment of war, and the bodies of the wounded, disabled and disfigured are physiological canvases on which war is portrayed. For some wounded people, simple daily activities such as working the land, going to the toilet, having sexual intercourse or going to church are nightmarish because of the excruciating pain caused by their injuries.

In an agricultural and largely self-sufficient society, where prosperity largely depends on one's physical strength, mobility and ability to work the land, wounds and physical injury negatively affect a person's ability to interact with their environment. Wounded men can no longer live up to their traditional masculine roles of providers and protectors. Injured women, already at a disadvantage because of the patriarchal nature of the society, risk divorce and isolation as they fail to fulfil the cultural requirements of their femininity. Severe physical and mental trauma impinges upon perceptions of self and creates friction between gender expectations and the lived reality of one's gender. At the same time, limited mobility generates greater dependency on caretakers, family and community networks. In a sense, the wounds cause a ripple effect that creates disturbances within families, clans and other social capital networks, leaving long-lasting intergenerational traces within the community as a whole. As one of the respondents to research I conducted with Indian scholar Bani Gill said, 'Every day, the war continues in my body.'[*]

---

[*] Hollander and Gill, 'Every Day the War Continues in My Body: Examining the Marked Body in Postconflict Northern Uganda'.

So, while northern Uganda is experiencing a general process of healing and post-conflict recovery, there are some wounds that heal faster than others, there are those that remain stagnant, and there are those that deteriorate over time. Many issues remain. There are problems regarding reburials of both mass graves and the graves of those who died in the IDP camps far away from their ancestral lands; there are land conflicts, partially a result of the long period of displacement and resulting lack of clarity about clan and family borders; there is a high level of suicide because of depression and hopelessness. These are just a small selection of the post-conflict challenges that Uganda is facing, and before they are addressed, the label 'peace' is contentious, to say the least.

Nonetheless, there are also many positive changes that are taking place. In 2010, the last IDP camp was dismantled, and people have returned to their homesteads to farm and rebuild their shattered lives. Villages destroyed by the LRA and the government are being restored to places of comfort and security. Cattle, which were nowhere to be seen by the end of the conflict, are once more dominating the landscape of northern Uganda, and traditional ox ploughs are cultivating land that was fallow during the conflict. A whole generation of children have been born who know of the conflict only through stories rather than personal experience. Gulu, the largest city in the region, is thriving and the rural areas are also developing.[*]

It may be trivial to some, but significant to others, that when one travels through northern Uganda today, you see people in beautiful clothes, living in very clean and well-kept homesteads that are sometimes decorated with flowers and neatly trimmed

---

[*] Lino Owor Ogora, 'Govt sowing seeds of unrest in north', Uganda *Daily Monitor*, 20 January 2013.

bushes. While a traveller who is new to the region might never take notice of this, or simply see it as something normal, for those who witnessed the horrors of the IDP camps, simple flowers in front of one's house signifies the restoration of human dignity that was all but lost during the course of the conflict. So while many war-affected people continue to deal with the legacies of the conflict, it is clear that in general, the Acholi people and other affected ethnic groups have begun their long road towards recovery and there is much to be positive and hopeful about, which can unfortunately not be said about all countries in the greater Horn of Africa, the Great Lakes region and Central Africa.

While the guns have fallen silent in Uganda, the LRA war has not yet ended. After a two-and-a-half-year interlude in hostilities from mid 2006 till late 2008 during the Juba peace talks, the war was breathed back to life on 14 December 2008 when Uganda launched Operation Lightning Thunder. The new theatre of war was in northeastern Democratic Republic of the Congo (DRC), southwestern South Sudan, and eastern Central African Republic (CAR), a vast area roughly the size of California, covered in thick jungle.

Operation Lightning Thunder was a joint Ugandan, Congolese and Southern Sudanese offensive in the Garamba Forest in Congo with the intention to kill or capture Kony and once and for all defeat the LRA, the same language heard earlier during Operation North and Operation Iron Fist. US President George Bush personally signed the directive to the United States Africa Command to provide financial and logistical assistance.

Despite the show of force, coordination problems, internal rivalries and secret hidden agendas undermined the operation and Kony and his top commanders escaped time and again. In line with the tradition of military offensives against the LRA, coalition forces failed horribly to protect the civilian population from the expected onslaught, which followed in late December 2008. Unable or unwilling to use conventional measures to fight back, Kony did what he does best, retaliating against unarmed civilians to show the world just how costly an attack on the LRA is. While the predominantly Christian Congo was celebrating Christmas, the Lord's Resistance Army attacked several villages in Haut-Uele Province in the northeast of the DRC. Human Rights Watch reported that the LRA killed 620 people in four days.*

The Christmas massacres have entered history as the LRA's deadliest massacre. Many of the casualties were hacked to pieces, decapitated or burned alive in their homes. The few eyewitnesses that survived had their lips cut off so that they couldn't speak ill of the rebels. Nine months after the offensive, various estimates indicated that the LRA had killed over 1,000 people, abducted many hundreds and displaced up to half a million across northeastern DRC, parts of western Equatoria in South Sudan and areas in the east of CAR.

With less intensity, these terror campaigns have continued in the decade following the Christmas massacres. According to the Crisis Tracker,† the LRA killed 2,479 people and abducted 7,579 between 2009 and 2019. From 1 May 2018 to 1 May 2019 there were 411 abductions, showing that the LRA continues to be a menace.

---

* DR Congo: LRA Slaughters 620 in 'Christmas Massacres', Human Rights Watch, 17 January 2009, available at www.hrw.org/news/2009/01/17/dr-congo-lra-slaughters-620-christmas-massacres

† Mapping Violence in Central Africa, Crisis Tracker, available at www.lracrisistracker.org

For almost a decade Uganda, with the support of the US and regional partners, conducted a well-funded but poorly coordinated manhunt to capture Kony and defeat the LRA. In May 2017, this mission fizzled out without achieving either objective. Kony, who has elevated escaping capture to an art form, has never been apprehended or killed and what has actually happened to him is shrouded in mystery. At various intervals between 2013 and 2017 it was rumoured that Kony was ill and that, increasingly, the day-to-day running of the LRA had been handed over to his sons Ali and Salim Saleh.* This would indicate that Joseph Kony is no longer fit to lead the LRA; however, the source of this information is unclear. Since 2017, there hasn't been any documented sighting of Kony.

Operating in a region wrecked by civil wars and where governments only exert very limited control, the LRA continues to exist. However, cut off from support and weakened by defections and internal struggles, it is no longer the formidable force it once was. There are now other security priorities, such as the civil war in South Sudan, sectarian violence and civil war in CAR, and ongoing civil conflicts and Ebola in DRC. According to a study published by the London School of Hygiene and Tropical Medicine, the civil war in South Sudan, which started in December 2013, claimed nearly 400,000 lives.† In CAR, the political and sectarian violence also claimed thousands of lives. Conflicts in the DRC have been the deadliest since World War II and insecurity

---

* Ridel Kasasira, 'Kony's son takes over LRA control', *Daily Monitor*, 17 May 2014, available at www.monitor.co.ug/News/National/Kony-s-son-takes-over-LRA-rebel-command/-/688334/2317056/-/4xjh87/-/index.html

† Checchi et al. (2018), 'Estimates of crisis-attributable mortality in South Sudan, December 2013–April 2018: A statistical analysis', London School of Hygiene and Tropical Medicine.

continues to persist. In this region, Uganda has become a beacon of relative stability, housing over a million refugees from the DRC and South Sudan.

At the time of writing, there is some cause for limited optimism for the region. Protests in Sudan have seen the ousting of long-time dictator and LRA supporter Omar al-Bashir and they could usher a period towards democratic reform. South Sudan is experiencing its longest ceasefire since violence broke out in 2013. In CAR, warring parties signed a peace agreement in February 2019 that at the time of writing continues to hold. Hopefully these positive trends can be sustained and replicated in other conflict-affected countries in the region so that experiences like those of Norman Okello can one day belong to the past.

Dr Theo Hollander, 2019

Acknowledgements

There are many people who have helped to bring Norman's story to life and who deserve our acknowledgement and gratitude. First and foremost, of course, there is Norman himself. Without his gift of storytelling, the enormous trust that he put into me to tell his story in the most open and honest way, and his courage to visit places that hold very deep traumas, I would have never been able to write his story in such vivid detail. Norman is without a doubt the most inspirational person I have ever met, and writing his story has been an absolute privilege. I also want to thank Norman's family – his mother and father who welcomed me to their house on numerous occasions, his wife, his children and his siblings. Their love and support have been a key pillar in Norman's recovery.

Second, Norman had critical friends who offered us support in the writing process. People who stand out include Victor, Richard and Pamela. Victor and Richard were Norman's colleagues at the War Affected Children Association. Pamela is a gospel singer from Gulu and a close friend to us both. They all share similar histories to Norman's, and they all shared their own war experiences with me, which added further context to Norman's story. Richard accompanied us on several trips we made to key locations in Norman's story, and his support and understanding made Norman's difficult confrontations with his past more bearable. Hervé Cheuzeville also deserves a special mention, not only for the very important role that he played in Norman's recovery, but also for his advice on the last chapters of the book and for providing additional detail. Overall, most people who played a significant role in Norman's recovery have been mentioned in this book. Norman conveys his deep gratitude to all who have helped him get to the stage where he was able to tell his story and recover from the traumatic events narrated in this book.

Various people have been critical in getting this book to the publishing stage. Ten years have passed since I finished the first draft and there have been numerous steps on the road towards publication. I want to extend my thanks to my former colleagues at the Refugee Law Project, especially Dr Chris Dolan, Moses Chrispus Okello and Steve Oola, who supported the publication of an earlier iteration of this book in separate chapters under the name 'In the Service of the Lord's Army'. This caught the attention of the UK charity Christian Aid, which used Norman's story for various media products, including the documentary *In Kony's Shadow – Norman Okello's Story*, which can be found on YouTube. Special thanks to the writer and freelance journalist Will Storr, who was involved in producing a story in the *Guardian* about Norman, and who introduced me to his literary agent Paul Moreton from the Lomax, Bell and Moreton Literary Agency. Paul Moreton put his trust in the book and hired editor Martin Fletcher, who provided a first round of extensive edits. At Martin's suggestion and with his help, several chapters were added to Norman's story to provide the historical and political context of the war.

Acknowledgements

I want to thank people at Unbound, without whom this book wouldn't have crossed the publishing finish line. Unbound believed in this book from the start and they provided critical support to raise funds, provide editorial services and help with the design and printing. I want to extend my thanks to DeAndra Lupu, Rachael Kerr, Katy Guest and Georgia Odd. Special thanks also to my old Refugee Law Project colleagues Patrick Otim and Shaffic Opiny, who helped put together Norman's promotional video, and my close friend Dr George Abongomera, who helped me with some of the logistics of the promotional video while I was living far away in Myanmar.

I want to acknowledge several people have reviewed the book on content and flow. They include key experts such as Ronald Atkinson, Rev Dr Andrew David Omona and Klaas Castelein, who reviewed the content, especially of the context chapters, and friends and colleagues such as Elsbeth van Wijk, Jane Danielson and Stephanie Schulze, who looked at the flow and structure. Many thanks for your support.

Thank you to all the people who backed the crowdfunding campaign. They include people who I have never met, but also many of my friends, colleagues and family. Without your support, this book wouldn't have been published, so my deep gratitude.

I want to thank people who are very dear to my heart and who have supported me in more ways then I can mention. They include my friends in Uganda – George, Niki, Klaas, Gijs, Britte, Andreas, Paola, Stephen, Lauren, Marije, Sham Lal, Jen, Carter, Sander, Rens, Natig, Moses, Patrick (RIP), Brenda, Deo, Bob, Francis, Kara, Jimmy, Loek, Matthijs, Rodney, Lucia and Marleen, among many others. My family supported me throughout my life, and without their love and support, I might have never met Norman in the first place. My mother and father came to Uganda twice and supported an agricultural project for former child soldiers and a project to help people with conflict-related injuries live more dignified lives. My sisters, Yvonne and Natasja, visited as well. I am happy that they all met Norman, who has had such a profound impact on my life. Norman named one of his children after Natasja, and Yvon accompanied Norman, Richard and me on several trips to places in Norman's story. Last but certainly not least, I want to thank the love of my life – Sarah Toner – for her incredible support over the last seven-plus years of our adventurous, loving and fun lives in Uganda, Myanmar and now Kenya.

A Note on the Authors

NORMAN OKELLO is a former child soldier from northern Uganda, abducted at the age of twelve and forced to fight in what was one of the most notoriously violent rebel forces in the world. He was both a victim and a perpetrator of violence. In 2004, he co-founded a charity that aimed to support former child soldiers, and for over six years he provided critical assistance to hundreds of abductees who escaped the LRA. Norman is now a family man who owns his own farm and serves the public as a civil servant. Having overcome hardship and hatred, his life now centres on helping others and serving his community. Norman's story is a testament to the strength of human resilience in the face of severe danger and deprivation. He hopes his story can educate people about the consequences of war, and that it can provide a human face to the conflict in northern Uganda.

DR THEO HOLLANDER is a peacebuilding professional with over a decade of experience working with child soldiers, reintegration of combatants, transitional justice, security and justice sector reform, and conflict mediation. Between 2007 and 2009, Theo spent many months working with Norman in Uganda and present-day South

Sudan to capture his story. Theo has documented hundreds of stories of victims of the LRA war as a research coordinator for a war and peace documentation centre in northern Uganda, which provided further insights and depth to this book. To date, writing Norman's story has been the most rewarding project Theo has worked on, and he hopes that it can serve as a source of inspiration for others.

Unbound is the world's first crowdfunding publisher, established in 2011.

We believe that wonderful things can happen when you clear a path for people who share a passion. That's why we've built a platform that brings together readers and authors to crowdfund books they believe in – and give fresh ideas that don't fit the traditional mould the chance they deserve.

This book is in your hands because readers made it possible. Everyone who pledged their support is listed below. Join them by visiting unbound.com and supporting a book today.

With special thanks to the following friends of this book: N F, Liza Hollander, Fiachra MacCléire, Ashish Pandey and Ton en José Smeenk.

Martha Adam-Bushell
Steve Ainsworth
Natig Alasgarov
Jose Maria Arraiza
Marian Baker
Robert Barclay
Robert Barkell
B Barrett

Laurie Bell
Henk Boelman
Thomas Boone
David Botteram
Dorien Braam
Jeanne Briggs
Tom Brimelow
Gareth Brinkworth

Marleen Brouwer

Neil Bruton

Ivan Campbell

Klaas Castelein

Herbert Cats

Chloé Cbd

Hervé Cheuzeville

Ben Clench

Mairead Condon

Michelle Crijns

Shelagh Daley

Caitlin Davies

Rob de Lange

Faustine de Monès

LA de Visser

Gavin Devitt

Tessa Diphoorn

Sonia Dixon

Thomas Donnelly

Keith Dudleston

Pauline Eloff

Mollie Fair

Annabel Falcon

Benedict Faria

Guillermo Farias

Catherine Fischl

Georg Frerks

Bridget Frost

John Gattorn

Daniele Gibney

Bani Gill

Margriet Goos

Deb Green

Mel Green

Katy Guest

Frea Haker

Lucian Harriman

Conor Hegarty

Philip Hewitt

Cheryl Heykoop

Natasja Hollander

Yvon Hollander

Roger Horton

Hanna Idema

Jodie Jackson

Thea Jansen-Smeenk

Niek Jansma

Jennifer Jokstad

Dan Kieran

Anneke Kneppers

Nikola Ladyton

Mit Lahiri

Sham Lal

Susan Law

Jess Lee

Jonny Lee

Anna Lickley

Thandar Lwin

Ariana Martini

Ellen Maynes

Supporters

Gavin McGillivray

Aidan McQuade

Bairbre Meade

Sarah Mendelsohn

Maurits Mens

John Mitchinson

Ali Moore

Linda Murgatroyd

Paul Murphy

Henri Myrttinen

Tun Tun Naing

Jana Naujoks

Carlo Navato

Kevin O'Connor

Robin Odriscoll

Nicola, Tom and Rosa
  Oldham

Gijs Opbroek

James Owen

Dokter Paardekut

Danielle Parry

Liz Patterson

Anne Peeters

Ian Plenderleith

Justin Pollard

Jessica Price

Jane Richardson

Robma

Usha Rowan

Abhilash Sarhadi

Ananda Schouten

Steffen Schwörer

Ojaswi Shah

Karen Simbulan

Alissa Skog

Oliver Slow

Stephanie Smale

Ben Smeenk

Truus Smeenk

Lili Soh

Claire Staunton

Billy Stewart

Daniel Szczepanski

Kim Tate Wistreich

Britte Tiem

Kloé Tricot O'Farrell

Emmy Troquete

Karlien Truyens

Rens Twijnstra

Nico Tyabji

Finny Underhill

Claire Vallings

Karin van Bemmel

Anne van den Heuvel

D van Geenen

Marleen van Seggelen

Elsbeth Van Wijk

Sander van Zanten

Matthijs Verbeek

Judith Verweijen